INTERCULTURAL SERVICES

INTERCULTURAL SERVICES

A Worldwide Buyer's Guide and Sourcebook

Gary M. Wederspahn

Routledge
Taylor & Francis Group

LONDON AND NEW YORK

INTERCULTURAL SERVICES
A Worldwide Buyer's Guide and Sourcebook

Copyright © 2000 by Taylor & Francis,
All rights reserved. This book, or
parts thereof, may not be reproduced in any form
without permission of the publisher.
First published in 2000 by Gulf Publishing Company
Subsequently published by Elsevier

This edition published 2011 by Routledge
2 Park Square, Milton Park, Abingdon, Oxon OX14 4RN
711 Third Avenue, New York, NY 10017, USA

Routledge is an imprint of the Taylor & Francis Group, an informa business

Library of Congress Cataloging-in-Publication Data
Wederspahn, Gary M.
   Intercultural services : a worldwide buyer's guide
and sourcebook / by Gary M. Wederspahn.
      p. cm.
   Includes index.
   ISBN 0-87719-344-4 (alk. paper)
   1. Business consultants.   2. Diversity in the
workplace—Study and teaching. 3. International
business enterprises—Management—Study and
teaching. 4. Multiculturalism—Study and
teaching. 5. Industrial sociology—Study and
teaching. 6. Employees—Training of. 7.
Corporate culture.   I. Title.

   HD69.C6 W434 2000
   305.8'0071'5—dc21   00-025064

This book is dedicated to Ann,
my lifelong partner
in cross-cultural adventures.

Contents

Acknowledgments

Many friends and colleagues have given me input and support during the writing of this book. They are far too numerous to mention individually. I have acknowledged their ideas and works throughout the text and the resource lists. However, I want to recognize George Renwick in particular. His example of freely sharing information and ideas in the intercultural field over the years strongly influenced my decision to undertake this project.

I owe Philip Harris special acknowledgment for being my mentor and advisor. I must thank Jack Condon, Bob Kohls, Robert Brown, Banu Golesorkhi, Peggy Pusch, and Toby Frank for encouraging me to write the book. Also, I am indebted to Raymond Saner and Lichia Yiu for generously allowing me to use their enormous private library in Geneva for research.

Along the way, I received permission to use visuals created by Alexander Patico, Terrence Brake, Danielle Walker, Sandra Fowler, Monica Mumford, Gary Ferraro, Philip Harris, William Stripp, Roger Kaufman, Alicia Rojas, Hanna Mayer, and Prudential Resources Management Intercultural Services. I am most grateful for these additions to the book, which enhance its clarity and comprehensibility.

Numerous clients gave me valuable information and examples of their successes, failures, and lessons learned. I could have not written the book without them. Besides this behind-the-scenes assistance, several clients reviewed my proposal for the book and gave me their recommendations for how to make it relevant and useful to buyers of intercultural services. I want to express appreciation to Alan Freeman of the Walt Disney Company, Kris Rainey of BellSouth International, and Joe McClure of General Motors Corporation for helping me in this way. Bill Sheridan of the National Foreign Trade Council is due special thanks for writing the foreword.

I am personally grateful to Lois Purdham-Kidane and Violeta Samonte for creating an excellent living environment for me in Switzerland in which to write this book.

Foreword

I have been involved in international human resources management for 30 years and have lived as an expatriate in the Caribbean and Middle East. Along the way, I have also been a business traveler, particularly to Europe, the Middle East, the Indian subcontinent, and Southeast Asia. In my role at the National Foreign Trade Council (NFTC), I have the good fortune to be at the crossroads of a wide range of expatriate management challenges, issues, and answers.

In reviewing Gary Wederspahn's *Intercultural Services: A Worldwide Buyer's Guide and Sourcebook*, I am very impressed by its thoroughness, balance, and relevance. Included in the book's comprehensive references are several studies that the NFTC has conducted on international relocation trends and issues. Although the primary sponsor-members of the NFTC have been involved in cross-border business for some time (in some instances for more than 100 years), all can learn valuable lessons and discover useful resources in this book.

As we enter the 21st century, we witness whole new industry groups crossing international borders (information technology, power and utility, and telecommunications companies are a few examples). Managers in these companies can certainly benefit from this guide and sourcebook by using it to rapidly gain knowledge and insight into intercultural services. They can receive immediate and long-term payoffs by becoming more sophisticated buyers and users of these services.

The author also recognizes that the USA is a significant destination location for direct investment and joint venturing, and that there are mutual cross-cultural challenges (such as those faced by Daimler Chrysler) in coming to the United States. The power of the Internet and CD-ROM–based tools provide a very exciting source of help on the myriad challenges faced by business-travelers, expatriates' families, and employers. Here too, Wedersphan has provided abundant information on these new resources.

The importance of cross-cultural awareness cannot be underestimated. Today, most employers understand the total cost involved in a cross-border assignment, which usually runs from two to four times the assignee's salary. However, employers still tend to pay more attention to the choice, care, and maintenance of a piece of capital equipment than they do the equivalent choice, preparation, and maintenance of the "million-dollar expatriate." Unfortunately, very few employers have focused on the significant return on investment that cross-cultural training delivers. This book offers useful information and guidance in that regard.

In closing, let me reiterate what a valuable resource I find *Intercultural Services: A Worldwide Buyer's Guide and Sourcebook* to be. It has alerted the NFTC and me to additional tools and resources of which we were unaware. It would be a good investment and useful asset for any organization or corporation venturing into the global arena.

> *William R. Sheridan*
> Director, International Compensation Services
> National Foreign Trade Council

Preface

The need for this book was clearly apparent during a recent telephone forum of international human resource managers for which I was a guest presenter. One of the participants said "I was just tossed into the situation of having to find intercultural services for my company's employees and didn't even know where to start!" Several others echoed her frustration and confusion. I understand their feelings, having been in that situation myself as a new training manager at the beginning of my career.

I share some of the responsibility for having increased the complexity of their task. By contributing to the development of the broad range of services now available, I helped create the cornucopia of choices they face. With this book, I hope to simplify their buying decisions somewhat by giving them objective information and practical advice for locating and selecting services and products that will meet their needs and fit their budgets.

I have been a user, purchaser, manager, evaluator, designer, and provider of intercultural services for the past 30 years—an exciting time during which the field has grown from its infancy to become a well-established and accepted source of resources for international companies and organizations. The driving forces behind the development of this new profession are the globalization of the missions of these corporations and organizations, plus the emergence of an increasingly diverse worldwide workforce.

The number of companies engaged in international business ventures and the number of expatriates assigned to support these operations increased greatly during the 1980s and 1990s. This trend will continue. A 1998 survey of 177 multinational corporations by the National Foreign Trade Council and Windham International reported that 81 percent of the respondents expected their expatriate populations to grow beyond the year 2000.

The worldwide corporate expatriate employee population is about 250,000, according to data from the UK-based Cranfield School of

Management's Centre for Research in Management of Expatriation as cited in the November 10, 1999 *International Herald Tribune*. This total does not include the employees' family members, nor does it count the many thousands of people who yearly travel across borders on business or who deal with foreign counterparts via long distance. The expatriates and international travelers of noncorporate organizations further swell the number.

All of these people face significant cross-cultural challenges for which they need to be prepared and equipped. Providing them with the awareness, knowledge, positive attitudes, and skills they require is an important responsibility of international human resource managers. That means doing the *right* thing for the people involved and doing the *smart* thing for the success of their organizations' and companies' cross-border ventures.

The proliferation of intercultural services, providers, and purchasers has kept pace with the internationalization of business. Thirty years ago, there were only a few providers offering some half-dozen services. By 1999, I had collected information on nearly 400 providers. I also gathered 34 surveys on the use of cross-cultural training by US-based international companies from 1981 to 1998. During that period, the number of companies surveyed who actually made use of the services grew from 33 to 70%. The range of services available today is a diverse, and often bewildering, array of programs, products, materials, and tools delivered in many different modes and formats.

This book is meant to be an introductory guide and reference for users and purchasers of intercultural services. It will help them understand the concepts underlying the designs of the various programs and products and will enable them to communicate more knowledgeably and confidently with potential providers. As well-informed consumers, they will be able to get the most from their investments and make more valuable contributions to the success of their organization's or company's international activities.

Also, by sharing more common points of reference with their suppliers, buyers will have better prospects for establishing mutually rewarding teamwork with them. I hope that expatriates, international employees, and other people who have cross-border responsibilities will be the ultimate beneficiaries of such teamwork and that this book will be used as a tool to achieve that end.

Gary Wederspahn

1

Exploring Intercultural Services

To say that the world is getting smaller is a cliché. To say that ultimately the only effective way to deal with it is through the development of intercultural skills is profound and revolutionary.

David S. Hoopes in *Global Guide to International Business*

Overview

This book is a guide and sourcebook designed to be used as a "job aid" by purchasers and users of intercultural services and products. It will give you the information and advice you need to make wise buying decisions and to establish effective working relationships with your providers. Business globalization and cultural diversity in the workplace have created significant challenges and opportunities for most corporations and organizations. Increasingly, they are seeking outside resources to confront, manage, and benefit from these new realities. Assistance is available in great abundance and variety. The following chapters will help you effectively select and use services and products appropriate to your needs and circumstances. This first chapter is aimed at introducing you to the book and to the intercultural field so you can get off to a good start.

About the Book

> Knowledge is of two kinds. We know a subject ourselves or we know
> where we can find information upon it.
>
> **Samuel Johnson** in James Boswell's
> *The Life of Samuel Johnson*

Why This Book Is Needed

Employees who have cross-border responsibilities and cross-cultural relationships must be prepared to effectively handle the inevitable intercultural tasks and challenges involved. Providing them with the awareness, knowledge, positive attitudes, and skills they require is an important responsibility of international human resource managers. In many cases, it also means finding appropriate intercultural services, products, and providers. Making the right choices and purchases often means the difference between success or failure and resources wisely spent or wasted.

The range of options available today is a diverse, and often bewildering, array of services, programs, products, materials, and tools delivered in many styles, modes, and formats. These resources often are based on different definitions of intercultural effectiveness and different philosophies and theories regarding how adults learn. An additional complication is that the range of offerings now includes various related services such as relocation assistance, career counseling, and international assignment policy consulting. The experience and competence of the providers vary greatly. However, their sales and marketing materials universally promise excellent results and customer satisfaction. These assurances must be taken with a healthy dose of caution.

As a buyer, especially if you are new to the intercultural field, you might need some help in sorting through this cornucopia of choices and claims. It is normal to be a bit uncomfortable pondering which of the many well-packaged services presented to you would best fit your organization's needs and budgets. This book is an impartial source of information and advice that can raise your level of knowledge and confidence. It will help you avoid the risk of false starts and "buyer's remorse" due to making purchasing decisions you may later regret.

The Aim of the Book

I wrote this book to give you an insider's view of the intercultural service profession and a behind-the-scenes introduction to what the field offers. The book is meant to be a practical guide and a sourcebook. It will help you understand the concepts underlying the designs of the various programs and products and will enable you to deal more knowledgeably and confidently with potential or current suppliers. As an informed consumer, you will be able to take a more active role in planning and managing the services you purchase and to be sure that you get the most from your investments.

My aim is to reduce the complexity and increase the transparency of the discussions between buyers and sellers. More knowledge on the part of purchasers will promote a healthy demand for good quality services and products. Higher client expectations will be welcomed by most providers as a stimulus for upgrading the performance standards of their profession. Also, having more common points of reference with your vendors will improve your communications and teamwork with them. The results should be positive collaborative efforts and outcomes for both you and your vendor. Successful programs and good relationships are mutually advantageous. Failures harm both buyers and sellers by undermining future support for intercultural services.

My intent is that you will use this book for the benefit of your expatriates, international business travelers, multicultural employees, and cross-border managers. I also hope that it will be a starting point of a personal learning quest that takes you far beyond the scope of the book.

Sources of the Book

Over the past 30 years I have been a purchaser, user, manager, evaluator, designer, provider, and seller of intercultural services. The advice offered and opinions expressed in this book come directly from my own experience. I am well aware that my perspective is western and American, but I have sought to represent, accurately and empathetically, the viewpoints of friends and associates from many countries. The book's factual information is derived from my academic studies, attendance at professional seminars, and the literature of the intercultural communications and relations field. Numerous clients and colleagues also contributed valuable tips and suggestions.

But the most essential input has been from the hundreds of expatriates, international business travelers, cross-border employees, and their local counterparts in many countries with whom I have had the great privilege of working. The lessons they learned and taught me are scattered throughout the book. Their successes and failures underlie most of the examples given and insights shared.

Intended Readers

This book is primarily for the people who locate, select, buy, and oversee the delivery of intercultural services and products to support their cross-border operations. In many cases, these are human resource and training managers of international corporations, governmental agencies, nongovernmental organizations, and nonprofit institutions. However, line managers and senior executives who are concerned about their employees' cross-cultural effectiveness also can use the book for identifying needs and raising critical issues. Likewise, professionals engaged in private business abroad can use it to gain practical tips and information for avoiding common cross-cultural pitfalls.

Diversity managers facing multicultural issues in the workplace will discover helpful concepts and resources in the book. Service providers may wish to share portions of it with their prospects and clients to facilitate their discussions of program objectives and designs. Likewise, the book will be a useful supplementary text or reading for courses on international business and international relations in colleges and universities.

The book is aimed at readers who are not familiar with the intercultural field. It will give them a broad introduction detailed enough to satisfy their immediate requirements and will establish a solid foundation for further learning. The subject matter is sufficiently in-depth to intellectually engage them, yet simple and straightforward enough to not require previous knowledge. To emphasize that my tips and advice are intended for readers on an individual and personal level, I refer to "you" throughout the book. Also, I hope that this more casual tone will help you feel that I am relating to you as a coach and colleague.

How the Book Is Organized

The book is both a guide and a sourcebook. The first chapter introduces you to the book and to the field of intercultural services. The top-

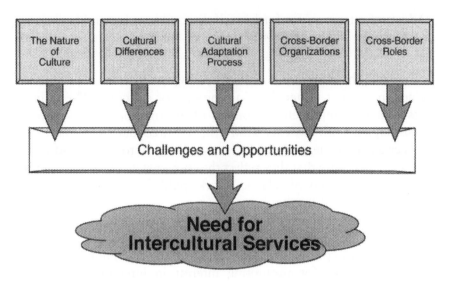

EXHIBIT 1–1. SOURCES OF INTERCULTURAL NEEDS.

ics in the rest of the book are presented in the sequence in which they typically occur in practice. Chapters 2–4 deal with the factors that generate the need for intercultural services. Exhibit 1–1 illustrates the major sources of the cultural challenges and opportunities that confront international organizations. These include the nature of culture itself, the impact of cultural differences, the demands of the cross-cultural adaptation process, and the requirements of cross-border organizations and roles.

Chapters 5–9 focus on techniques, tools, and resources for meeting the cross-cultural challenges and leveraging the opportunities present in the international environment. This section of the book contains descriptions of services and products, plus tips on when and how best to use them. The final chapter gives you a rationale and evidence with which you can build in-house support for the use of intercultural services.

The sequence of the chapters reflects a progression from general to more specific topics. However, they can be read in any order that best meets your needs and interests. Major sections within the chapters are designed as separate units suitable for group discussion. Each chapter has

❑ Sets of focus questions to facilitate reflection on the significance and implications of the topics.
❑ Practical recommendations on how to use the content of the chapter.

❑ Lists of references for further self-directed learning and for locating resources.

To make the book more reader-friendly, specific references are contained in the text rather than in footnotes or endnotes. The resource lists contain comprehensive sources of information on the topics in each chapter. With few exceptions, the resources date from the 1990s. This criterion is meant to make it easier for you to locate and obtain them and to ensure that they reflect the current state of the intercultural field. A bibliography of "classic" works published prior to 1990 is located at the end of this book.

The resource lists are intended to be extensive enough to accommodate a wide range of interests and a variety of uses. They include references for exploring the topics on a deeper level, nontechnical articles and books for promoting interest in intercultural concepts among your colleagues, links to sources of additional help and information, and surveys and scholarly works to validate the substantive content of the book. Most importantly, the resource lists are meant to enable you to research specific intercultural needs and services prior to making purchases.

How to Use the Book

Each chapter offers suggestions on how to use the book by yourself, with colleagues, or with suppliers. In general, the book can be used in the following ways:

For Yourself

❑ *Learning:* Become acquainted with the key concepts and issues underlying the cross-cultural field. Make yourself familiar with the ideas and terminology until you feel you are a well-informed lay person. Use the suggested resources to broaden and deepen your knowledge of any aspect of intercultural services that interests you.

❑ *Value creation:* Apply the criteria and recommendations in the book to identify tangible ways to enable your company or organization to avoid wasting resources or missing opportunities due to intercultural incompetence. Employ the savings and gains to make additional improvements.

❑ *Skill enhancement:* Improve your own cross-cultural communications and relationships by practicing the principles and using the insights offered in the book. Make cultural awareness and sensitivity a part of your skills "tool kit."

❑ *Astute purchasing:* Use the guidelines and the resource lists in Chapters 6, 7, and 8 to compare services, products, and providers before making purchases.

With Colleagues

❑ *Awareness building:* Share information, check lists, examples and exercises with coworkers who have cross-cultural roles and responsibilities. Ask them to assess the validity of concepts and observations contained in the book.

❑ *Education:* Sponsor informal seminars and focus groups on intercultural topics relevant to your organization's international activities. Use portions of the book for handouts, readings, and discussion papers.

❑ *Gaining support:* Gather evidence of the need for intercultural services from employees and business units. Provide this information, along with rationale and recommendations from the book, to key decision-makers. Enlist their support for acquiring needed services.

With Suppliers

❑ *Conveying needs:* Share excerpts that describe your organization or company's intercultural needs and challenges with potential or current providers. Ask them to propose appropriate services or products and explain how these will meet your needs. Seek their help in identifying and specifying any needs that remain unclear.

❑ *Defining objectives:* Show providers the section on setting objectives as a means of encouraging them to develop achievable and measurable goals for the programs they propose to you. Work with them to sharpen the focus of the objectives.

❑ *Selling the concept:* Use providers to help you sell the idea of intercultural service internally. Tell them which portions of the book sparked the most interest among your employees. Plan promotional activities and events together.

❑ *Assessing services, products, and providers:* Use the book to establish your own criteria for quality service and standards for supplier performance. Make your expectations explicit and transparent by indicating the criteria upon which they are based.

About the Intercultural Field

> If we seek to understand a people, we have to try to put ourselves, as far
> as we can, in their particular historical and cultural background. One
> has to recognize that countries and people differ in their approach to life
> and their ways of living and thinking . . . We have to use their language,
> not language in the narrow sense, but the language of the mind.
>
> Jawaharla Nehru in *Visit to America*

Origins of the Field

People always have had reasons to learn about other cultures. Cross-
cultural trade and commerce have existed since ancient times. The conflict between Christian and Moslem beliefs and values that preoccupied
much of Europe and the Middle East from the Crusades until about the
16th century was a negative type of cross-cultural encounter. Marco
Polo's account of his trip through Asia in 1274 sparked new interest in
foreign lands and customs on the part of Westerners. The Age of Exploration that began around 1400 brought many societies throughout
the world into sudden contact with each other. The establishment of
commercial and colonial empires by western powers in the 1700s intensified the day-to-day interaction between people from vastly different backgrounds.

The Protestant missionary movement of the 1800s created new interest in the customs and lifestyles of other civilizations. The emergence
of the modern nation-state raised awareness of cultural identity as borders were drawn between and around various ethnic groups. And ultimately, the revolution in transportation and communications during
the past century radically reduced the psychological boundaries between all countries.

Unfortunately, the history of cross-cultural relations is filled with
misunderstandings, intolerance, friction, and conflict. Seeing others as
adversaries, exploitable labor, or potential religious converts seems to
have long been the norm. Only recently have the knowledge and the intellectual tools needed to systematically promote mutual acceptance
and positive interaction among people from different cultures been
available.

During the past 50 years, the academic disciplines of anthropology,
sociology, psychology, linguistics, comparative management, and communications all have contributed to the development of the intercul-

tural field. The international experience of corporations and humanitarian, religious, and development organizations also has provided important input. The twin engines of business globalization and the communications technology revolution are currently spurring the growth of intercultural services.

The field is a relatively new area of endeavor being defined by a fledgling profession. Providers are typically rushing to meet the pressing needs of their clients. They also have the challenge of working with their colleagues to establish a generally accepted set of qualifications, approaches, tools, and standards that is the hallmark of a fully recognized profession. At this stage of its development, the field is still very malleable and open to fresh ideas, innovative techniques, and new practitioners. To comprehend these dynamics and to understand the interculturalists with whom you will deal, it is useful to have a basic grasp of the history of the field.

History of the Field

The profession began shortly after World War II. There have been three major periods in its history. Prior to about 1980, cross-cultural services were delivered mostly to nonprofit or governmental organizations. From 1980 to 1990, the market for corporate intercultural training emerged and developed. In the post–1990 period, the field has matured considerably and has gained increasing acceptance and sophistication.

The Early Years

The Experiment for International Living (now World Learning), founded in 1932, was an early pioneer in the field. "Thunderbird" (The American Graduate School of International Management) and the US State Department's Foreign Service Institute were established in 1946. These organizations were the first to focus on the cross-cultural challenges facing expatriates and international travelers. By the late 1950s, they were joined by the Centre for International Briefing in England and the Business Council For International Understanding in the United States. Academic-style orientation programs and briefings were the norm for the preparation of expatriates during this era. It was not until the establishment of the Peace Corps in 1962 that systematic cross-cultural training was designed.

During the 1960s, feedback from former Peace Corps volunteers and other expatriates dramatized the difficulties of overseas adaptation and performance. This "reality check" motivated training designers and trainers to experiment with a wide variety of nontraditional approaches that went beyond lecture-based instruction. Role playing, feedback, simulations, case studies, sensitivity groups, personal encounter sessions, and experiential cultural exploration activities such as village visits and home stays were tried. The Center for Research and Education, a major Peace Corps training contractor at the time, helped legitimatize and popularize many of these new methods.

The lessons learned during this creative era were summarized in the four-volume *Guidelines for Peace Corps Cross-Cultural Training* written by Albert R. Wight, Mary Anne Hammons, and William L. White in 1970. This was the seminal work that sparked much interest in intercultural services and became a model for the practitioners and organizations that established the new field. A major step toward the development of the profession was the founding of the Society for Intercultural Education Training and Research (SIETAR) in 1975. It has held annual conferences since then and has become the worldwide association of intercultural specialists.

The vast majority of the training during the 1970s in the United States was done in noncorporate settings such as the US Navy, the Department of State, and the Peace Corps. During this period, several universities started cross-cultural communications programs. Articles and books on intercultural topics began to appear. The Stanford Institute for Intercultural Communication was founded in 1976 and began offering workshops for business consultants, counselors, and educators. Also during that year, the *International Journal of Intercultural Relations* and its editor, Dan Landis, sought to bring a scholarly influence to the field.

The need for predeparture preparation of expatriates was gradually becoming recognized. In 1977, the Overseas Briefing Center was established to train US government employees and their families assigned abroad. The publication of the landmark books *The Cultural Environment of International Business* by Vern Terpstra in 1978, *Managing Cultural Differences* by Philip Harris and Robert Moran in 1979, and *Culture's Consequences* by Geert Hofstede in 1980 helped bring the intercultural field to the attention of the corporate world.

The Emerging Corporate Market

Although a few multinational corporations made use of the orientation programs available in the 1960s and 1970s, intercultural services did not start to gain momentum in the private sector until about 1980. Major companies doing business internationally became more aware of and concerned about the high cost of failed expatriate assignments. They were also receiving feedback from their returning expatriates regarding the difficulties of life and work abroad. Systematic international assignee selection and structured cross-cultural training were seen by these corporations as potential ways to increase their competitiveness and the cost-effectiveness of their cross-border operations while simultaneously improving employee morale.

At the same time, providers developed new training models more appropriate for a corporate clientele. These designs included a combination of practical information, cultural awareness building, feedback, and the development of communication and relationship skills. Interactive techniques, such as case-study analysis, problem-solving exercises, and role-plays were added, but the excesses of sensitivity and encounter group training (fairly common in the 1960s) were avoided. Seminars were shortened in length and made more intensive than the earlier academic-style orientations. This new generation of programs was based more directly on business situations and examples. Focus on country-specific culture became the norm. Most providers tried to tailor their training to the requirements of individual clients.

During the 1980s, many more articles on cross-cultural business topics appeared in the popular press, academic journals, and professional association magazines. This was also a time when numerous books on globalization and international management were being published. In 1982, the Intercultural Press was founded and made a variety of cross-cultural learning resources easily available to end-users and service providers. Likewise, many professional and business conferences featured presentations and workshops that raised the level of cultural awareness in the private sector.

Despite the increased publicity, the level of usage of cross-cultural training rose only slowly. Most corporate clients during the 1980s were large companies long engaged in overseas business. A survey of major US international firms by the Center for Research and Education in 1981 indicated that 33 percent of the respondents purchased training for their expatriates. A similar survey by Runzheimer International 10 years later reported a figure of 43 percent. The market undoubtedly would have appeared much smaller if a representative sample of companies of all types and sizes had been surveyed rather than only large, international ones.

Nevertheless, the demand was sufficiently strong to attract many new practitioners to the field. By 1987, the Intercultural Communication Institute was established to continue and expand the work of the Stanford Institute. It soon became the preeminent provider of intensive professional training for trainers and consultants. There was a proliferation of new cross-cultural training companies. Most of today's leading intercultural training and consulting firms got their start during the 1980s.

Growth and Diversification

The field began to come of age during the 1990s. The challenge of globalization increased the demand for intercultural services of all types on the part of international organizations and corporations. In 1991, Gulf Publishing Company launched the Managing Cultural Differences series to meet the needs of cross-border personnel. At the beginning of this 21st century, this series encompasses some 12 titles, of which this book is one.

The number and variety of books and other resources for intercultural learning increased dramatically during the decade. The creation of BAFA BAFA, a popular cross-cultural simulation game, by Garry Shirts and the production of the seven-part *Going Global* video series by Lenny Copeland and Lewis Griggs made intercultural learning more accessible and enjoyable for many people. These products were the forerunners of many other tools and resources.

During the 1990s, providers gradually established a solid record of well-received programs. A survey of 177 corporations by Windham International and NFTC in 1998 found that 70 percent of them were using some form of cross-cultural training and that 85 percent of the respondents viewed these programs positively. Another survey the same year by Prudential Relocation International reported that 89 percent of the respondents felt cross-cultural preparation should be made mandatory by their companies.

The continual growth in demand attracted still more providers. Vendors have had to differentiate themselves from their competitors. Consequently, the types of services and products offered have diversified, and the materials used to sell and deliver them have become more sophisticated and professional-looking. Likewise, the standard of customer service was raised. Competitive pressure has promoted quality awareness, innovation, and specialization. Unfortunately, the abundance of options has also caused some purchasers to view the services as interchangeable commodities and has made it more necessary than ever for the buyer to be discriminating.

As the field gained acceptance and popularity, a number of companies that provide language training, moving and storage, relocation, insurance, and accounting assistance to international assignees entered the marketplace. These providers "bundled" intercultural services with their own by forming consortia with cross-cultural training firms, using them as subcontractors or, in some cases, buying them outright. These new middlemen increased the usage of intercultural services by selling them to their existing clients. However, they also made the market more complex by creating another tier of sellers that acted as intermediaries between end-users and the primary providers.

The decade of the 90s also saw the rapid growth of a related field in the United States—domestic diversity training. It has roots in the US legal environment and has been oriented toward Equal Opportunity and Affirmative Action legislation and sexual harassment and racial prejudice issues. Nevertheless, many of its fundamental concerns pertain to cultural and ethnic differences. Therefore, a growing overlap exists between diversity training and the intercultural field. A few practitioners work in both fields, and some books and instructional tools are designed to apply to both. More importantly, the blending of global intercultural challenges with domestic diversity issues in the workplace has set the stage for productive cross-fertilization and collaboration. This development is addressed by Dr. Philip R. Harris is his article, "Diversity in the Global Work Culture," in *Equal Opportunities International*, Volume 15, Number 2, 1996.

During the 1990s, many corporations experienced major downsizing that resulted in the shrinking of their international human resource and training departments. In response, several vendors introduced the concept of outsourcing intercultural services. Under this arrangement, the providers were delegated the responsibility of managing and administering their clients' programs in addition to delivering them. This solution was promoted as a means of giving essential support to expatriates and international business travelers despite the reduced head counts of the human resources and training departments. In some instances, providers established on-site centers or placed employees at their clients' locations to manage the delivery of these services.

New Developments and Trends

Several developments during the 1990s will likely influence the direction of the intercultural field during the next decade. Being aware of these trends will enable you to anticipate new ways your company or organization can make use of intercultural services.

Although the worldwide expatriate population is expected to continue to rise, the average number of expatriates per company is declining as progressively smaller companies enter the global business arena. The Windham/NFTC survey mentioned earlier reported that the number of responding companies with 25 or fewer expatriates (54 percent of the total) was substantially larger than in previous years. These smaller companies usually have less international sophistication and smaller training budgets than do larger firms. Therefore, providers will need to offer them more basic services.

Political turmoil and natural disasters have increased the need for peacekeeping forces and for relief and refugee assistance agencies to deploy their personnel on short notice to very difficult locations around the world. These people usually face extreme cross-cultural challenges. Finding feasible ways to help prepare them for that aspect of their humanitarian missions is an important task confronting the intercultural service field.

The profession is expanding into new areas. Providers have discovered applications for intercultural insights and techniques to fields such as law enforcement (see Shusta, Levine, Harris, and Wong *Multicultural Law Enforcement—Strategies for Peacekeeping in a Diverse Society,* Prentice Hall, 1995), conflict resolution, executive recruitment, marketing and sales, electronic communications, entertainment, the travel industry, and health care.

A 1998 survey of medical schools conducted by the Association of Medical Colleges found that 67 percent of the schools responding had established courses in cultural competence and that 15 percent planned to add it to their curricula. The Cultural Competence Initiative of the American Medical Association (AMA) has as its goal " . . . to create behavioral and institutional changes that will enable physicians to provide individualized, patient-centered care that reflects the multiple cultures of their patients." An important step in that direction was the publication, in 1999, of the AMA's *Cultural Competence Compendium*, a comprehensive collection of cross-cultural guidelines and resources for physicians.

The Society for Human Performance in Extreme Environments is considering the impact of cultural issues on multinational technical teams operating in isolated, confined environments on land and under the sea. Dr. Philip R. Harris even anticipates a need for intercultural services in space with the establishment of culturally diverse off-planet colonies and space exploration crews. See his *Living and Working in Space*, Chinchester, UK: Wiley-Praxis, 1996, for details. This process of finding new uses for intercultural knowledge and expertise is very likely to continue into the foreseeable future.

All the developments mentioned previously encourage segmentation of the market. Providers will need to establish niches for themselves in which they can best meet the diverse requirements of clients of different sizes and types. The vendors that offer to accept any and all assignments will find themselves becoming increasingly "generic" and vulnerable to competitors that specialize in a particular area.

Another significant change is that training program designs now tend to rely more on research than they have in the past. With the exception of Geert Hofstede's work, little scientifically rigorous research on intercultural topics relevant to business was available until the 1990s. A review of cross-cultural management research from 1971 to 1980 by Dr. Nancy J. Adler of McGill University was reported in the *Academy of Management Review* in 1983. She concluded that this type of research was in its infancy. A review of similar studies conducted between 1982 and 1992 was published in the Spring 1994 *Human Resources Quarterly* in which Carol D. Hansen and Ann K. Brooks still used the term "infancy" to describe the level of the research being done. However, a recent increase in the quantity and quality of research should help enhance the credibility and relevance of intercultural services available in the next decade.

New technologies undoubtedly also will have an impact on the field. In particular, they will influence the modes of delivery and the accessibility of services. The first generation of interactive CD-ROMs is already on the market. Country-specific orientation programs are being offered online. Expatriate counseling and coaching services may be obtained via teleconferencing and e-mail. Virtual multicultural teams are being formed and supported globally within many international companies. The Internet has become a rich source of useful information on all countries worldwide. Standardized or custom-tailored documents on business protocol and practices in different cultures can be posted on company intranets. These new options are not likely to replace face-to-face training programs, but they are sure to compete with them. Ultimately, perhaps, they will generate still more demand for intercultural services.

A development that may have far-reaching impact on intercultural training in the future is the recent establishment of worldwide guidelines for quality management of training by the International Organization for Standardization (ISO). This non-governmental organization based in Geneva, Switzerland, has developed globally accepted quality standards in the manufacturing and service industries. Its new 14-page ISO 10015: 1999 document undoubtedly will influence the requirements that international corporations and organizations set for their training providers. Intercultural training firms that become ISO-certified may have a competitive advantage.

Learning About the Field

SIETAR, the professional society, divides the field into education, training, and research. This segmentation accurately reflects the main interests of its members although individual practitioners may fall into more than one of the categories. Nevertheless, distinguishing between these three areas is a useful starting point if you want to become oriented to the intercultural field.

Educators

Intercultural educators, of course, are located at academic institutions. Although they may work as consultants, trainers, or speakers from time to time, their main contributions to the field are through their thinking, writing, and teaching. Many universities and colleges use their facilities and faculty members to offer courses and seminars on intercultural business topics. Book publishers have responded to the professors' need for cross-cultural teaching aids. For example, Gulf Publishing has issued instructor's guides for both its *Managing Cultural Differences* and *International Business Cases*, and Prentice Hall has an instructor's manual for its text, *Multicultural Law Enforcement*.

Courses at universities and colleges generally have academic rather than pragmatic perspectives. Nevertheless, attending these classes may be a useful way for you to become broadly acquainted with the concepts and content of the field. Drawbacks for many business people are that the courses typically are somewhat prolonged, that they are given on the educational institutions' premises, and that they have fixed schedules not set for the convenience of a particular client. For these reasons, busy international managers with intensive travel demands may find academic programs difficult to use.

Trainers and Consultants

Intercultural trainers and consultants are a much more diverse group. They may work as independent practitioners, collaborate on projects with a few colleagues on an ad hoc basis, participate full-time in small entrepreneurial enterprises, or become employees of established training and consulting companies. Their backgrounds, experience, and credentials vary greatly. The training companies also have very different organizational cultures, philosophies, and management styles. It is important that you find trainers who are compatible with your company's or organization's mode of operation.

The programs they offer tend to be relatively brief, intensive, practical, and flexible. These usually are scheduled at the client's convenience. They can be delivered at the provider's site, at your facilities, and at other locations. Most suppliers are happy to make presentations or do demonstrations for potential buyers. However, the heterogeneity of the training providers may make it difficult for you to identify the most suitable ones.

Researchers

Intercultural researchers are more difficult to identify as a group. With a few notable exceptions, they work in academic settings. Their research topics range from the practical to the esoteric. During recent years, however, many surveys and studies have focused on ways to improve cross-cultural learning and to increase intercultural business effectiveness.

Researchers normally have the knowledge and skills required to design and conduct needs assessments, survey expatriates' and international employees' opinions and morale, and to audit a company's overall intercultural performance. They can give you sound advice to help avoid the common mistakes new purchasers make when selecting services. But their level of expertise and expense may be more than is required if your needs are simple and straightforward. Qualified researchers are often found in the departments of anthropology, communications, sociology, and international business. Increasingly, the title "professor of cross-cultural management" is found in business schools.

Other Alternatives
In addition to consulting with members of the three groups already listed, you have other alternatives for exploring the intercultural field. These include attending the public seminars and presentations offered by World Trade Centers, state, regional and local international trade organizations, chambers of commerce, and other international business associations, many of which are focused on specific countries or regions of the world.

Likewise, you have opportunities to attend workshops and presentations on intercultural business topics at the conferences of professional associations. Several of these, such as the American Society for Training and Development, the Society for Human Resource Management, and the Employee Relocation Council, have established international interest groups that have their own meetings and conferences. In addition, service providers occasionally present public demonstrations of their programs as a marketing technique.

The most direct way for you to become acquainted with the intercultural field, however, is to attend the annual SIETAR conference. These conferences are usually held in the spring at interesting locations around the globe. The conference is a week in length and additional preconference workshops are available. A wide variety of presentations and demonstrations are available. Perhaps more importantly, you will have many opportunities to network informally with practitioners of all types.

Explorers who are interested in a more in-depth and rigorous introduction to the field may find the week-long intensive workshops of the Summer Institute for Intercultural Communication suitable. The Intercultural Communication Institute offers these learning experiences during a three-week period in July. Workshops at different levels are available on many topics. These workshops are taught by some of the leading specialists in the field.

Terminology and Jargon

The beginning of wisdom is to call things by their right names.

Chinese proverb

Before starting to use this book or beginning to explore the intercultural field, you should familiarize yourself with frequently used words and expressions. Some of these have special meanings and particular connotations among intercultural practitioners. The task of interpreting and understanding the materials given to you and presentations made to you will be much easier if you share a "common language" with providers. The most common jargon in the field is defined in the following list. Most of the terms are explained in much greater depth in Chapters 2–4.

Common Intercultural Terms

✦ *Culture:* The shared set of learned beliefs, values, assumptions, attitudes, and behaviors that differentiates a particular group of people from others. In practice, interculturalists often have their own preferred definitions of culture and enjoy debating the meaning of the word.

✦ *Physical culture:* Those creations, artifacts, products, tools, structures, and other material things made by a people which express their unique cultural identity.

✦ *Surface culture:* The readily apparent aspects of a culture such as social customs, mannerisms, dress, music, cuisine, and business rituals.

✦ *Deep culture:* The hidden, intangible dimension of culture that underlies and "drives" the surface culture. It includes beliefs, values, assumptions, and expectations.

✦ *Cross-cultural:* Pertaining to interactions, transactions, and communications between different cultures, usually referring to two cultures.

✦ *Multicultural:* Same as *Cross-cultural* but pertaining to more than two cultures.

✦ *Transcultural:* Transcending or going beyond a particular set of cultural boundaries.

✦ *Intercultural:* Among or between cultures. This term is often used interchangeably with cross-cultural and multicultural or may combine them.

✦ *Interculturalist:* A person who specializes professionally in the intercultural field.

✦ *Culture shock:* A sudden onset of symptoms of stress caused by tension accumulated during the cultural adjustment process.

+ *Cross-border:* Referring to transactions, communications, and relations across national borders. This term is interchangeable with international.

+ *Multinational corporation:* A company that has largely autonomous operations in multiple countries while providing general direction and control from a worldwide headquarters.

+ *Global/transnational corporation:* A company having a worldwide network of operations among which traditional headquarters functions are distributed.

+ *Globalization:* The trend toward the creation of an interdependent world economy.

+ *Foreign/foreigner:* These terms literally mean "from another country," but they tend to have the negative connotations of "alien" or "outsider" among practitioners in the intercultural field. Consequently, these terms have become somewhat politically incorrect.

+ *Expatriate:* Anyone who is living and working temporarily outside of his or her own country. This term applies to people of all nationalities regardless of where they may be assigned and is preferred over "third-country national" and "inpatriate" as these words imply that a particular country is the center of the world.

+ *Host-country nationals:* The local people with whom an expatriate lives and works in his or her country of assignment.

+ *Repatriation/re-entry:* Returning to one's own country following an international assignment.

+ *Overseas/abroad:* Terms meaning "in another country," not necessarily "beyond an ocean." They have a rather old-fashioned connotation.

+ *Third Culture Kids (TCKs):* Children of expatriates, who tend to mix the cultural values of their homeland with those of the host countries to which their parents were assigned.

+ *Accompanying partner:* A person who has a primary relationship with an expatriate and who lives abroad with him or her. This may be a spouse or a companion of either sex. The term replaces the expressions "trailing" or "following" spouse and recognizes the possibility that the partner may be of the same sex as the expatriate.

Mini-Case: One Company's Experience

All experience is an arch to build upon.

Henry Brooks Adams in *The Education of Henry Adams*

A practical way for you to start your exploration of the intercultural field is to consider the actual experience of an international corporation and try to determine which services would have helped it handle its cross-cultural challenges and opportunities more effectively. The case described in the following paragraphs is based on well-documented information and first-hand accounts. It includes, in a highly summarized way, situations the company faced in several countries over an extended period of time. The managers of this company used a variety of intercultural services from different providers to successfully confront the cultural issues in their cross-border operations.

Which services and products would you have selected and why? As you read the case story, I suggest that you make a list of your choices and the reasons for them. It may be interesting to compare your observations and conclusions with the recommendations I would give to the company. A summary of these is located in the appendix.

Details of the Case

During the past 30 years, the international business of a major US clothing manufacturer grew briskly. The worldwide demand for its products was strong, and overseas sales became a significant part of its annual income. Like most companies in the industry, it moved much of its purchasing and manufacturing offshore to reduce production costs. Senior managers had to continually rush to keep abreast of the rapid globalization of the corporation's business.

Large numbers of international travelers were required to negotiate agreements, establish commercial relationships, oversee suppliers, provide technical and management support, train local employees, monitor operations, and troubleshoot problems. In addition, they and many home office staff were in constant phone, fax, and e-mail communication with people in other countries, some of whom they had never met face-to-face. They also had frequent visits from international customers, vendors, partners, and employees. Some of them admitted that they felt like they were "winging it" much of the time during their intercultural interactions.

Many US expatriates from a wide variety of technical and business backgrounds were deployed to manage its widespread interests and ventures. They and their families encountered the normal range of challenges and difficulties in adjusting to life and work abroad. Most of them adapted to the cultures of their host countries well enough to be productive and were generally satisfied with their assignments. However, some reached only a marginal level of performance, and a few returned home early due to cultural maladjustment. Several of these returnees and even some others who had completed successful overseas assignments left the company.

A certain amount of expatriate failure and turnover was considered normal. But the burgeoning costs of international assignments made even a small number of aborted ones seem like a large waste of corporate resources. Furthermore, the retention of employees who had experience abroad was important to the company's future global business goals. Avoiding their loss was considered a way to protect the considerable investment the company had made to enable them to gain that experience.

For many years, the company treated its off-shore suppliers as mere vendors. Long-standing problems of missed delivery dates, as well as quantity and quality variances, existed. Despite its clout as a major buyer, the company discovered that suppliers occasionally gave priority to the orders of their other customers, including competitors. More seriously, there were reasons to believe that some of them were failing to live up to the company's ethical standards regarding the workplace environment and the treatment of employees. The company decided to promote closer teamwork with its providers. It renamed the purchasers (all expatriates) Local Partner Relationship Managers and gave them appropriate new job descriptions and objectives.

Mini-Case Analysis Questions
1. What global business strategy and planning issues are involved in this case? _____

   How have they contributed to circumstances faced by the company? _____

2. Who are the key players? _____
   What are their responsibilities for improving the intercultural effectiveness of the firm? _____
   _____

   What are their needs? _____
   _____

3. Who are the stakeholders? _____
   What benefits can they receive by improving the company's intercultural performance? _____
   _____

   What are the risks and costs of not doing so? _____
   _____

4. What business opportunities are present? _____
   _____

   How can they be leveraged? _____
   _____

5. What are the major constraints and obstacles? _____
   _____

   How can these be removed? _____
   _____

6. Which intercultural services seem appropriate? _____
   _____

   Which ones do you most recommend? _____
   _____

7. What is the rationale for employing the services you recommend? _____
   _____

The cross-cultural issues and challenges in this case are not unique or exotic. In fact, they are quite typical of those faced by any organization "going international." What is notable are the creative and the effective ways in which the company dealt with them by combining in-house resources and assistance from intercultural service providers. Successfully managing the cultural dimension of its business has made it a stronger competitor and a more attractive international employer. How these results can be achieved by your company or organization is the subject of the rest of this book.

Focus Questions
- ☑ Why are you interested in intercultural services? For practical application to an immediate need, long-range strategic planning, or personal learning and professional development? Another reason? A combination of these?
- ☑ Are you sure that cultural factors significantly contribute to your company's international business difficulties?
- ☑ Which chapters or sections of the book seem most relevant to your needs and interests? How do they relate to your job? Which ones should you read first?
- ☑ Who else in your organization might be interested in discussing the topics contained in the book? What is the best way to invite them to join you?
- ☑ Does it also make sense to involve intercultural service providers in your discussions? If so, how?
- ☑ Are there any internal or external resources you could use to supplement or expand on the topics in the book?
- ☑ What does the history of the intercultural field tell you about the practitioners, the profession, and the marketplace for services? How can you apply these insights to your role as a purchaser?
- ☑ How many needs for intercultural services did you identify in the case description? Which ones?
- ☑ Does your organization or company have similar needs? If so, how can you use this book to make your colleagues aware of those needs?

Summary and Suggested Action Steps

This chapter is an introduction to the book as a tool for your use as a buyer of intercultural services. It includes the language you need to better understand the book itself and to communicate more effectively with providers and practitioners. The chapter is meant to open the door to the field by giving you a bit of its lore, history, and jargon. By presenting a realistic case description, it also offers you an opportunity to contemplate the actual issues and challenges that underlie the need for intercultural services and poses questions to consider as you read the rest of the book.

Here are some ways you can use the content of this chapter:

✓ Follow the suggestion to browse through the chapters and identify the topics of most interest to you. Make a check list of these and use them to guide your reading of the book.
✓ Review the list of terminology and jargon before reading proposals and marketing materials from vendors or attending presentations by them.
✓ Discuss the history of the intercultural field and its current state-of-the-art with service providers. Form your own picture of what the field has to offer your company or organization.
✓ Invite a few colleagues to meet with you occasionally to discuss the issues or ideas raised during your reading of the book.
✓ Do the exercise of trying to identify all the intercultural services that would have been helpful to the company in the case description.
✓ Review the resource list at the end of the chapter and highlight the references or organizations you may want to use to go beyond the scope of this book. Assign an assistant or an intern to scan the resource lists in all the chapters and to locate those of most interest to you.
✓ Make a personal plan for exploring the intercultural field. Contact the appropriate organizations and people and arrange to attend conferences or seminars that will enable you to deepen and broaden your knowledge.

Resources

The following are suggestions for further information on intercultural learning.

Organizations for Networking

American Citizens Abroad (ACA), 5 Bis rue Liotard, CH–1202, Geneva, Switzerland, tel: (41–22) 340–0233, e-mail: acage@aca.ch and Web site: http://www.aca.ch. This is a nonprofit association dedicated to serving and defending the interests of US citizens worldwide. It is useful for networking and exchanging practical information about issues affecting expatriates.

American Society for Training and Development (ASTD), 1604 King Street, PO Box 1443, Alexandria, VA 22313–2043, tel: (703)

683–8100, e-mail: csc4@astd.org and Web site: http://www.astd.
org/. The members of this organization are mostly trainers and training
managers from the private and public sectors. It has an international
professional practice group and sponsors an annual conference focused
on international and intercultural training issues and topics.

Employee Relocation Council (ERC), 1720 North Street, NW,
Washington, DC 20036, tel: (202) 857–0857, fax: (202) 467–4012,
e-mail: info@erc.org and Web site: http//www.erc.org/. ERC is a professional membership organization composed mostly of corporate relocation managers and service providers. It sponsors an annual
conference on international relocation at which intercultural service
providers frequently make presentations.

The Federation of American Women's Clubs Overseas (FAWCO), a
not-for-profit organization with clubs in 34 countries, FAWCO USA,
PO Box 448, Marfa, TX 79843, e-mail: arconinn@iglobal.net and Web
site: http://www.fawco.org/ on the Internet. International headquarters
are at Nassaulaan 1, 3818 GM Amersfoort, the Netherlands, tel: 31–
33–4–618–211 and fax: 31–33–4–652–937. This organization informally assists expatriate women with cultural orientation and
adjustment.

International Association for Cross-Cultural Psychology, Dr.
Theodore Singelis, Department of Psychology, California State University, Chico, CA 95929–0234, tel: (530) 898–4009, fax: (530) 898–
4740, e-mail: iaccp@csuchico.edu and Web site: http://www.fit.edu/
campuslife/clubs-orgfs/iaccp/. This professional organization has more
than 700 members in more than 65 countries and may be a source of
cross-cultural counselors.

*The International Society for Intercultural Education, Training, and
Research* (SIETAR USA), 573 Bayview Street, Yarmouth, ME 04096–
9751, tel: (207) 846–9598, fax: (207) 846–0763, e-mail: ici@inter
cultural.org and mdpusch@aol.com, Web site: http://208.215.167.139/
index.html. SIETAR is the worldwide professional association of interculturalists. It hosts conferences that offer the opportunity for learning at all levels and for networking with practitioners. It also publishes
a referral directory.

National Foreign Trade Council, Inc. (NFTC), founded in 1914, is an
organization composed of some 550 major multinational employers including corporations, law firms, accounting firms, and international
business and human resource advisory companies. It is located at 1270

Avenue of the Americas, New York, NY 10020–1700, tel: (212) 399–7128, fax: (212) 399–7144, e-mail: BJFONT@aol.com and Web site: www.usaengage.org/background/nftc.html. Among its services, the NFTC offers presentations on expatriate policies and practices for senior-level international human resources executives and sponsors surveys on topics of interest to them.

Society for Cross-Cultural Research, c/o Leigh Minturn, Department of Psychology, University of Colorado, Boulder, CO 80302, tel: (303) 440–4342, fax: (303) 492–297, e-mail: lminturn@psych.colorado.edu and Web site: http://www.fit.edu/campuslife/clubs-org/sccr/. This organization is composed of social scientists engaged in cross-cultural research from a multidisciplinary perspective.

Society for Human Resource Management (SHRM), 1800 Duke Street, Alexandria, VA 22314, tel: (703) 548–3440, fax: (703) 535–6490, e-mail: shrm@shrm.org and Web site: http://www.shrm.org/. This organization has an Institute for International Human Resources that hosts an annual conference that includes presentations on intercultural issues and topics.

The Summer Institute for Intercultural Communication, 8835 SW Canyon Lane, Suite 238, Portland, OR 97225; tel: (503) 297–4622, fax: (503) 297–4695, e-mail: ici@intercultural.org and Web site: http://www.intercultural.org. A variety of open enrollment seminars on intercultural topics at all levels is offered by the Intercultural Communication Institute.

Publishers

HRD Press, 22 Amherst Road, Amherst, MA 01002–970, tel: (800) 822–2801, fax: (413) 253–3490, e-mail: info@hrdpress.com and Web site: http://www.hrdpress.com/. This publisher is a good source of books on international human resources topics.

HR Press, PO Box 28, Fredonia, NY 14063, tel: (800) 444–7139 and (716) 672–4254, fax: (716) 697–3177, e-mail: hrpress@netsync.net and Web site: http://www.hrpress-software.com/index.html. This publishing house has numerous books and instructional aids in the area of workforce diversity.

Gulf Publishing Company, PO Box 2608, 3301 Allen Parkway, Houston, TX 77019–1805, tel: (800) 231–6275 and (713) 529–4494, fax: (713) 520–4433, e-mail publications@gulfpub.com and Web site:

http://www.gulfpub.com/book/mcd/mcd.html. Gulf Publishing offers books on a variety of intercultural business topics through its Managing Cultural Differences series.

Intercultural Press, Inc., PO Box 700, Yarmouth, ME 04096, tel: (800) 370–2665, fax: (207) 846–5181, e-mail: interculturalpress@ internetmci.com and Web site: http://www.bookmasters.com/interclt/ index.html/. Intercultural Press sells a wide range of books, videos, games, simulations, and other intercultural learning materials.

MCB University Press, 60/62 Toller Lane, Bradford, West Yorkshire, UK, BD8 9BY, tel: 44–0–1277–777700, fax: 44–1274–785200, e-mail: dmartinex@mcb.co.uk and Web site: http://www.mcb.co.uk. This publisher offers more than 100 journals, many of which are oriented toward international management and human resources topics. It has numerous electronic databases and online resources.

Sage Publications, 2455 Teller Road, Thousand Oaks, CA 91320, tel: (805) 499–0721, fax: (805) 499–0871, e-mail: customer-service@ sagepub.com and Web site http://www.sagepub.com. Sage publishes intercultural titles, many of which are texts or reference books for academic courses.

A Few Introductory References

Black, S. J., and Gregersen, H. B. *So You're Going Overseas: A Handbook for Personal & Professional Success*, San Diego, CA: Global Business Publishers, 1998.

Copeland, L., and Griggs, L. *Going International: How to Make Friends and Deal Effectively in the International Marketplace*, New York: Random House, 1985.

Dahlén, T. *Among the Interculturalists: An Emergent Profession and Its Packaging of Knowledge*, Stockholm, Sweden: Stockholm University Press, 1997.

Harris, P. R., and Moran, R. T. *Managing Cultural Differences.* (5th ed.) Houston: Gulf Publishing Company, 2000.

Hess, D. J. *The Whole World Guide to Cultural Learning*, Yarmouth, ME: Intercultural Press, 1994.

Kohls, L. R. *Survival Kit for Overseas Living* (3rd ed.) Yarmouth, ME: Intercultural Press, 1996.

Storti, C. *Figuring Foreigners Out: A Practical Guide*, Yarmouth, ME: Intercultural Press, 1998.

Periodicals

The Art of International Living, 12427 Hedges Run Dr. #107, Woodbridge, VA 22192, tel: (703) 494–9757 fax: (703) 494–6487, e-mail: ArtIntLvng@aol.com and Web site: http://www.artintlving.com. This bimonthly publication is dedicated to topics of interest to expatriates and their families.

Cross Cultural Letter to International Managers is a pamphlet-style newsletter on intercultural business topics. It is published 10 times per year by the Institute of Cross Culture Communication, Riversdown House, Warnford, Hampshire, SO32 3LH, UK, tel: 44–1962–771–111, fax: 44–1962–771–105, e-mail: iccc@crossculture.com.

Cross-Cultural Research, Sage Periodicals Press, 2455 Teller Road, Thousand Oaks, CA 91320, tel: (805) 499–0721, fax: (805) 499–0871, e-mail: customer-service@sagepub.com and Web site: http://www.sagepub.com. This academically oriented quarterly journal is dedicated to research in the intercultural field.

Cultural Diversity at Work, The GilDeane Group, 13751 Lake City Way N.E., Suite 106, Seattle, WA 98125–3615, tel: (206) 362–0336, fax: (206) 363–5028, e-mail: editors@diversityhotwire.com and Web site: http://www.diversityhotwire.com/index.htm. This bimonthly publication features articles on domestic diversity and international cross-cultural topics.

Cultural Dynamics is an interdisciplinary journal published by Sage Publications, 2455 Teller Road, Thousand Oaks, CA 91320, tel: (805) 499–0721, fax: (805) 499–0871, e-mail: customer-service@sagepub.com and Web site: http://www.sagepub.com. It includes articles from sociology, psychology, philosophy, and communication studies that relate to socio-cultural issues.

Culture and Psychology is an interdisciplinary journal published quarterly by Sage Publications, 2455 Teller Road, Thousand Oaks, CA 91320, tel: (805) 499–0721, fax: (805) 499–0871, e-mail: customer-service@sagepub.com and Web site: http://www.sagepub.com. It focuses on individual and societal dimensions of psychology within the context of culture.

The Edge: The E-Journal of Intercultural Relations, is a quarterly online publication from HART-LI Communications, c/o William Hart, Department of Communication, Old Dominion University, Norfolk, VA 23529. It contains articles, essays, interviews, and reviews on a broad range of intercultural topics. You may contact HART-LI Communications via telephone (575) 683–3834, fax: (575) 683–4799, by e-mail at wbhart@hart-li.com and view the journal at its Web site: http://kumo.swep.com/biz/theedge/.

European Journal of Cultural Studies is published by Sage Publications, 2455 Teller Road, Thousand Oaks, CA 91320, tel: (805) 499–0721, fax: (805) 499–0871, e-mail: customer-service@sagepub.com and Web site: http://www.sagepub.com. It is an interdisciplinary forum focused on European cultural issues and cross-cultural relations.

The Expatriate Management Update, 100 Euclid Avenue, Hastings, NY 10706, tel: (914) 478–4616, fax: (914) 478–4509, e-mail: llyn clague@aol.com and Web site: http://members.aol.com/expatmgmt/index.htm/. This monthly newsletter provides information on expatriate program management topics and frequently highlights intercultural service providers.

The Expatriate Observer, Organization Resources Counselors, Inc., Rockefeller Center, 1211 Avenue of the Americas, New York, NY 10036, tel: (212) 719–3400, fax: (202) 729–5625, e-mail: info@orc.com and Web site: http://www.orcinc.com/. This quarterly newsletter deals with issues and concerns of international assignees and their families.

International Journal of Cultural Studies is published by Sage Publications, 2455 Teller Road, Thousand Oaks, CA 91320, tel: (805) 499–0721, fax: (805) 499–0871, e-mail: customer-service@sagepub.com and Web site: http://www.sagepub.com. It is an academic journal that features research on cultural realities from a multidisciplinary perspective.

The International Journal of Intercultural Relations, Elsevier Science, PO Box 882, New York, NY 10159, tel: (888) 437–4636 or (212) 633–3730, fax: (212) 633–3680 and e-mail: ijir@olemiss.edu and Web site: http://www.elsevier.nl/locate/ijintrel/. This quarterly journal contains mostly scholarly articles on intercultural communications and relations.

Journal of Cross-Cultural Psychology is published by Sage Publications, 2455 Teller Road, Thousand Oaks, CA 91320, tel: (805) 499–0721, fax: (805) 499–0871, e-mail: customer-service@sagepub.com and Web site: http://www.sagepub.com. This academic journal is published six times annually.

Journal of Transcultural Nursing is published in association with the Transcultural Nursing Society by Sage Publications, 2455 Teller Road, Thousand Oaks, CA 91320, tel: (805) 499–0721, fax: (805) 499–0871, e-mail: customer-service@sagepub.com and Web site: http://www. sagepub.com. It includes articles on the relationship between culture and health care.

Transcultural Psychiatry is a quarterly research-based journal published by Sage Publications, 2455 Teller Road, Thousand Oaks, CA 91320, tel: (805) 499–0721, fax: (805) 499–0871, e-mail: customer service@sagepub.com and Web site: http://www.sagepub.com. It is aimed at mental health professionals.

Worldwide Business Practices Report, International Cultural Enterprises, Inc., PO Box 514, Deerfield, IL 60015, tel: (800) 626–2772 and (708) 945–9516, fax: (708) 945–9614, e-mail: ice@mcs.com and Web site: http://www.businessculture.com/. This monthly publication features practical articles on the cross-cultural aspects of doing business in many different countries.

2

Key Intercultural Concepts

A nation's culture resides in the hearts and in the souls of its people.

Mahatma Gandhi

Culture: Whats, Hows, and Whys

The all-pervasive power of culture shapes what people believe and value, how they think and feel about themselves, others, and the world, and why they act toward each other the way they do. Yet culture is invisible, unless one has the knowledge, concepts, and categories necessary to make it reveal itself. These intellectual tools are essential professional assets of today's global business people and international managers. They are also the keys that open the door to success within an intercultural environment.

Understanding the Core Concepts

Culture hides more than what it reveals, and strangely enough what it hides, it hides most effectively from its own participants.

Edward Hall

This chapter is an introduction to the fundamental concepts that will help you recognize your company's international cross-cultural business challenges and opportunities. It will give you a basic understanding of the core ideas that underlie the programs and products that have been developed to help clients meet their challenges and benefit from their opportunities in the global business environment. Also, it will enhance your communication with service providers by establishing essential common points of reference with them.

The impact of culture on international business ventures is felt in many ways. The broadest issues have to do with the nature of culture itself, the specific cultural differences confronted in the particular countries or regions where your company or organization's projects are located, the challenge of cross-cultural communications, and the process of cultural adaptation. Gaining awareness of these four fundamental areas is a solid basis for appreciating culture as a critical factor and for recognizing when there is a need for intercultural services.

What Is Culture?

Within your home culture, there is little or no incentive or need to focus on culture consciously. It is normally accepted, without reflection, as "just the way things are." Yet culture has a potent impact on all the stakeholders in the international business environment. Therefore, the first step in gaining cultural awareness is simply to recognize culture's presence and power. Failure to confront this basic reality allows it to continue being an invisible but omnipresent obstacle undermining even the best-intentioned efforts to achieve international business success.

It is useful for you, as a buyer of services, to know how the term "culture" is used in the intercultural field. Academics and practitioners have defined culture in many ways. A comprehensive definition would include the following elements:

❑ Culture encompasses an identifiable group of people who share common values, beliefs, customs, and a distinctive way of life.
❑ Culture explains why these people tend to think, feel, communicate, and act the way they do.
❑ Culture is learned, mostly informally, within the social environment.

❑ Culture also includes the unique artifacts, language, art, music, drama, literature, folklore, cuisine, architecture, and other products of a people.
❑ Culture is an integrated whole, coherent and internally logical. It creates a unified worldview and mindset.
❑ Culture is not static but changes slowly due to the influence of other cultures and internal developments and innovations.

A common technique used to bring culture into conscious awareness and explore its implications is to depict it symbolically as a tree, pyramid, or iceberg (see Exhibit 2–1). These are simple and useful ways to address the general issues that culture raises.

The cultural iceberg model is used in Prudential's intercultural training programs. It contains a sequence of interdependent factors: perception, beliefs, values, assumptions, attitudes, expectations, and behaviors.

The key points illustrated by the iceberg model are

1. Most of culture is beneath the surface where it cannot be seen or easily understood. This "deep culture" can be an unforeseen and dangerous obstacle in a cross-cultural setting, just as it was the submerged part of the iceberg that sank the ship *Titanic*. A culture is hidden even from the people within it. Its shape and structure can be surmised only by observation and analysis of evidence that is accessible above the surface.
2. At the surface level, superficial similarities and patterns of behavior may belie significant differences between cultures at the deeper level. Such similarities include the use of English in international business, the adoption of western-style clothing in the office environment, the presence of worldwide fads and fashions, and the availability of fast foods, popular music, and commercial products from one's home culture. These apparent commonalities may mislead an expatriate or international business traveler into discounting important cultural differences.
3. A third lesson provided by the iceberg analogy is that the deep cultural forces that drive human behavior are linked to each other. Values (qualities generally accepted as good and worthwhile) shape many of the other attributes of culture. Perceptions are colored by

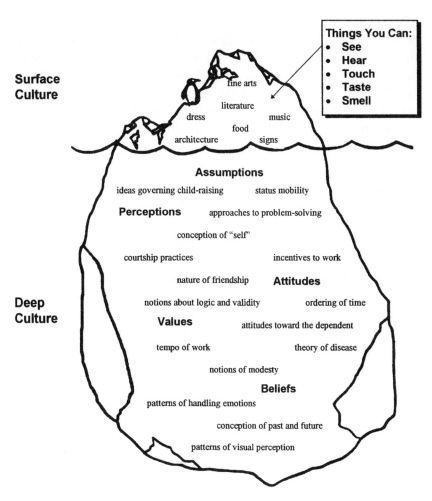

Things You Can:
• See
• Hear
• Touch
• Taste
• Smell

Surface Culture

fine arts

literature

dress   music

food

architecture   signs

Assumptions

ideas governing child-raising   status mobility

Perceptions   approaches to problem-solving

conception of "self"

courtship practices   incentives to work

nature of friendship   **Attitudes**

Deep Culture

notions about logic and validity   ordering of time

Values   attitudes toward the dependent

tempo of work   theory of disease

notions of modesty

Beliefs

patterns of handling emotions

conception of past and future

patterns of visual perception

EXHIBIT 2–1. THE ICEBERG CONCEPT OF CULTURE. (Source: Prudential Resources Management, intercultural program materials, Valhalla, NY, 1997.

beliefs and vice versa. For example, a loud, animated verbal exchange between two people in another country may be perceived by an American observer as a hostile encounter when it may actually be a friendly but excited conversation.

Beliefs and values mutually influence each other. In some cultures, the belief that the knowledge and wisdom of previous generations are still relevant today promotes the value of venerating elders and showing them a great deal of deference and respect. Assumptions reflect the attitudes and values that underlie them. One assumes meetings will start on time if there is a shared positive attitude toward punctuality. Gaining insight into how these hidden cultural factors work lays a systematic foundation for learning about any culture, including one's own.

Cultural Self-Awareness

An essential part of understanding culture and having a point of reference for confronting cultural differences is being aware of your own "cultural baggage." Introspection and self-contemplation are not stressed in the outward-looking and action-oriented US culture. Therefore, it is especially important that intercultural services for US Americans include an emphasis on cultural self-awareness.

Authors L. Robert Kohls, Edward C. Stewart, and Milton J. Bennett have contributed very useful insights into US cultural values. A list of the typical content of American "cultural baggage" includes

Individualism	Informality
Task/goal focus	Efficiency/productivity
Directness	Openness to change
Self-determination	Egalitarianism
Competitiveness	Content-focused communication
Punctuality	Bias for action
Pragmatism	Optimism

Individual Differences, Culture, and Human Nature

Discussions of culture are sometimes hampered by objections from those who resist the notion that culture is a significant influence on behavior. Some argue that individual differences, not cultural ones, explain why people act the way they do. Others stress that, "Underneath, we are all the same," so cultural differences do not really matter. Both of these viewpoints are flawed because they overstate the portion of truth each contains. Individual differences do explain much of human behavior, and at a biological level, all people do share common needs and drives. However, these facts in no way erase or reduce the importance of understanding the cultural roots of behavior. These twin objections may be resolved, and fruitless debate can be avoided by recognizing that all three factors play a role, as Exhibit 2–2 illustrates.

The following focus questions relate to the broad cultural context in which international business is conducted. These questions will help you apply the concepts and ideas presented in this chapter. Answers to these

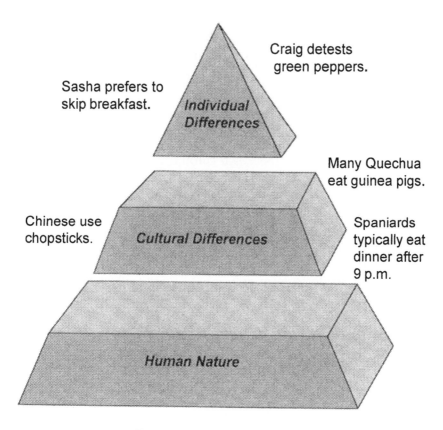

Craig detests green peppers.

Sasha prefers to skip breakfast.

Individual Differences

Many Quechua eat guinea pigs.

Chinese use chopsticks.

Cultural Differences

Spaniards typically eat dinner after 9 p.m.

Human Nature

Everyone needs to eat

EXHIBIT 2–2. INDIVIDUAL DIFFERENCES, CULTURE, AND HUMAN NATURE.

questions will give you a good starting point for discussing your company's needs with colleagues and potential intercultural service suppliers.

Core Concepts Focus Questions
- ☑ How well do the senior executives responsible for your company's global business ventures understand the nature of culture and its implications for cross-border business outcomes?
- ☑ Likewise, what is the level of cultural awareness and understanding of the employees who directly conduct international operations and those who interact and communicate, at long distance, with employees, partners, suppliers, and customers overseas?
- ☑ How seriously do they take culture as a significant factor contributing to their success or failure in managing international transactions?
- ☑ Are they unrealistically optimistic and overconfident about the ease of conducting cross-cultural business? Have they been misled by superficial similarities between cultures?
- ☑ Do they recognize individual versus cultural differences?
- ☑ Are they aware of their own cultural values, biases, assumptions, and expectations?
- ☑ Do they understand to what extent and how their "cultural baggage" influences the ways in which they communicate with and relate to people from other cultures?
- ☑ Do they realize how others are likely to view and respond to them?
- ☑ Are they interested in culture and motivated to learn more about it?

Understanding Cultural Differences

> By nature people are much alike. It is only their learning and habits that are so different.
>
> Confucius

The second area in which culture influences the success or failure of cross-border business is where interactions between the home culture and particular host cultures produce various kinds of mutual misunderstandings, friction, and stress. A prerequisite for comprehending the dynamics of cross-cultural differences and considering possible ways to manage them is to understand how and why cultures differ. It requires little perceptiveness to notice obvious differences in business and social etiquette or practices. However, such superficial observations do not provide much useful information about the underlying differences in expectations, intentions, and behaviors that are so disruptive in relations between people from different cultures.

A 1995 survey conducted by the NFTC and Selection Research International documented the impact of these kinds of differences on failed international assignments. The inability to adjust to new and novel conditions and the failure to communicate and interact effectively with local people were rated by 96 percent of the respondents as the leading causes of unsuccessful assignments. A similar study done the same year by Living Abroad Publishing, Inc. reported that the three most critical factors in failed expatriate assignments were the individual's inability to adjust to the host culture, the family's maladjustment, and cross-cultural difficulties on the job.

A 1997 Arthur Andersen survey of more than 400 expatriates looked at traits that contributed to successful international assignments. This survey found that the respondents rated the ability to combine the best elements of both the home and host cultures and to conform and adapt to the norms of the host country as the two most significant requirements for success. Therefore, both the positive and negative indicators clearly point to the need to manage cultural differences effectively.

How Cultures Differ

Most efforts by intercultural specialists to provide insights into cultural differences involve a process of contrasting cultural values. Several re-searched-based studies on the ways in which cultural values differ are available. These include the works of Geert Hofstede, Fons Trompenaars, and André Laurent. They reflect different approaches and methods, but they all compare particular value dimensions of specific countries.

Basic Value Contrasts

Some of the more important cultural value contrasts are

❑ Individualism versus group orientation
❑ Hierarchical versus egalitarian distribution of power

❑ Content-focused versus context-focused communication style
❑ Formality versus informality
❑ Punctuality versus flexible sense of time
❑ Task and goal orientation versus relationship orientation
❑ Holistic/deductive versus linear/inductive thinking
❑ Confrontation versus diplomacy
❑ Short-term versus long-term viewpoint
❑ Competition versus cooperation
❑ Self-determination versus acceptance of fate/circumstance
❑ Permissiveness versus strict rules
❑ Pragmatic flexibility versus adherence to detailed plans
❑ Achieved versus ascribed status
❑ Change as positive versus being undesirable
❑ Youth-orientation versus age-veneration
❑ Dominance over nature versus harmony with nature
❑ Male dominance versus gender equality
❑ Rigid class structure versus social mobility
❑ Favoring action and doing versus just being

Other value contrasts can be made. However, this list of 20 dimensions is sufficient to demonstrate the richness of comparisons possible. Awareness of the existence of these areas of potential misunderstanding and conflict is only a starting point for determining the specific differences likely to cause problems in a particular cross-cultural setting. For further details on cultural contrasts, you may want to read *Multicultural Management 2000* from Gulf Publishing Company's Managing Cultural Differences series.

The actual interaction difficulties depend entirely upon the unique set of values each culture brings to the interaction between them. One or more contrasts may emerge as key issues. For instance, US international business travelers and expatriates are likely to encounter characteristic value clashes in various countries as detailed here.

Typical US Cross-Culture Clashes	
Host Country Value	**USA Value**
Japan: Group orientation	Individualism
Guatemala: Flexible time sense	Punctuality
Saudi Arabia: Relationship focus	Task/goal orientation
Switzerland: Formality	Informality

India: Stratified class structure	Egalitarianism
China: Long-term view	Short-term view
Germany: Structured orderliness	Flexible pragmatism
France: Deductive thinking	Inductive thinking
Sweden: Individual cooperation	Individual competition
Malaysia: Modesty	Self-promotion

Valid Generalizations, Not Stereotypes

Although it is useful to make well-substantiated generalizations about the characteristic values of different cultures, it is dangerous to over-generalize and engage in stereotyping. An effective way to avoid this pitfall is to stay acutely aware of the fact that generalizations are valid only as statistical statements about large numbers of people. You should keep in mind that value contrasts are not either/or dichotomies, but rather descriptions of two cultures' overall tendencies to be nearer to or farther from a particular value orientation. Likewise, it is important to recognize that many countries, such as Belgium, Indonesia, South Africa, Spain, India, Russia, China, and Switzerland, have distinctive multiple cultures within their national borders.

Another good reason to have a bit of healthy skepticism regarding cultural generalizations is the fact that nearly all of the research upon which they are based has been designed and conducted by westerners, primarily in the United States and Europe. An exception is a survey of global values done by the Dentsu Institute of Human Studies, which is based in Japan. Between 1996 and 1998, the Dentsu Institute surveyed urban households in Britain, France, Germany, Sweden, the United States, Japan, China, Korea, Singapore, and India.

These studies seemed to confirm a few conventional western perceptions of Asian cultural values (group orientation, for example), but called others into question. Also, the overall similarities between western and Asian respondents were much greater than is usually presumed to be the case. In addition, in some cases, the differences between countries in Asia were larger than between them and the United States and countries in Europe. This data was reported in an article by Charles Wolfe, Jr. in the November 10, 1999, *International Herald Tribune* entitled "Asians' Values Seem Much Like Everyone Else's." This survey's results are a good caution against relying too heavily on cultural generalizations.

The strength of a value in any culture is distributed over a bell-shaped curve. In another culture, the same value dimension also will adhere to a bell curve. However, the norms between the two may be quite different. Noting the relative distance between the norms enables you to generalize about the potential difficulty members of one culture may have relating to members of the other culture along that dimension. Remaining aware of the exceptions to the norms at the ends of the curves and the possible overlap between the curves helps you to avoid stereotyping. The illustration in Exhibit 2–3 comparing two cultures' values regarding group identity and individualism makes this point graphically.

Scanning for Differences

It is advisable for you to scan to identify the particular cultural value contrasts that have the most bearing upon your company's international business activities. The list of 20 value contrasts mentioned previously in this chapter can be used as framework for conducting such a scan. This scan would reveal not only the types of differences encountered, but also in which countries the greatest cross-cultural obstacles are likely to be faced. A 1999 survey of 264 companies by Windham International, the NFTC, and the Institute for International Human Resources assessed which countries were most difficult for US expatriate assignments. Their rankings are listed here.

Difficult Assignment Countries

1. China	10. France
2. Russia	11. Saudi Arabia
3. India	12. Philippines
4. Indonesia	13. South Korea
5. Brazil	14. Malaysia
6. Japan	15. Nigeria
7. Mexico	16. Poland
8. Colombia	17. Singapore
9. South Africa	18. United Kingdom

A survey of 112 US leaders of business ventures in countries in eastern Europe and the Balkans was reported by Edward Dunbar in the

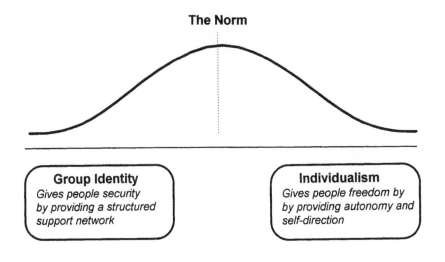

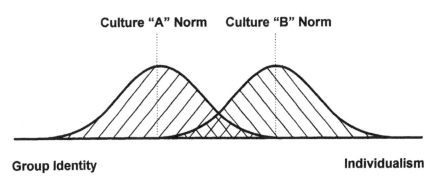

EXHIBIT 2-3. VALUE CONTRAST CURVES.

Handbook of Intercultural Training (Landis D., and Bhagat R. S.: Sage Publications, 1996). The respondents rated the difficulty presented by work-related cultural differences in the various countries on a five-point scale ranging from one being "not very challenging" to five being "very challenging." Their ratings show that they felt it was quite challenging to work in all of the countries:

Romania: 4.22   Latvia: 3.86
Czech Republic: 3.96   Bulgaria: 3.85
Poland: 3.92   Hungary: 3.84
Lithuania: 3.92   Finland: 3.72
Slovakia: 3.89   Estonia: 3.62

These two surveys clearly demonstrate the impact of cultural differences on both expatriate adaptation and cross-border business performance. This kind of data may convince decision-makers of the importance of identifying the major culture gaps faced in their organizations or companies' international operations. It also might help you gain approval to conduct a scan for cultural differences and to explore the necessity of acquiring intercultural services.

A scan may be conducted in-house, contracted to an outside consultant, or done via a combination of the two approaches. It can be based on written surveys, interviews, or focus groups of knowledgeable and representative international business travelers, host-country employees, and expatriates. If adequate cultural studies are available on the particular countries, they also may be used. In any case, the key to the usefulness of a scan is that it be systematic, thorough, and specific.

The scan should identify which cross-cultural situations need priority attention due to the presence of broader cultural gaps. It should provide practical input for the training and development of your international assignees, business travelers, and home office staff who routinely deal face-to-face or at long distance with people from other countries. Doing a country-by-country scan with external service providers is a good opportunity for you to test their qualifications and to start developing working relationships with them. In addition, a scan will contribute a great deal to your own learning and professional development.

Transcending Cross-Cultural Differences

The point of recognizing cultural differences and understanding the key concepts underlying intercultural services is to be able to transcend the differences for the benefit of your organization or company and its employees. Comprehending the ideas, gaining the knowledge, and mastering the skills will allow you to not only solve cross-cultural problems and overcome obstacles, but also to proactively develop powerful new tools for achieving international success. These new assets include techniques for effective cross-cultural communications, which are presented in the following list, intercultural synergy, which is covered in Chapter 3, and multicultural teamwork, which is discussed in Chapter 4.

Cultural Differences Focus Questions
- ☑ In which host countries are the cultural gaps the broadest?
- ☑ Have there been reports of misunderstandings, disagreements, or friction between international employees and their local counterparts?
- ☑ What particular themes or issues are most frequently mentioned?
- ☑ Have opportunities been lost due to failure to account for cultural differences?
- ☑ Are unexpected difficulties with the local workforce being encountered?
- ☑ Do expatriates and international business travelers frequently complain about host-country cultural values?
- ☑ Is their morale and productivity being negatively affected by cultural differences?
- ☑ Have host-country employees, partners, customers, or suppliers complained or hinted about problems with the expatriates, international business travelers, or home office staff who communicate with them via telephone, e-mail, and fax?
- ☑ If so, what are the specific issues and which value differences are involved?
- ☑ Do host national employees and expatriates claim that the home office does not understand the cross-cultural realities they face in their countries?

Cross-Cultural Communications

An understanding of cross-cultural communications can easily affect business transactions in the international marketplace. When an individual is familiar with a particular culture's mores and customs, he or she will earn the client's trust, avoid misunderstandings, and strengthen and expand business relationships.

William E. Simon
former US Treasury Secretary

One skill required to perform all cross-border functions is effective cross-cultural communication. Therefore, it is worthwhile to give this topic special attention. Understanding the concepts and issues that underlie communication across cultural boundaries will give you a better appreciation of the complexity and subtlety of the communication tasks your international employees face. Also, because it is a common need, it is likely to be a practical starting point for introducing intercultural services to your company for the first time.

The Communication Process

The word "communication" comes from the Latin *communicare*, meaning to share or make common. Sharing a common cultural background with another person makes communication relatively easy. Cross-cultural communication is far more challenging. A major part of the difficulty is that the focus and style of communications are strongly influenced by deeply held cultural perceptions and values. The parties communicating with each other take much for granted and rely on mutually shared assumptions about what to communicate to whom and when, where, and how. In the absence of a common set of cultural values and assumptions, miscommunication is frequently the result. Exhibit 2–4 contains a simplified model illustrating the challenge of effective cross-cultural communication.

In this illustration, a person from one culture conceives an idea and "encodes" it in a verbal and nonverbal message, and then transmits it to a person who has a different cultural background. The second person receives and "decodes" the message in order to grasp the thought intended. The encoding process includes considering the status and background of the recipient (friend, parent, boss, child, and so on) and selecting the words or gestures most likely to be understood accurately. This process is normally done without consciously thinking about it. Often people are not aware of all the messages they are sending, especially the nonverbal ones.

When the message is sent across the cultural boundary, a communications breakdown is likely because the message is "filtered" through a different set of beliefs, values, attitudes, perceptions, and assump-

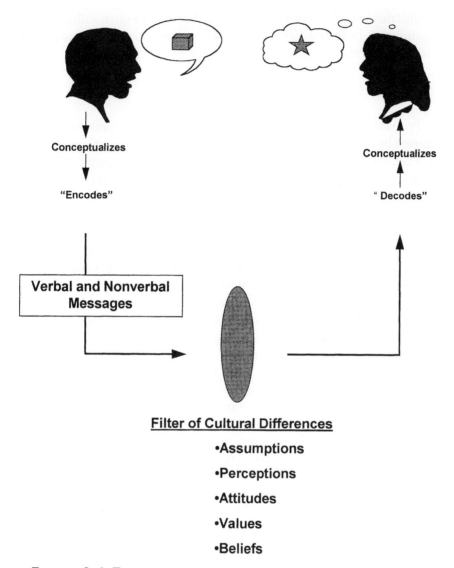

EXHIBIT 2–4. THE CROSS-CULTURAL COMMUNICATION CHALLENGE.

tions. Both the encoding and decoding are done in reference to one's own culture. Therefore, the message frequently is distorted during transmission. The communication challenge is identical when a message is sent in the opposite direction, which is usually going on simultaneously. Two of the most basic barriers to cross-cultural communication include differences in context versus content focus and the use of nonverbal language.

Context versus Content Focus

Probably the greatest impact on cross-cultural communication is caused by cultural differences in the focus of communications. Edward T. Hall, one of the founders of the intercultural field, classified the communications patterns of different cultures along a continuum from high-context and low-context. This concept is a powerful tool for understanding the dynamics of cross-border communications.

In high-context societies, the *context* (the external setting and the internalized cultural commonalties) in which the communications are taking place carries most of the meaning. The location, situation, and occasion plus the relationships, status, and roles of the people involved determine, to a great extent, what can be said to whom and where and how. Messages generally are implicit, symbolic, subtle, and indirect. They often rely on unspoken understandings, hints, social rituals, and nonverbal cues. The focus on the context is analogous to using a floodlight to broadly illuminate the scene in order to see all the surrounding details.

At the other end of the spectrum, low-context cultures focus intensely on the *content* of the communication. In these cultures, the facts, data, concrete information, numbers, dates, and unambiguous words carry most of the meaning. Communications generally are simple, explicit, precise, and direct. Message content is usually organized in a logical, linear way. Good communicators are clear and straightforward. There is much reliance on written documents and contracts. This type of communication is like using a spotlight to brightly illuminate a limited area in order to see small details.

Drawing from the work of Edward Hall, Robert Kohls, and others, Gary P. Ferraro has ranked 12 countries on the high-context versus low-context spectrum in *The Cultural Dimension of International Business* 2nd ed., Upper Saddle River, NJ: Prentice-Hall, 1994. His findings are illustrated in Exhibit 2–5.

These differences in the focus of communications have important implications for communications between people from different countries. For example, in the United States, communication tends to be relatively low-context. Common expressions and sayings such as "Don't beat

Low Context

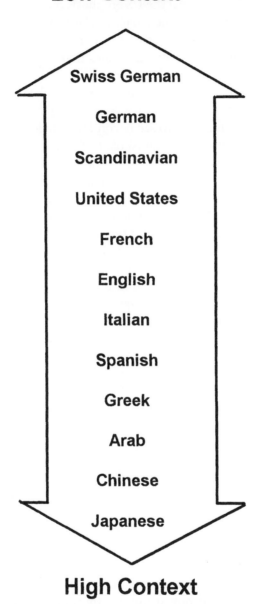

Swiss German

German

Scandinavian

United States

French

English

Italian

Spanish

Greek

Arab

Chinese

Japanese

High Context

EXHIBIT 2–5. THE CONTEXT FACTOR IN CROSS-CULTURAL COMMUNICATION. (Source: The Cultural Dimension of International Business, 2nd edition, by Gary P. Ferraro, ©1994. Reprinted by permission of Prentice-Hall, Inc., Upper Saddle River, NJ.)

around the bush," "Get to the point," and "Say what you mean and mean what you say" reveal the US emphasis on content above context.

In contrast, Mexico, which has a relatively high-context focus in communications, has a proverb, "Only drunks and small children always tell the truth." This saying implies that unless one is in an uninhibited condition or childishly naive, it is normal to avoid being totally candid. The Chinese sayings "Be aware of people's faces and observe the color hue of their voices" and "Those who keep on smiling seldom lose their teeth" stress the need to see beyond the obvious and to be discreet and diplomatic rather than plainspoken. When contextual factors such as personal relationships, image, and reputation are highly important in one's culture, a high-context communication focus makes sense.

This difference in communication styles explains why US managers often consider their Mexican counterparts overly rhetorical and "flowery" in the way they speak and write and why they complain that the Mexicans always tell them what they want to hear. It also contributes to westerners' impression that the Chinese are "inscrutable." On the other hand, the Mexicans frequently find their US counterparts impersonal and "cold," and complain that they are too single-minded and blunt. The Chinese are likely to consider US Americans somewhat simplistic and naive. This kind of communications gap is also characteristic of relations between US business people and their Japanese, Malaysian, Indonesian, and Arab colleagues. Likewise, it often causes US managers to be surprised by the frankness of the Germans and Dutch who often are even more low-context focused in their communications than they are.

Nonverbal Communication Differences

The second major barrier to cross-cultural communication is due to cultural differences in "body language." It is important to understand the impact of nonverbal communications on cross-border roles and relationships because a great deal of valuable information is sent and received on the nonverbal channel, especially in high-context societies. In these cultures, how people feel about themselves and others, how they reveal their emotions, motivations and intentions, and how they signal their status and power are mostly transmitted nonverbally. To understand these messages and respond to them appropriately, you need to be aware of the nature of nonverbal communications, have adequate observation skills for detecting the unspoken cues, and know the meaning of the culturally specific signals and gestures.

Nonverbal communication can be called a language because it has a structure and set of rules analogous to a grammar and a "vocabulary" of generally accepted meaning-bearing gestures and cues that function like words. The structure of nonverbal language consists of categories that may be used to observe and analyze nonverbal interactions, as illustrated in the following examples.

Nonverbal Communication Dimensions

❑ Eye contact: Avoidance of eye contact in Japan is used to show respect and deference. However, Arabs often establish and maintain intense eye contact as a sign of interest and respect.

❑ Facial expressions: Venezuelans may squint and wrinkle their noses to indicate lack of understanding. Filipinos raise their eyebrows to signal "yes." Smiles in Japan may express embarrassment and discomfort rather than happiness.

❑ Hand/arm gestures: In many cultures, it is impolite to point with the index finger. The OK sign made by forming a circle of the thumb and index finger is obscene in Brazil, as is the two-fingered victory gesture in England and Australia.

❑ Posture: The Japanese have an elaborate ritual of bowing to display status and acknowledge relationships. Crossing one's legs in a way that allows the bottom of the shoe to be seen by others is offensive in Saudi Arabia.

❑ Interpersonal physical distance: In the Middle East, people tend to stand very close to one another in face-to-face conversations. Northern Europeans need a lot more space.

❑ Touching and body contact: In Latin America and the Middle East, touching others while talking to them is a sign of acceptance and friendliness. Men and men and women and women often walk arm-in-arm. Touching another person with the left hand is taboo in parts of Asia and the Middle East.

❑ Use of space: The location of desks in an office and the seating arrangement in meetings in Japan indicate hierarchy. In many countries in Europe and the United States, the size and location of one's office display status.

❑ Personal appearance, dress, and grooming: Wearing shorts in public, except at the beach, is considered inappropriate in many countries in Asia. Women in much of the Middle East show virtue by dressing modestly. Beards are an indication of radicalism in some cultures and conservatism in others.

❏ Time-related signals: High-level Latin American officials or executives may arrive late to a meeting to indirectly demonstrate their importance. In Scandinavia, strict punctuality is a required sign of responsibility and respect in social and business situations.
❏ Meaning of symbols, objects, and colors: In Japan and Korea, the number four is considered unlucky and the color white represents death. The Chinese consider letter openers or scissors inappropriate gifts because they would symbolize severing a relationship. Some cultures use only certain kinds or colors of flowers to express romantic intentions, condolences, or congratulations.
❏ Use of silence: In the United States, long silences in conversation are awkward and uncomfortable. During meetings in Japan, silence may be a positive sign of reflection and concentration.

Nonverbal Business Interactions

Situations involving greetings and business protocol inevitably have many nonverbal gestures and cues. There may be elaborate rules for the order of introductions, shaking hands, bowing or embracing, the seating arrangement, the exchange of business cards, and the giving and receiving of gifts. Other important areas of business such as conducting negotiations, selling, interviewing, making presentations, and giving feedback also require cross-cultural nonverbal communications awareness and skill.

The examples in the preceding list only begin to point to a few of the abundant risks of confusion, misunderstanding, and hurt feelings arising from faulty nonverbal communications between cross-border business counterparts. As a purchaser of intercultural services, you should be sure that your providers' programs and materials include the full range of nonverbal communication dimensions, cover the major pitfalls, and that they are country-specific.

Cross-Cultural Communications Focus Questions
☑ Are your employees who have cross-border roles and responsibilities aware of the cross-cultural communications requirements involved? If not, is this lack of awareness an obstacle in the performance of their roles?
☑ Do they understand the impact of cultural differences in context versus content focus and nonverbal language?

☑ Have communication problems been caused by these differences?

☑ If so, are these problems recognized as being serious enough to require remedy?

☑ Would more knowledge and skills in these areas be helpful to your employees?

☑ Are they motivated to receive training and development in cross-cultural communications?

☑ Does your company or organization provide this type of training and development? If not, why not? Does it have plans to do so?

Cross-Cultural Transitional Experiences

When one is uprooted, transplanted, there is a temporary withering.

Anais Nin

It is difficult to adapt to living and working in another country or to deal regularly and intensively with people from a different culture. Many unavoidable and frequently unexpected challenges, pitfalls, and obstacles are encountered. Both the inevitability of the challenges and the surprising aspect of them are due to the nature of culture itself. The unique, deep, and largely hidden cultural programming of the individual makes it likely that any *other* culture will seem strange, incomprehensible, and even somewhat threatening at first.

Stages of Intercultural Sensitivity

In a 1986 article in *the International Journal of Intercultural Relations*, Milton J. Bennett identified six distinct developmental stages of intercultural sensitivity. This model illustrates how an individual may gradually evolve from an ethnocentric viewpoint to one of "ethnorelativism." Each stage represents a way of experiencing and reacting to cultural differences. The stages are

1. Denial of the existence of differences
2. Defense against the perceived threat of the differences

3. Minimization of the significance of the differences
4. Acceptance of the reality and importance of the differences
5. Adaptation of one's thinking and behavior in confronting the differences
6. Integration of the differences into one's own viewpoint and behavioral patterns

For cross-border businesses, this adaptation process is much more than a matter of academic interest. A 1995 survey of human resource managers of 72 major international companies by Prudential Intercultural Services found that the respondents ranked cross-cultural adaptability the most critical factor in success of expatriate assignments. Significantly, it was ranked even above job, technical, and management skills.

Therefore, it is helpful for you to examine the adaptation process for specific challenges that may be addressed by intercultural services or products. A common approach to the issue of cross-cultural adaptation includes the presentation and discussion of the causes and symptoms of cross-cultural stress plus an explanation of "culture shock" and the adjustment pattern that expatriates typically go through during an international assignment.

Cross-Cultural Stress

According to well-accepted theories and research in the field of psychology, stress is the inevitable result of any change that requires a new adaptive response on the part of the individual. Within one's familiar cultural environment, the magnitude and pace of change are normally manageable by the individual. However, in a new cultural environment, the frequency and intensity of the changes dramatically increase. As a consequence of these new demands, the level of stress increases.

A classic study of life changes by psychologists T. H. Holmes and R. H. Rahe found that even positive and welcomed changes cause stress. They determined that people who experienced too many changes, of any kind, in too short a period of time, had significantly higher risks of developing psychological and physical illness. On a physiological or emotional level, cross-cultural stress is no different than the ordinary stress present in one's home culture. It is the causes that differ. The cross-cultural sojourner typically is surprised by these novel stresses and unprepared to deal with them. In addition, familiar and reliable strategies and techniques for dealing with stress may be unavailable or inappropriate in the new environment.

Causes of Cross-Cultural Stress

Cross-cultural stress is caused by a combination of challenges in the external environment and the expatriates' emotional reactions to them. Listed here are examples of both kinds of stresses commonly reported by people living and working abroad.

Environmental Challenges

❏ The challenge of adjusting to a new physical environment including different climate, sanitation, and health conditions
❏ The impact of unfamiliar sights, sounds, smells, and foods
❏ Being confronted with differences in language and communication styles
❏ Having to adapt to unaccustomed schedules and routines for eating, sleeping, working, resting, and socializing
❏ Encounters with different cultural values and beliefs that may be confusing or contrary to one's own

Emotional Challenges

❏ Missing emotional support resources from home, especially people and activities important to one's happiness
❏ Discomfort with local "body language," especially interpersonal touching and use of space
❏ Feeling awkward handling local etiquette in social and business settings
❏ Distress about the decline in one's level of competence and productivity due to cross-cultural obstacles
❏ Sense of isolation from being an outsider and having no clear niche in the culture

Common Symptoms of Cross-Cultural Stress

Some symptoms of cross-cultural stress can be felt subjectively, and others are apparent to the people around the expatriate.

Subjective Signals

❑ Negative feelings about the local culture and people including irritability, hostility, and defensiveness
❑ Physical reactions such as changes in appetite, lack of energy, insomnia, excessive need for sleep, sexual dysfunction, stomach/digestive problems, and increased bodily tension
❑ Emotional symptoms like homesickness, nervousness, depression, uncharacteristic mood swings, anxiety, and anger
❑ Self-directed negativity including feeling overwhelmed and losing one's sense of confidence or self-worth

Visible Signs

❑ Self-damaging behavior such as reduced exercise, over-eating, sexual adventurism, and alcohol or drug abuse
❑ Social interaction problems such as increased marital friction and family conflict, withdrawal or exaggerated dependence, aggressiveness and domineering behavior, and inappropriate attention-seeking
❑ Dysfunctional work-related behaviors including indecisiveness, inflexibility, close-mindedness, hypersensitivity to criticism, impatience, boastfulness, and ridicule or excessive criticism of local counterparts and coworkers

Culture Shock

Kalervo Oberg, an anthropologist who served with a missionary organization in Brazil, coined the term "culture shock" in 1960. Since then, it has come into popular use far beyond the intercultural field. In the process, it has acquired so many different meanings that it has little precision. Various intercultural specialists have preferred words such as transition shock, ecoshock, culture fatigue, and role shock in attempts to give the concept more specific content. However, "culture shock" persists as the predominant term used to refer to the dramatic low period often experienced during the cultural adaptation process.

As a purchaser or user of intercultural services, you undoubtedly will read about "culture shock" and hear the term frequently. Therefore, you need to understand it. A practical definition is that culture shock is the point at which the normal functioning of an individual is significantly impaired by the accumulation of cross-cultural stress. Culture shock goes well beyond the shockingly exotic incidents or encounters that international travelers seem to enjoy recounting. Former expatriates often remember it as a major low point in their assignments.

Despite its popularity and face validity, the notion of "culture shock" should be tempered by an awareness of its limitations. The term emphasizes the negative and difficult aspects of cross-cultural adaptation. The implication is that "culture shock" is a kind of illness that may be prevented or cured rather than an essential and integral part of a transitional experience. And, this negative connotation obscures the consistently favorable feedback from expatriates about their international assignments.

The Arthur Andersen survey mentioned earlier found that respondents rated their overall satisfaction with their expatriate experiences an average of 4.1 on a 5-point scale. Keeping this essentially positive picture in mind will help prevent you from overreacting to "horror stories" of maladjustment that may be presented by some vendors to sell intercultural services.

Cultural Adjustment Patterns

Certainly not every international assignee experiences "culture shock." But it is clear from feedback from overseas transferees and international business travelers that the great majority of these people are affected by many cross-cultural stresses at some point. The emotional ups and downs of a typical expatriate assignment have been compared to a roller coaster ride. As a purchaser of intercultural services, you should be aware of these predictable mood swings.

Stages of Adjustment

You can identify several stages of adjustment in a typical assignment. The first phase is usually a high point reflecting the anticipation of excitement and adventure in the new environment. This point is often followed by a honeymoon period during which the newcomers are usually welcomed and assisted by local people or fellow expatriates. This high point may be maintained for a while by the stimulating novelty of the new sights, sounds, tastes, and experiences offered by the local culture. However, the difficulties and daunting challenges that lie ahead gradually become apparent, and the emotional pain of missing special people and lifestyle rewards left at home start to be felt more intensely.

These factors often lead to a marked drop in morale. The decline may be abrupt or not and may be deep or shallow at its low point. This phase tends to occur when the sobering realities of the hard work required to learn how to function personally and professionally in the new culture are confronted. This point is normally followed by a gradual upswing in spirit and self-confidence as cross-cultural insights and skills are gained and the cultural environment seems more comprehensible and familiar. However, numerous setbacks and breakthroughs are likely to happen along the way.

This recovery process has three major levels that you may be able to recognize and remember as the "three Cs." At the first level, expatriates tend to focus their energy on *coping* with the day-to-day challenges. The second level is reached when they are basically *comfortable* in the new environment. On the third level, they have gained the *competence* required to fulfill personal and job-related goals in culturally appropriate ways. Individual patterns of adjustment may differ considerably, but all expatriates discover that it takes time and effort to feel at home in the new culture. The Arthur Andersen survey mentioned previously found that the greatest number of respondents reported that it took 6 to 12 months for them to feel comfortable in their life and work in the host country.

Toward the end of the assignment, another high point often occurs that is caused by the anticipation of enjoying the pleasures of homecoming. However, unexpected adjustment challenges and disappointments frequently encountered after returning home contribute to another low point referred to as "re-entry shock." Expatriates are not fully reintegrated into their home cultures until this final phase of adjustment is completed. A 1996 study by the Conference Board reported that 40% to 50% of them leave their companies within three years of their return. This high attrition rate is due, in part, to the impact of repatriation stress.

Expatriate Adaptation Factors

The highs and lows of an international assignment are normal responses to the multiple and inevitable stresses involved. The cycles may be moderate or severe depending on many internal and external factors.

Internal Factors

❏ The psychological suitability of the employee and family members for an international assignment
❏ The extent to which their expectations are realistic
❏ The level and quality of their cross-cultural knowledge and skills
❏ Their family and marital stability
❏ Their ability to provide support to each other
❏ The quality of career path planning the employee has done

External Factors

❏ The kind and degree of cultural differences and novelty encountered
❏ The intercultural complexity of the job
❏ The living and working conditions
❏ The depth of involvement in the local culture required
❏ The presence or absence of satisfying lifestyles for the family members
❏ The level of adjustment support received in-country

By understanding the dynamics of the life-changing transition through which your international assignees are going, you will be able to offer empathetic and effective support to them. In many cases, merely helping them gain a better perspective of the process of cultural adaptation is very reassuring to expatriates and enables them to make sense of the powerful experience.

Cultural Adaptation Focus Questions

☑ Are there frequent complaints from expatriates and international business travelers regarding the local people or the working and living conditions in host countries?
☑ Are there hints of problems or criticism of their performance or social behavior from local colleagues and counterparts?
☑ Have home office supervisors noticed a significant drop in the productivity and morale of the expatriates and international travelers?
☑ Are they well selected and prepared for adapting to life and work abroad?

☑ Do they avoid socializing with the local people?

☑ Are the expatriates experiencing unusually high levels of emotional, marital, and family problems?

☑ Must international and local human resource managers invest an inordinate amount of time and energy dealing with their adjustment problems?

☑ Do they too frequently fail to complete their international assignments?

☑ Is an international assignment considered a positive career move?

☑ Are there excessive demands for salary, prequisites, and benefits to compensate for the challenges and difficulties of an international assignment?

☑ Do returning expatriates express overall satisfaction with their assignments?

☑ Do they report personal and professional learning and growth as a result of the international experience?

Summary and Suggested Action Steps

This chapter is an overview of the main concepts and ideas that underlie the intercultural field. It provides a set of mental tools and an introduction to the body of knowledge purchasers of intercultural services need in order to start to identify the cross-cultural issues and challenges faced by their companies. The nature of culture, cultural differences, cross-cultural communication, and the expatriate adaptation process are presented in sufficient detail to enable you to discuss these topics competently with colleagues and potential providers of services. The chapter also lays a foundation for understanding the cross-border organizational issues and roles presented in the following two chapters.

Here are some ways you can use the content of this chapter:

1. Reflect on the impact of culture on your organization or company's international operations and on its various business units. Recall significant past incidents of success and failure and assess them in terms of cross-cultural effectiveness.

2. Establish formal or informal groups of internationally experienced employees and use the focus questions as a basis for group discussions.
3. Use the list of 20 cultural differences to scan the host-countries in which your organization or company is operating to determine the specific cultural differences faced in each one. Interview host-country counterparts and employees well acquainted with the countries. Keep a record of their comments and reactions.
4. Debrief returned expatriates and international travelers to determine the extent to which cross-cultural stress affected their morale and performance abroad. Share the book's information on cross-cultural stress and adaptation with them. Gather feedback on their patterns of cultural adaptation and ask for their recommendations regarding the preparation of future expatriates and travelers.
5. Start a file of cross-cultural challenges and opportunities. Use the data from the country scan and the discussion groups as input for this file. Share this information with appropriate senior executives and human resource managers if you feel it is relevant to your organization or company's international performance.
6. Propose cultural awareness events such as sack lunch seminars featuring guest speakers, videos, and panel discussions involving international employees and visitors from the host-countries. Focus on the topics in this chapter. Also promote country awareness days on the special holidays of host-countries with cultural entertainment, food, and music, plus articles and announcements in your in-house newsletter and intranet.

Resources

General Intercultural Concepts

Bhawuk, D.P.S., and Triandis, H. C. "The Role of Culture Theory in the Study of Culture and Intercultural Training." In D. Landis and R. S. Bhagat (eds.), *Handbook of Intercultural Training*. (2nd ed.) Thousand Oaks, CA: Sage Publications, 1996, pp. 17–34.

Brake, T., and Walker, D. *Doing Business Internationally.* Princeton, NJ: Princeton Training Press, 1995, Chapter 2A, pp. 4–38.

"Bridging the Culture Gap," and "Beyond Culture Shock" from *Going International*, a seven-part video series completed in 1983 by

Griggs Productions, 5616 Geary Boulevard, San Francisco, CA 94121; tel: (800) 210–4200 and (415) 668–4200, fax: (415) 668–6004, e-mail Griggs@griggs.com and Web site: http://www.griggs.com. These videos are somewhat dated but are still useful on an introductory level.

Cavanaugh, G. F., Fisher, C. T., and Cavanaugh G. E. *American Business Values: with International Perspectives*. Englewoods Cliffs, NJ: Prentice Hall, 1997.

Cusher K., and Brislin, R. "Key Concepts in the Field of Cross-Cultural Training: An Introduction." In *Improving Intercultural Interactions: Modules for Cross-Cultural Training Programs*, Thousand Oaks, CA: Sage Publications, Inc., 1997, pp. 1–20.

Fontaine, G. *Successfully Meeting the Three Challenges of All International Assignments* is an online book posted on his Web site: http://www2.hawaii.edu/~fontaine/garyspage.html in 1998 by Gary Fontaine, University of Hawaii, Honolulu, HI 96822, tel: (808) 956–3335. See Chapters 1 and 2.

Marx, E. *Breaking Through Culture Shock: What You Need to Succeed in International Business*. Sonoma, CA: Nicholas Brealey Publishing Ltd., 1999.

Odenwald, S. B. *Global Training: How To Design a Program for the Multinational Corporation*. Homewood, IL: Business One Irwin, 1993, pp. 46–56.

Schwartz, S. H. "Values and Culture." In D. Munro, F. Schumaker, and S.C. Carr (eds.), *Motivation and Culture*. New York: Routledge, 1997, pp. 69–84.

Stewart, E. C., and Bennett, M. J. *American Cultural Patterns*. (Rev. ed.) Yarmouth, ME: Intercultural Press, 1991.

Cultural Differences

Axtell, R. A. *Do's and Taboos Around the World*. (3rd ed.) New York: John Wiley & Sons, Inc., 1993.

Dana, R. H. *Understanding Cultural Identity in Intervention and Assessment*. Portland, OR: Portland University Press, 1998.

Gannon, M. J., et al. *Understanding Global Cultures*. Thousand Oaks, CA: Sage Publications, 1994.

Giger, J. N., and Davidhizar, R. E. *Transcultural Nursing: Assessment and Intervention*. St. Louis, MO: Mosby-Year Book Inc., 1995.

"Global Contrasts." Video and workbook produced in 1996 by Griggs Productions, cited above and "Managing the Overseas Assignment" from the original *Going International* video series.

Gropper, R. C. *Culture and the Clinical Encounter: An Intercultural Sensitizer for the Health Professions.* Yarmouth, ME: Intercultural Press, 1996.

Hampden-Turner, C., and Trompenaars, A. *The Seven Cultures of Capitalism: Value Systems for Creating Wealth.* New York: Doubleday, 1993.

Harris, P. R., and Moran, R. T. *Managing Cultural Differences.* (5th ed.) Houston, TX: Gulf Publishing Company, 2000.

Hellman, C. *Culture, Health, and Illness,* Newton, MA: Butterworth & Heinemann, 1995.

Hickson, D. J., and Pugh, D. S. *Management Worldwide: The Impact of Societal Culture on Organizations around the Globe.* New York: Penguin Press, 1996.

Hofstede, G. *Cultures and Organizations: Software of the Mind.* (Rev. ed.) New York: McGraw-Hill Inc., 1997.

Inglehart, R., Basanez, M., and Moreno A. *Human Values and Beliefs: A Cross-Cultural Sourcebook.* Ann Arbor, MI: University of Michigan Press, 1998.

Irish, D. P., Lundquist, K. F. and Nelsen, V. J. (eds.), *Ethnic Variations in Dying, Death and Grief.* London: Taylor & Francis, 1993.

Klopf, G. F. *Intercultural Encounters.* Englewood, CO: Morton Publishing Company, 1991.

Laurent, A., and Van Maanen, J. "The Flow of Culture: Some Notes on Globalization and the Multinational Corporation." In S. Ghoshal and D.E. Westney (eds.), *Organizational Theory and the Multinational Corporation.* New York: St. Martins Press, 1993, pp. 275–312.

Lewis, R. L. *When Cultures Collide: Managing Successfully Across Cultures.* Sanoma, CA: Nicholas Brealey, 1996.

Martloustaunau, M. O., and Sobo, E. J. *Cultural Context of Health, Illness, and Medicine.* Westport, CT: Bergen & Garvey, 1998.

Morden, T. "International Culture and Management." *Management Decision,* No. 35, 1995, pp. 16–21.

Peterson, R. B. (ed.). *Managers and National Culture: A Global Perspective.* Westport, CT: Quorum Books, 1993.

Schneider, S. C., and Barsoux, J. L. *Managing Across Cultures.* London: Prentice Hall Europe, 1997.

Thiedermann, S. *Bridging Cultural Barriers for Corporate Success.* New York: Lexington Books, 1991.

Trompenaars, F. *Riding the Waves of Culture.* Burr Ridge, IL: Irwin Professional Publishing, 1994.

Cross-Cultural Communications

Axtell, R. A. *Gestures: The Do's and Taboos of Body Language Around the World.* New York: John Wiley & Sons, Inc., 1998.

Bennett, M. J. *Basic Concepts of Intercultural Communication: Selected Readings.* Yarmouth, ME: Intercultural Press, 1998.

Chan-Herur, K. C. *Communicating with Customers Around the World: A Practical Guide to Effective Cross-Cultural Business Communications.* San Francisco, CA: AuMonde International Publishing, 1994.

Gallois, C. and Callan, V. *Communication and Culture: A Guide for Practice.* New York: John Wiley & Sons, 1997.

Gudykunst, W. B., Ting-Toomey, S., and Nishida, T. (eds.). *Communication in Personal Relationships Across Cultures*, Thousand Oaks, CA: Sage Publications, 1996.

Lewis, R. D. *Cross Cultural Communication: A Visual Approach.* London: Transcreen Publications, 1999.

Lustig, M. W., and Koester, J. *Intercultural Competence: Interpersonal Communications Across Cultures.* (3rd ed.) New York: Harper Collins, 1996.

Munter, M. "Cross-Cultural Communications for Managers." Business Horizons, No. 36, 1993, pp. 69–78.

Niemeier, S., Campbell, C. P., and Driven, R. (eds.). *The Cultural Context in Business Communication.* Amsterdam: John Benjamins Press, 1998.

Ricard, V. *Developing Intercultural Communication Skills*, Melbourne, FL: Krieger Publishing Company, 1993.

Samovar, L. A., and Porter R. E. *Communication Between Cultures*, Belmont, CA: Wadsworth Publishing, 1991.

Samovar, L. A., and Porter R. E. (eds.). *Intercultural Communications: A Reader.* (7th ed.) Belmont, CA: Wadsworth Publishing, 1994, pp. 4–26.

Singer, M. S. *Perception & Identity in Intercultural Communications.* Yarmouth, ME: Intercultural Press, 1998.

Ting-Toomey, S. *Communicating Across Cultures.* New York: Guilford Publications, 1998.

Ulijn, J. M., and Campbell, C. P. "International Paragraphing: What Can Cultures Learn from Each Other in the Communicative and Managerial Field?" In B. Smieja and M. Tasch (eds.), *Human Contact Through Language and Linguistics,* Frankfort: Lang Verlag, 1997, pp. 491–500.

Urech, E. *Speaking Globally: Effective Presentations across International and Cultural Boundaries.* London: Kogan Page, Ltd., 1998.

Varner, I. I., and Beamer, L. *Intercultural Communication in the Global Workplace,* Burr Ridge, IL: Irwin Professional Publishing, 1995.

Wiseman, R. L. (ed.). *Intercultural Communication Theory.* Thousand Oaks, CA: Sage Publications, 1995.

Wiseman, R. L., Hammer, M. R., and Hishida, H. "Predictors of Intercultural Communication Competence." *Journal of Intercultural Relations,* Vol. 13, 1989, pp. 349–370.

Wiseman, R. L., and Koester, J. (eds.). *Intercultural Communication Competence,* Thousand Oaks, CA: Sage Publications, 1993.

Expatriate Adaptation

Anderson, L. E. "A New Look at an Old Construct: Cross-Cultural Adaptation" *International Journal of Intercultural Relations,* Vol. 18, No. 3, 1994, pp. 293–328.

Arthur Andersen, *A Study of the Expatriation/Repatriation Process,* New York: Arthur Andersen Worldwide, SC, 1997.

Arthur Andersen and Bennett Associates, *Global Best in Class Study,* New York: Arthur Andersen Worldwide, SC, 1997.

Aycan, Z. (ed.). *Expatriate Management: Theory and Research,* Greenwich, CT: JAI Press, 1997.

Bachler, C. J. "Global Inpats: Don't Let Them Surprise You." *Personnel Journal,* June 1996, pp. 54–58.

Bennett, R. "Family: The 'Make or Break' Issue in the International Assignment." *Mobility,* Feb. 1995, pp. 35–39.

Blohm, J. M. *Where in the World Are You Going?* Yarmouth, ME: Intercultural Press, 1996.

Brett, J. M., and Stroh, K. M. "Willingness To Relocate Internationally." *Human Resource Management,* Fall 1995, Vol. 34, No. 3, pp. 405–424.

Brewster, C. "The Paradox of Expatriate Adjustment." In J. Selmer (ed.), *Expatriate Management: New Ideas for International Business.* Westport, CT: Quorum Books, 1995, pp. 137–156.

Conway, B. *Expatriate Effectiveness: A Study of European Expatriates in South-East Asia*, New York: John Wiley & Sons, 1998.

Digh, P. "The (Really) New Expatriates: Planning for the Changing Face and Mindset of Tomorrow's Global Employees." *Mobility*, Mar. 1998, pp. 41–45.

Expatriate Roundtable is a free monthly teleconference on expatriate issues offered by Integrated Resources Group, Bank One Building, Suite 505, 3444 North First Street, Abilene, TX 79603; tel: (915) 676–2290, e-mail: irg@expat-repat.com and Web site: http://www.expatforum.com.

Fishman, S. R. "Global Assignments: A Family Affair." *Canadian Business Review*, Vol. 23, Apr. 1, 1996, pp. 18–22.

Frazee, V. "Expert Help for Dual-Career Spouses." *Workforce*, Vol. 78, No.3, Mar. 1999, pp. 18–23.

Hepworth, J. C. *Things to Know About Americans*, Denver, CO: University Center, Inc., 1991.

Kalb, K., and Welch, P. *Moving Your Family Overseas*, Yarmouth, ME: Intercultural Press, 1992.

Khoury, J. "Ruminations from 'The Other Half': Expatriate Partners Tell It Like It Is." *Mobility*, Apr. 1999, pp. 39–42.

Kohls, L. R. *Survival Kit for Overseas Living.* (3rd ed.) Yarmouth, ME: Intercultural Press, 1996.

Lanier, A. *Living in the U.S.A.* (5th ed.) Yarmouth, ME: Intercultural Press, 1996.

McEvoy, G. M., and Parker, B. "Expatriate Adjustment: Causes and Consequences." In J. Selmer (ed.), *Expatriate Management: New Ideas for International Business*, Westport, CT: Quorum Books, 1995, pp. 97–114.

Means, L. K. "Unhappy in Paris? How Can That Be?" *Mobility*, July 1998, pp. 49–51.

Organization Resources Counselors, *1998 North American Survey of International Assignment Policies and Practices*, New York: ORC, 1998.

Pascoe, R. *Culture Shock: A Wife's Guide*, Portland, OR: Graphic Arts Publishing Company, 1992.

Peit-Pelon, N. J., and Hornby, B. *Women's Guide to Overseas Living.* (2nd ed.) Yarmouth, ME: Intercultural Press, 1992.

Perraud, P. B. "Career and Lifestyle Options for Relocating Spouses or Partners of Expatriated Employees." *Expatriate Observer*, Vol. 18, No. 3, Fall 1995, pp. 1–18.

Piker, F. K. "Attracting, Retaining, Motivating Senior-Level Expatriates." *Innovations in International HR*, Vol. 23, No. 3, Summer 1997, pp. 1–5.

Pollock, D. C., and Van Reken, R. E. *The Third Culture Kid Experience*, Yarmouth, ME: Intercultural Press, 1999.

Schell, M. S., and Solomon, C. M. *Capitalizing on the Global Workforce: A Strategic Guide for Expatriate Management*, Burr Ridge, IL: Irwin Professional Publishing, 1996.

Shepard, S. *Managing Cross-Cultural Transition*, Bayside, NY: Aletheia Publications, 1998.

Storti, C. *The Art of Crossing Cultures*, Yarmouth, ME: Intercultural Press, 1990.

Swaak, R. A. "Today's Expatriate Family: Dual Careers and Other Obstacles." *Compensation and Benefits Review*, May/June, 1995, pp. 21–26.

Wederspahn, G. M. "Foreign Assignment: USA." *Mobility*, Oct. 1995, pp. 87–90.

Wederspahn, G. M., and Wederspahn, A. "Overseas Assignment Without One's Spouse." *Mobility*, March/April 1998, pp. 67–70.

Wederspahn, G. M., and Wederspahn, A. "Single-Status Assignments: 9 Key Questions for Couples." *Expatriate Management Update*, Oct. 1996, pp. 3.

Repatriation

Austin, C. N. *Cross-Cultural Reentry: A Book of Readings*. Abilene, TX: Abilene Christian University Press, 1986.

Austin, C. N. *Cross-Cultural Reentry: An Annotated Bibliography*. Abilene, TX: Abilene Christian University Press, 1983.

Baughn, C. "Personal and Organizational Factors Associated with Effective Repatriation." In J. Selmer (ed.), *Expatriate Management: New Ideas for International Business*. Westport, CT: Quorum Books, 1995, pp. 215–230.

Berg, L. S. "Repatriation: The Expatriate Challenge," *Expatriate Observer*, Vol. 20, No. 2, Spring, 1997, pp. 1–9.

Black, S. J., Gregersen, H. B., and Mendenhall, M. E. *Global Assignments: Successfully Expatriating and Repatriating International Managers*. San Francisco: Jossey-Bass Publishers, Inc., 1992.

Bryson, B. *I'm a Stranger Here Myself: Notes on Returning to America After Twenty Years Away*. New York: Broadway Books, 1999.

The Conference Board. *Managing Expatriates' Return: A Research Report*. Report Number 1148–96-RR, New York: The Conference Board, Inc., 1996.

Engen, J. R. "Coming Home." *Training*, Mar. 1995, pp. 37–40.

RHR International "Repatriation: The Challenge of Coming Home." *Executive Insights*, Vol. 10, No. 1, 1997.

Shilling, M. "How to Win at Repatriation." *Personnel Journal*, Vol. 40, Sep. 1993, pp. 43–46.

Smith, C. D. *Strangers at Home: Essays on the Effects of Living Overseas and Coming "Home" to a Strange Land*. Bayside, NY: Aletheia Publications, 1996.

Soloman, C. M. "Repatriation: Up, Down or Out?" *Personnel Journal*, Jan. 1995, pp. 28–37.

Stoltz-Loike, M. "Ensuring Successful Repatriation: Solutions." *International HR Journal*, Winter, 1999, Vol. 7, No. 4, pp. 11–16.

Storti, C. *The Art of Coming Home*. Yarmouth, ME: Intercultural Press, 1997.

Wederspahn, G. M. "Home After the Range." *Export Today*, Apr. 1998, pp. 18–20.

3

Cross-Border Organizations

Globalization requires the inclusion of all cultural groups within the organizational framework.

> **Robert T. Moran, Philip R. Harris, and William G. Stripp** in *Developing the Global Organization: Strategies for Human Resource Professionals*

Organizational Border Crossing

As a result of the globalization of business, US firms are extending their organizations across national borders in ever greater numbers. Different stages of corporate globalization and various types of international relationships between companies present unique sets of cross-cultural challenges and opportunities. Cross-border joint ventures, alliances, and other intercompany enterprises all require managing cultural differences in organizational culture, structure, and practices. Likewise, the interface between these companies is laden with intercultural pitfalls. How well corporations manage the differences and avoid the pitfalls often makes the difference between global business success and failure.

Risks and Opportunities

> When globalization efforts fail, chances are it is because of a mistaken
> vision of the organization and the values needed for success. Too often
> we do not properly plant for the global harvest.
>
> **Kenichi Ohmae** in *The Borderless World*

Recognizing the Risk Factors

The cross-border reach of corporations has been growing rapidly for
the past two decades, and no end seems to be in sight. A 1996 survey
of 250 manufacturing and service companies by Cushman & Wake-
field Worldwide found that 70% of them were more likely to consider
international expansion than they were five years previously. This unprecedented international movement of commercial organizations is a
result of their quest for business opportunities on a global scale. However, significant risks also are involved. These are reflected by the high
failure rate of international alliances and joint ventures that has been
documented by several studies in recent years.

According to a 1995 Columbia University study, 57% of cross-
cultural joint ventures end in failure. Their average life span was only
three and a half years. A survey of 200 companies in 60 industries conducted by Larraine Segil, reported in the November 1998 issue of
Global Workforce magazine, stressed that cross-border alliances are
much more challenging than domestic ones. She found that they take
two to three times longer to create and at least half of them fail.
Seventy-five percent of the companies surveyed believed the failures
were caused by incompatibility of national or corporate cultures.

Many intercultural services are designed to help companies deal with
the cross-cultural consequences of transferring organizational cultures,
structures, and practices to other countries. Providers often stress the
importance of these kinds of services in their sales presentations and
marketing materials. Therefore, you should be acquainted with the cultural risks and challenges, as well as the opportunities that emerge in
cross-border organizational relationships.

On an organizational level, you must consider several factors when
deciding whether and how intercultural services can make a contribution to the success of your company's business ventures abroad. The
first of these is to understand why your organization or company is

"going international." Secondly, it is important to determine the stage of globalization that the company or business unit has reached. Another consideration is the nature and type of organizational relations and arrangements that are involved abroad. You should also be aware of the common cross-cultural issues and problems that surface when your employees must work in the corporate cultures of other countries. In addition, it is essential that you have a viable vision of a healthy intercultural organization.

Seeking Global Opportunities

Understanding why your company is engaging in cross-border business lays a foundation for considering how intercultural services may contribute to achieving your company's goals. Many motivations push or pull companies into the international business arena:

Market-Oriented
❑ Escaping limited growth opportunity in a mature domestic market
❑ Entering emerging affluent consumer markets abroad
❑ Establishing a presence in regional Free Trade zones
❑ Gaining distribution capacity through international joint ventures and alliances
❑ Following customers and clients abroad
❑ Confronting foreign competitors in their own markets
❑ Gaining global business experience
❑ Increasing product or service life-cycle through international sales

Production-Oriented
❑ Seeking lower production costs abroad
❑ Gaining access to international technology, capital, and human and natural resources
❑ Achieving greater economies of scale in production, logistics, and marketing
❑ Responding to investment inducements and tax advantages
❑ Lowering international transportation time and costs
❑ Sharing costs of research and development
❑ Making greater use of employees' expertise and skills
❑ Obtaining broader applications for current technologies

Few of these aspirations can be fulfilled without the effective use of appropriate cross-cultural awareness, knowledge, skills, and attitudes. Many of the requirements for different intercultural competencies depend on your company's international organizational relationships and stage of globalization.

The Globalizing Organization

> Global organizations . . . have shed their national identity, are highly adaptive to changes in the environment, and are extremely sensitive to all global trends that may affect the future. This is a very different and sophisticated form of organization, as well as business strategy. It requires a completely different mindset and very adaptable managers and corporate cultures.
>
> **Patricia Galagan** in "Executive Development in a Changing World" in *Training & Development Journal,* June 1990.

It has become very common for companies and organizations to claim in their annual reports and publicity materials that they are "global" or are "going global." It is much more rare for them to support this rhetoric with solid evidence that they understand what is entailed in the process of becoming global. Unfortunately, not all providers of intercultural services have sufficient clarity of understanding of the issues, challenges, and requirements to help effectively in their clients' efforts to globalize. Therefore, you need to have a fairly good grasp of the process yourself in order to evaluate globalization seminars that may be offered to you.

Stages of Globalization

In 1990, researcher and author Nancy J. Adler identified several stages through which a company or business unit goes as it becomes increasingly globalized. Many interculturalists have elaborated on these phases and explored their implications. They usually describe four or five transitional steps a company takes when evolving from a domestic to a global corporation.

The Domestic Stage

At the purely domestic stage, cross-cultural issues are limited to those caused by the ethnic diversity of the workforce and the marketplace. The company's goods and services are designed for the domestic market and produced by a domestic workforce. It functions in a national environment of standards, rules, and regulations. It may face competition and may purchase raw materials or subproducts from other countries, but these factors have little influence on the way it views itself or how it is organized and does its work.

The Export/Import Stage

As the company engages in import and export business deals, communications and relations with nondomestic customers, franchisees, suppliers, and distributors are new concerns. Knowing the rules regarding the international transfer of goods and services and dealing with the host national officials who interpret and enforce them become important to the company's success. Managers travel between the home-country and overseas locations. Cultural values pertaining to business relations and diplomacy, consumer tastes and preferences, quality assurance, and delivery deadlines are critical issues. Cross-cultural selling and vendor relations skills are needed. Hosting international visitors at the home office becomes necessary.

The International Stage

A third stage of internationalization occurs when a company begins moving production or assembly to other countries and has to deal with the local employees, labor leaders, and government agencies responsible for labor relations, environmental protection, and workplace safety. However, power remains concentrated at the home-country headquarters, and the company retains a strong national identity. Virtually all of the highest positions in the company are filled with people from the home culture. At this stage, expatriates may be assigned to the host-countries to set up and manage production, deliver technical training, and penetrate the local market. International business travel becomes more frequent and more culturally demanding. Frequently, the parent company initiates joint ventures and other types of business alliances with local corporations.

At this level, additional challenges, such as establishing and maintaining good relations with international partners and host-country community and business leaders, become important. More information about the history, culture, and political and economic conditions of the host countries is necessary. New cross-cultural skills are required to conduct international marketing, technology transfer, business protocol, and negotiations. Expatriate employee and family cultural adjustment issues become business concerns.

The Multinational Stage

At this stage of globalization, the company has established nearly self-sufficient operations in multiple countries or regions. The national entities act quite independently of one another. They are concerned, primarily, with the domestic business environment in their own countries. The major flow of communication is between each country and the corporate headquarters in the home country. The central parent company generally controls overall strategy, major policies, and resource allocation.

Decisions regarding local marketing, sales, manufacturing, distribution, customer service, and competitive tactics are made in the individual countries. The organizational structure, management style, business practices, and procedures conform to host-country cultural norms. For this reason, this stage is sometimes referred to as multidomestic. The local company's name and the brand names of its products may reveal its international origin, but efforts are made to "nationalize" its image. The national language is likely to be used most of the time in the workplace.

In mature multinational corporations, somewhat less need exists for international travelers and expatriates because of the relatively high degree of autonomy of the national operations. Those expatriates in-country generally are there to "work themselves out of a job" and not to perform ongoing functions. Recruiting and retaining local managers are high priorities. With less of a cultural gap between the local company and the host-country, there is not quite as much need for intercultural services as there is at the earlier international company stage. Nevertheless, important issues must still be addressed, such as improving cross-cultural understanding and communications between the corporate headquarters and the field, encouraging the local managers to adopt the home company's core vision, values, and ethics, transferring key technologies and skills, and dealing with problems of divided loyalties.

The Global/Transnational Stage

The global or transnational corporation is characterized by having multiple centers worldwide that are all networked with each other. Its identity and self-concept transcend its national origins. Its executive leadership, technical and managerial talent, manufacturing facilities, research and development centers, capitalization sources, labor, raw materials, and markets are located anywhere there is a significant competitive advantage. Power is relatively decentralized. There is a high level of cultural diversity within the worldwide senior management. A very large amount of information flows freely in all directions among the different centers. Strategic planning, new product development, and high-level decision-making are often done by multicultural teams. Cross-cultural joint ventures and business alliances become more complex and commonplace.

Given the importance and high frequency of the multiple cross-cultural interfaces among the employees and the organizations in the global corporation, there is an increased need for intercultural services. In addition to the cross-cultural skills and international knowledge required by companies at other stages, a truly transnational corporation has new demands. It must have a clear global vision and articulate a strategy to implement the vision. It has to promulgate global thinking among its top executives, develop global managers, create and sustain a worldwide corporate culture, and conduct a very high level of business diplomacy.

The global corporation also needs to train and support virtual and face-to-face multicultural teams. It has to reduce the cross-cultural barriers to long-distance communication via telephone, fax, Internet, e-mail, and other forms of electronic and computer-based networking. Due to the dynamic and highly competitive nature of this stage of globalization, capturing intercultural learning and retaining globally experienced employees are high priorities. The successful global corporation is able to transcend cultural differences, create cross-cultural synergy, and sustain a commitment to ongoing global learning.

Organizational Forms and Cultural Requirements

Contrary to the expectations of some naive commentators, cultural differences are not erased or diminished by the process of globalization. Authors Stephen Cornell and Douglas Hartman make this point in their book *Ethnicity and Race: Making Identities in a Changing World* (Thousand Oaks, CA: Pine Forge Press, 1998). They write, "Although the effects of globalization have been in some ways integrative and homogenizing, in other ways they have had the opposite effect. They variously resuscitated old identities and inspired new ones, differentiating people from each other in new or altered ways or, at the very least, introducing new conceptions of difference."

It seems clear that global organizations are never free from the need to manage differences. However, at each stage of globalization, managers' intercultural competence requirements do change. The amount and type of knowledge and skills needed depend, to a large extent, on the set of issues and challenges that characterize a particular level. As Exhibit 3–1 illustrates, each one has implications regarding the importance of culture to a transnational organization's or company's success.

Globalization Focus Questions
- ☑ Why is your company "going global?" Is it a common vision shared by all those involved? Does it have the support of all the required players and stakeholders?
- ☑ At which stage of globalization is your company or business unit currently functioning? Is it in transition to another stage? Is this transition part of an intentional corporate strategy?
- ☑ Does your senior management understand the process of globalization? How well-developed are their global thinking and intercultural business skills?
- ☑ Are they aware of the transcultural organizational issues and challenges encountered at the different stages of globalization? Do they realize the potential business impact of these issues and challenges? If not, why not?
- ☑ Do your international employees have the cross-cultural capabilities required to support your company's current and next stage of globalization? If not, are they being provided with them?

Organizational Form

Domestic	Export	International	Multinational	Global/Transnational
Domestic multi-culturalism making an impact.	Ability required to negotiate and do business with foreign distributors.	Must adapt approach and products and services to local cultures. Cultural diversity strongly affects external relationships, especially with potential buyers and foreign workers.	Localized structure reduces need for cross-cultural awareness.	Need to manage cultural diversity inside and outside the company. All levels need cross-cultural management skills for maximum flexibility.

EXHIBIT 3–1. ORGANIZATIONAL FORM AND THE IMPORTANCE OF CULTURE. (Source: Training Management Corporation, Doing Business Internationally: The Workbook to Cross-Cultural Success, Princeton Training Press, Princeton, NJ, USA 1992. Used with permission.)

Cross-Border Organizational Relationships and Issues

The globalization of markets poses new challenges to organizations . . . These developments give rise to new organizations that bring together individuals and groups from different national and organizational cultures. In the process, unprecedented cross-cultural puzzles get created that may result in the most confusing disasters or develop highly creative synergies.

Andre Laurant in "The Cross-Cultural Puzzle of Global Human Resource Management" from *Globalizing Management*

Transnational Organizational Relationships

Many forms of collaboration between corporations have evolved in today's global business environment. Joint ventures, multicompany alliances, licensing agreements, project-based cooperative networks, and franchises are becoming commonplace cross-border arrangements. Even serious competitors have entered limited cooperative ventures for specific purposes in some locations. Each of these organizational relationships generates various kinds of cross-cultural issues and challenges.

Given the poor record of success of transnational intercompany ventures, the effective use of intercultural services can make a valuable contribution. As a purchaser of intercultural services, you should be aware of the wide variety of alternative international organizational arrangements and identify which ones pertain to your company. Some of the different organizational relationships are as follows:

Cross-Border Organizational Relationships*
Strategic Alternatives in World Trade & Investment
❑ Strategic alliances
❑ Transnational ownership of equity securities
❑ Transnational management organization
❑ Wholly-owned manufacturing branch plant or subsidiaries
❑ Consortium
❑ Joint ventures
❑ Cross-production agreements
❑ Turnkey operations
❑ Manufacturer's contracts
❑ Research consortium
❑ Outsourcing agreements
❑ Franchising
❑ Licensing with partial ownership

---

*Source: Robert T. Moran, Philip R. Harris, and William G. Stripp, *Developing the Global Organization: Strategies for Human Resource Professionals*, Houston, TX: Gulf Publishing Company, 1993. Used with permission.

❑ Cross-licensing agreements
❑ Licensing
❑ Management or technical assistance contracts
❑ Cross-distribution agreements
❑ International barter and countertrade
❑ Foreign branch sales office
❑ Foreign warehouse
❑ Export directly to the "end user"
❑ Export directly to a "foreign distributor"
❑ Export directly through a "foreign sales agent"
❑ Export indirectly through an "export management company"
❑ Export indirectly by hiring an "export agent"
❑ Export indirectly by "piggybacking" on an international company
❑ Export indirectly by selling to an "export merchant"
❑ Export indirectly by selling to a "commission buying agent"

Common Organizational Issues

Differences in organizational culture, structure, and behavior can be serious pitfalls in cross-border business ventures, even in the case of wholly owned subsidiaries. These problems are compounded and intensified in the kinds of interfirm relationships listed previously. They include, but are not limited to, the following areas.

Dissimilar Stages of Work Culture

Work in different locations throughout the world is at various stages of development. For example, First World economies tend to be in the industrial stage or in transition to the post-industrial stage. Second World countries, formerly in the communist block, are moving from centrally planned command economies to more open freemarket ones. Third World nations may be in the agricultural stage of development with a few industrial or post-industrial enterprises. Each of these stages has it own characteristic ways of organizing and performing work. They also use different tools and technologies in the work environment.

People and organizations moving from one stage of work culture into another encounter a kind of culture shock related to the nature of work and the level of technology used. A First World corporation that has its work organized around the availability of instant access to worldwide communications is frustrated at the "shortage" of fax machines, voice mail, intranets, e-mail, and reliable telephone lines in Third World countries. Likewise, the passage of managers and employees from those countries into the Information Age work culture (either abroad or in their home countries) often causes them tremendous stress. They are likely to be ill-prepared to function in a radically changed work environment dominated by communications and information technology. For further information on this subject, see *The New Work Culture* by Philip R. Harris listed in the resources at the end of this chapter.

Differences in Corporate Culture

The reason for the existence of a business organization and how it should function seems self-evident in most Western corporations. It is generally assumed that a company exists to generate profits as efficiently as possible in order to increase stockowners' earnings. However, managers and employees of companies in other parts of the world may have vastly different views regarding an organization's purpose and style of operation. In his book *Riding the Waves of Culture*, intercultural specialist Fons Trompenaars has identified four types of corporate culture that reflect national cultural differences. He uses the metaphorical terms "the family," "the Eiffel Tower," "the guided missile," and "the incubator" to describe them. Each type has its own reasons for being and its own ways of fulfilling its purposes.

The Family Model

A "family"-style corporate culture is a highly personal environment in which the members' main concern is to belong. It is hierarchical, with a father figure at top and "elder brother" managers at senior levels who care for the employees. Showing benevolent personal concern for employees is expected. In return, they are expected to give unquestioning loyalty to the boss and the firm.

Power and status within this organizational context are ascribed by one's position in the "family." The nature and quality of personal relationships are more important than the performance of tasks and the achievement of objectives. Rewards are based on one's loyalty and connections. Job security is strong and protected by a sense of family obligation. The main purposes of the organization are to preserve the family's interests and protect its members. This type of corporate culture is found frequently in Asia, the Middle East, and parts of Latin America.

The Eiffel Tower Model

This type of corporate culture is characterized by a bureaucratic division of labor with well-defined roles and functions at all levels. The hierarchy is relatively formal and inflexible. Power is exercised top-down in an impersonal way. Authority derives from the role one performs rather than one's personal attributes or qualities. Rules and procedures are explicit and detailed. All employees are expected to abide by them.

In return, employees expect to be treated equally and fairly. Rewards are based on the importance of one's role. Job security often is protected by law. The purpose of this type of corporate culture is to create a structure in which roles and functions are systematically and efficiently organized. The Eiffel Tower model is found most frequently in France, Belgium, Switzerland, Germany, and other countries in northeastern Europe.

The Guided Missile Model

A "guided missile" corporate culture is targeted at clearly defined goals and outcomes. It is focused on tasks, typically undertaken by teams and project groups. It is relatively egalitarian. Roles and functions are flexible and depend on the nature of the projects. Work is conducted in a highly pragmatic way with little concern for formal hierarchical structures.

Employees' power and status are often determined by their skills and the priority and visibility of the projects for which they are responsible. Reward is based on performance, problems solved, and results achieved.

Job security and loyalty to the company are not very strong. The purpose of this type of organization is to attain a specific goal. Examples of the "guided missile" model are found especially in high-technology companies in the United States, Canada, and northern Europe.

The Incubator Model

This kind of corporate culture is based on the philosophy that an organization's needs and interests are secondary to the fulfillment and well-being of the individuals in it. Its hierarchical structure is quite flat. There is a high level of informality and egalitarianism in the workplace. The "incubator" creates a protective environment in which employees' needs are met and their potential is developed. This humanistic concern is expressed in personal ways.

Employee benefits are generous, and policies are liberal and flexible. Status is achieved by demonstrating creativity and personal and professional growth. Rewards may be based on one's ownership position in the firm or on the company's performance. Job security is relatively strong. The purposes of this organizational model are to maximize the attainment of its members' potentials and the development and exploitation of their talents. This type of organization is not very common, but examples do exist among entrepreneurial companies, especially in the computer and biotechnology industries in Europe and North America.

A similar set of organizational types is presented in *Managing Across Cultures*, a book published by Prentice-Hall in 1997. In it, authors Susan C. Schneider and Jean-Louis Barsoux describe the results of recent studies of corporate cultures of companies in Europe, Asia, and Latin America. They identified four major models, which they call the "village market" (Anglo/Nordic), "family or tribe" (Asian), "well-oiled machine" (Germanic), and "pyramid of people" (Latin).

Such models are interesting and useful tools for understanding the reasons how and why the nature and purpose of organizations are defined so differently by cultures. The importance of these model-building efforts is that they are based on empirical data from the real world of international business rather than merely reflecting academic theories and speculation. They offer practical insights by accurately capturing the "flavor" of the different types of national corporate cultures.

Conflicting Practices and Behavior

People accustomed to different national corporate cultures naturally have significantly different management styles, work habits, expectations, and motivations. When they are required to function outside of their familiar cultural frameworks, much of what they have learned is not useful and may even be a liability. In addition, the behaviors for which they were rewarded in the past are likely to be inappropriate or ineffective in the new environment.

The following list highlights some of the difficulties when people from different countries try to manage the relationships between their companies. Various cultures are mentioned here to illustrate important differences in organizational behavior. Please keep in mind that these contrasts are not either/or dichotomies. Each dimension covers a spectrum of possible orientations. Furthermore, individual managers may differ significantly from their national cultural norms.

Leadership Style

In many Middle Eastern cultures, the boss is a powerful authority figure who should not be questioned or challenged. In Scandinavia, the boss tends to be seen as a team leader who seeks input from employees and delegates authority and accountability to subordinates.

Decision-Making

In Japan, decisions normally are reached through a participative process involving a high degree of consultation and consensus-building. In Latin American companies (especially family businesses), the boss personally makes virtually all important decisions.

Boss-Subordinate Relations

Companies in Switzerland and Germany typically have considerable distance in power and status between levels in the hierarchy. Subordinates are expected to show deference and respect toward their bosses. Companies in Australia and Israel tend to recognize less distinction between levels and allow familiarity and informal interactions among people of different status.

Workplace Decorum

Formality in dress and demeanor at the office are generally required in most northern European countries. Titles and family names rather than personal names typically are used between coworkers. In the Caribbean, companies permit much more casualness and informality in the workplace. First names and nicknames are commonly used among colleagues.

Employee Motivation

Job security is a very strong employee motivation in many cultures in eastern Europe. In the United States, opportunity for personal achievement via initiative, creativity, and risk-taking tends to be a significant motivator.

Task/Relationship Orientation

In Germany, employees typically focus narrowly on the goal of a project and the tasks necessary to accomplish it. Frequent socializing with coworkers is considered a distraction and a waste of time. In Latin America, establishing comfortable relationships must precede starting on the task and there is a great deal of socializing to facilitate the process of reaching the goal or completing the task.

Teamwork

Cooperative group effort is the norm in Japan. Teamwork is used to accomplish most projects and major tasks. The US culture often rewards competitive, high-performance individual efforts more than group endeavors. See the discussion of cross-border team roles in Chapter 4 for more details.

Time Management

The Swiss and Germans usually insist on strict adherence to schedules, appointments, and deadlines. Punctuality and efficient and productive use of time are expected of employees. In the Caribbean, Central and South America, and the Middle East, different values may take precedence over efficient time management, resulting in a more flexible sense of time in the workplace.

Interpersonal Communications

In Malaysia, Indonesia, Japan, and the Philippines, harmony in the workplace is a very high priority. Communication among employees and between the boss and subordinates tends to be indirect, subtle, and diplomatic with the goal of saving face and avoiding embarrassment. Mild hints and nonverbal cues may be used to convey negative messages. In the Netherlands, frankness and directness are important values. Confrontation and constructive face-to-face criticism and feedback are common in the workplace.

Rule Enforcement

In Switzerland, rules, regulations, and policies are explicit and they are strictly enforced. They apply equally to all employees. Exceptions are rare and difficult to obtain. In many places in Asia, the Middle East, and Latin America, rules may be overlooked and infractions ignored. Unwritten rules may carry more weight than official ones.

Role Definition

Companies in France normally define employees' roles and functions in great detail. Titles and job descriptions are clearly determined and taken seriously. In the United States, formal job descriptions may be less of an indication of an employee's actual role. Recognizing what needs to be done and responding to it without regard to one's official role are valued and reinforced.

Employee Evaluation

In Japan, employees are constantly being evaluated informally by their peers and supervisors. Structured formal evaluations are not emphasized. In many western cultures, employee performance is measured in quantifiable terms and assessed periodically through a clearly defined process.

Rewarding Employees

Companies in the United States tend to reward employees primarily for performance. Tangible accomplishments and results are considered to be the most important factor in determining compensation. However, companies in Japan usually base pay and benefits mostly on an employee's seniority and conformity to the corporate culture.

These areas of incompatibility in organizational practices and behaviors are stressful for both international managers and their counterparts in other countries. Intercultural services have been developed to deal with the issues arising from these differences. To understand the services and select the most appropriate ones, you should be aware of which of these issues most seriously affect your company's cross-border organizational relationships.

Divergent Assumptions and Expectations

Another set of pitfalls affecting cross-cultural business ventures results from the collaborating companies' divergent assumptions and expectations. What a company is looking for in a relationship with another company, what it hopes to get out of the arrangement, and how it expects the relationship to work are strongly influenced by culture.

Premises and Approaches

A common problem is that the companies start from incompatible premises when seeking a relationship. In some cultures, the rationale for entering into a joint venture is the belief that there is a natural community of interest shared by the companies. This reasoning was common in traditional Japanese business culture. Western companies, however, tend to focus on the practical competitive advantages they believe they can create through an alliance. This contrast between seeking to discover and nurture something that already exists potentially and actively creating something that does not yet exist reveals basic unshared premises. Consequently, the parties may unintentionally undermine the relationship from the very beginning because of differences in the assumptions underlying their approaches.

Identity and Loyalties

The questions "Who are we?" and "To what group do I belong?" often plague cross-border organizational relationships. One partner may consciously or unconsciously seek to impose its cultural identity on the other. In these cases, power struggles behind the scenes cause tension in the organization. This friction may exacerbate the divided loyalties that representatives of each culture naturally tend to feel toward the cross-border organization and their home company.

Risks and Rewards

Another issue stems from conflicting expectations regarding the risks and rewards implicit in the agreement. In group-oriented societies in Asia, the Middle East, and Latin America, it is often assumed that business relationships will be win-win or lose-lose. Thus, both anticipated rewards and unforeseen losses should be shared by the partners as they would be in a marriage. In northern European and in North American countries, however, a more narrow sense of individual corporate self-interest is usually brought into the relationship. Business people in these countries generally assume that a partner's loss or gain depends entirely on the conditions agreed upon in the contract—a strictly commercial transaction. This kind of discrepancy in expectations may cause irreparable damage if the joint enterprise encounters serious setbacks.

Time Perspective

Different cultural assumptions regarding time frames may also have a negative impact. Short-term thinking is common in the western post-industrial world. Frequently, interfirm business deals are expected to have a limited life span. They may be created to take advantage of a temporary business opportunity or undertaken as a defense move against a threat by a competitor. Their longevity often depends on annual or even quarterly profits and returns on investment. However, in Japan and other Asian countries, there is a tendency to have a much longer-term viewpoint. The care and effort invested in establishing a relationship with another company is expected to have payoffs for many years. The immediate set of circumstances and the current deals negotiated often are seen as merely open doors to a shared future.

Meaning of Contracts

Misunderstandings regarding the nature of a contract may cause another set of problems. In Latin America, for example, it is generally assumed that the real essence of the agreement and the contractual arrangement lies in the personal relationship between the contracting parties and not in a written document. In the United States, however, faith is placed in a formal, legal contract. When one party trusts in friendship and the other trusts in the law, difficulties are bound to arise. Disagreements over the role of lawyers and the need to negotiate every conceivable contingency in exhaustive detail signal the presence of conflicting values and expectations.

An additional issue pertaining to the nature of the contract is encountered in Asia. Unforeseen developments that negatively affect the local partner's benefits under the contract are often seen as legitimate grounds for renegotiating the contract. In western business practice, the terms of a contract are usually considered binding regardless of changing circumstances.

Proprietary Information

Cultural differences regarding the sanctity of intellectual property and proprietary information frequently become an issue in cross-border organizational relationships. Western corporations generally assume that ownership and control of their intellectual property is a legal right. However, the cultures of some countries support the belief that knowledge exists for the benefit of all people and not just for the profit of a few. Furthermore, in group-oriented societies, insider information is routinely shared among members of the group. Likewise, commitment to the group and one's fellow citizens may be stronger than loyalty to outsiders from another country. These cultural values can make it difficult to protect proprietary information in many parts of Asia.

Ethical Standards

Conflicting standards of corporate ethics also pose serious problems in cross-cultural business relationships, especially when a new organizational entity is created by the partners. Each party naturally considers itself a good corporate citizen and believes that it conducts business in an ethical way. It often comes as a surprise when the partners discover that their ethical standards are not only different, but that they conflict in important ways. All these issues hinge on deep cultural values, and they must be dealt with before the ethical guidelines of a new joint venture can be determined.

Typical Areas of Ethics Clash
- ❏ The meaning of rules and laws
- ❏ The definition of gifts and bribes
- ❏ The acceptability of nepotism and favoritism in hiring and promotion
- ❏ What constitutes conflict of interest in dealing with the suppliers and vendors
- ❏ Setting environmental protection standards
- ❏ Agreeing on acceptable conditions for workers

Interfirm Communications

Unshared assumptions and expectations regarding the nature, frequency, and type of communications between organizations may also cause friction between companies from different cultural environments. In Japan, for example, the concept of parallel hierarchies is very important. It requires that only managers of equal levels in two organizations deal with each other (allowing for company size and importance). Crossing status levels would be a serious breach of business etiquette and would very likely damage the interfirm relationship. Formality and ritual also characterize communications between companies in Japan. However, informality in business communications between people in different organizations is relatively common and accepted in the United States and Australia, for example.

In Latin America and much of Asia, personal ties between individuals in different organizations are assumed to be essential. Frequent, friendly communications beyond the exchange of routine business information are expected. Communications will break down and have to be entirely rebuilt if either counterpart is changed.

Therefore, staff turnover is highly disruptive to interfirm communications. In the US and many western countries, communications tends to be more impersonal and content-focused. Consequently, changing the individuals handling communications between companies (a purchaser and a vendor, for instance) causes little or no disruption.

As a purchaser of intercultural services, you should be aware of the impact of these cross-border organizational relationship problems. That knowledge enables you to highlight specific areas of need and to point out real risks and costs likely to be incurred if nothing is done to solve the cross-cultural "puzzles."

Organizational Relationship Issues Focus Questions
- ☑ Do your organization or company's reasons for international expansion require entering into new interfirm relationships in other cultures? If so, which types of relationships are they?
- ☑ What cross-cultural knowledge, attitudes, and skills on the part of your managers are required to make these relationships work?
- ☑ Do your colleagues have experience with cross-border organizational relationships? If so, were they successful? If not, why not?
- ☑ Do the international managers understand the organizational behaviors and practices of associates and partners from other countries?
- ☑ Are they familiar with the high failure rate of international joint ventures and alliances? Do they understand the cross-cultural pitfalls that cause these failures?
- ☑ Do they have strategies and plans for overcoming these difficulties? Are their strategies and plans realistic?
- ☑ Do they have the capabilities required to build successful organizational relationships within the corporate culture of another country?
- ☑ Are they willing and able to adapt their management styles enough to deal effectively with the management practices of their counterparts abroad?

The Intercultural Synergy Model

> Culturally synergistic organizations reflect the best aspects of all members' cultures in their structure and process without violating the norms of any single culture. Managers in synergistic organizations use diversity to solve problems.
>
> Nancy Adler in *International Dimensions of Organizational Behavior*

Despite the many pitfalls, problems, and difficulties generated by differences in the way organizations function in different countries, such differences can be assets to a corporation. Adopting and using a broader array of perspectives and approaches is a competitive advantage in the global marketplace. However, in order to leverage cultural diversity for a company's advantage, there must first be a vision of how this goal can be accomplished. The concept *cultural synergy*, described by Nancy J. Adler in her book *International Dimensions of Organizational Behavior,* is often used by interculturalists as a paradigm for describing optimal collaboration between cross-border organizations and companies. It is an important antidote to the discouragement and pessimism managers may feel in the face of seemingly overwhelming cross-cultural obstacles. More importantly, it is also a practical model and development goal for international organizations.

Stages of Synergy

Synergy can be defined as a synthesis of different elements into a whole that is greater than the sum of its components. Cross-cultural organizations typically evolve through at least two levels of integration before they are able to function synergistically. These stages are illustrated graphically in Exhibit 3–2.

Cultural Dominance

The first stage may be called *cultural dominance*. This level of collaboration is characterized by a large disparity in the power of the participants from each culture. Cultural differences are ignored or denied. One group imposes its national corporate culture on the other and

Cultural Dominance
Options: Limited to one culture's contributions
Power: Very unequal
Cultural Differences: Ignored or denied
Outcome: Win vs. lose
Workplace Ethic: "One culture dominates."

Cultural Compromise
Options: Limited to shared area
Power: Generally equal
Cultural Differences: Recognized but minimized
Outcome: Lowest common denominator
Workplace Ethic: "Let's find common ground.""

Cultural Synergy
Options: Greatly expanded   Power: Mutually multiplied
Cultural Differences: Valued and used   Outcome: Win/Win
Workplace Ethic: "Let's use your way, my way and our way."

EXHIBIT 3–2. STEPS TOWARD SYNERGY.

tends to dictate the way that their joint business is conducted. Therefore, the range of options available to their enterprise is limited mostly to the contributions of the dominant partner. It is also likely that the subordinate partner will feel undervalued and become resentful and poorly motivated.

Cultural Compromise

The second stage is referred to as *cultural compromise*. In it, the partners seek a common ground where their cultural values happen to be similar. Differences are recognized, but efforts are made to minimize them and exclude them from their mutual corporate culture. Power is shared more equally, and there are fewer causes of friction. In the interest of harmony, the partners avoid using many techniques unique to their own cultural backgrounds that might seem strange or questionable to their counterparts. This compromise on both sides restricts the scope of the options available, and the organization is limited to the partners' set of common practices. This stage results in a relatively impoverished range of potential responses to their business challenges.

Intercultural Synergy

At the *intercultural synergy* stage, cultural differences are valued and welcomed. The partners believe that the broadest possible diversity of values, viewpoints, and approaches is desirable. This variety significantly multiplies the number of possible avenues available for identifying and solving problems and reaching the organization's goals. Consequently, the enterprise can respond more creatively to the risks and opportunities present in the global business arena. This broader scope of responsiveness is a competitive advantage. The participants in a culturally synergistic organization seek to understand each other's cultures in order to discover and use the potential resources that their different backgrounds may contain. In this mutually validating environment, all parties are empowered for the benefit of the enterprise.

Making Synergy Work

Skeptics may doubt that cultural synergy is anything more than an ideal. Nevertheless, practical examples do exist in some cross-border business ventures. The experience of a Swedish manufacturer of high-precision metal products is a case in point. It has production and sales facilities in 15 countries on 5 continents, including a factory in the United States. It designed and developed a state-of-the-art assembly line in Sweden that was to be replicated in the US plant.

However, the US production managers had misgivings about the suitability of certain technical features of the assembly line for local conditions. When they raised questions, the initial Swedish response (demonstrating cultural dominance) was, "We invented the product and know it best. Do it exactly our way." After continued objections and requests for technical assistance from the Americans, a group of Swedish engineers was sent to fix the problems. A team of US and Swedish counterparts was formed. Gradually, they developed good working and social relationships and began to trust and respect each other.

At this point in the project, the Swedes agreed to some local adaptations and modifications, which demonstrates the cultural compromise stage. After a few months, the US assembly line was making products that equaled, then exceeded, the Swedish plant's output. The Swedish engineers were so impressed by these gains that they invited their US team members to Sweden to help introduce their jointly created improvements that integrated the two approaches. In Sweden, the social bonds and team performance continued to grow. Cultural synergy was the result. The production figures tell the story. The original Swedish output was 800 units per day, and the original US record was 500 units per day. According to an intercultural consultant familiar with the project, the ultimate output of the Swedish/US collaboration was about 1,000 units per day in each of the factories. Furthermore, a greatly strengthened multicultural technical team had been created. Both the increased production and the company's enhanced technical capability are tangible benefits of having made cultural synergy work.

As a purchaser of intercultural services, you should keep the concept of synergy in mind as a model for cross-border organizational relationships. Most providers of these services are familiar with the concept and are more than willing to help your company move in the direction of cultural synergy.

Cultural Synergy Focus Questions
- ☑ What is the current level of your company's cooperation with its international partners: cultural dominance, compromise, or synergy?
- ☑ Do your international managers understand the concept of cultural synergy? Do they recognize its benefits?
- ☑ Are opportunities for synergy being overlooked?
- ☑ Is synergy a goal to which they are committed? If not, why not?
- ☑ Are they able to communicate the concept of cultural synergy to their counterparts in other cultures? How well? Are their counterparts receptive to the idea of synergy?
- ☑ Are they capable of helping to build cultural synergy? If so, do they have the support of the senior management in their efforts? If not, are they being trained in the appropriate skills?

Summary and Suggested Action Steps

This chapter describes many of the ways in which culture affects the outcome of the cross-border relationships between organizations and the people in them. It provides a framework for considering the intercultural knowledge and skill requirements of different international organizational arrangements and stages of globalization. The impact of differences in national corporate culture and practices are explored, and a positive model for synergistic cross-cultural collaboration is presented and explained.

Here are some ways you can use the content of this chapter:

1. Form a focus group of international managers (formally or informally) to consider the intercultural implications of the company's current stage of globalization and types of cross-border organizational relationships. Share appropriate sections from this chapter and selected readings from the resource list with them.
2. Lead discussions of these materials and take notes of ideas and recommendations that emerge from the discussions. Share this information with senior executives and human resource managers.
3. Host sack lunch "globalization awareness" sessions featuring videos, presenters, or visiting colleagues and counterparts from other countries.
4. Identify those employees most directly responsible for establishing and managing cross-border joint ventures and business alliances. Ask them to review the cross-cultural organizational issues presented in this chapter and use them to assess the health of your organization's transnational relationships.
5. Keep a record of their responses and comments and share this information with key international decision-makers.
6. Assess your cross-border organizational relationships in other countries in terms of the cultural synergy model. Consider the business implications of your conclusions.
7. Identify specific opportunities to work toward cross-synergy and define appropriate action steps. Promote the synergy concept to those employees most involved in multinational teamwork. Offer them encouragement and support.
8. Announce new cross-border organizational relationships and other important events relating to international joint-ventures and business alliances in your newsletter and on your intranet.
9. Continue to add to your file of your organization or company's intercultural issues, needs, challenges, and opportunities. Discuss the contents of this file with potential providers of intercultural services when you feel you have sufficiently compelling "evidence" of need.

Resources

The Global Business Environment

Amin, S. *Capitalism in the Age of Globalization.* London: Zed Books, 1997.

Appadurai, A. *Modernity at Large: Cultural Dimensions of Globalization.* Minneapolis, MN: University of Minnesota Press, 1996.

Cornell, S., and Hartmann, D. *Ethnicity and Race: Making Identities in a Changing World.* Thousand Oaks, CA: Pine Forge Press, 1998.

Cvetkovich, A., and Kellner, D. *Articulating the Global and the Local: Globalization and Cultural Studies.* Boulder, CO: Westview Press, 1997.

David, K. *Cultural Environment of International Business.* Cincinnati, OH: South-Western Publishing, 2000.

Hill, C.W.L., *International Business: Competing in the Global Marketplace.* (3rd ed.) New York: McGraw-Hill, 1999.

Huntington, S. *The Clash of Civilizations and the Remaking of World Order.* New York: Simon and Schuster, 1996.

Institute of Directors, *Understanding Global Business*, London: Kogan Page, Ltd., 1999.

Kanter, R. M. *World Class: Thriving Locally in the Global Economy.* New York: Simon & Schuster, 1995.

Kozul-Wright, R. (ed.). *Transnational Corporations and the Global Economy.* New York: St. Martins Press, 1998.

Omae, K. (ed.). *The Evolving Global Economy: Making Sense of the New World Order.* Cambridge, MA: Harvard Business School Press, 1995.

Ohmae, K. *The Borderless World.* New York: Harper Business Press, 1990.

Tuller, L. W. *Going Global.* Homewood, IL: Business One Irwin, 1991.

Yankelovich, D. "Tomorrow's Global Businesses." *The Futurist,* July-Aug. 1991, pp. 60.

The Globalizing Organization

Adler, N. J., and Ghadar, F. "Strategic Human Resource Management: A Global Perspective." In P. Rudiger (ed.), *Human Resource*

Management in International Comparison. Berlin: de Gruyter, 1990, pp. 235–260.

Bharat-Ram, V. *The Theory of the Global Firm*. Oxford, UK: Oxford University Press, 1997.

Buckley, P. J., and Ghauri P. N. (eds.). *The Internationalization of the Firm: A Reader*. San Diego, CA: Academic Press, Inc., 1993.

Business Week, *Preparing Your Business for the Global Economy*. McGraw-Hill, 1997.

Davidson, W. H. *Managing the Global Corporation: Case Studies in Strategy and Management*. New York: McGraw-Hill, 1999.

Feist, W. R. (ed.). *Managing a Global Enterprise*. Westport, CT: Quorum Books, 1999.

Fombrun, C. J., and Wally S. "Global Entanglements: The Structure of Corporate Transnationalism." In V. Pucik, N. M. Tichy, and C. K. Barnett (eds.), *Globalizing Management: Creating and Leading the Competitive Organization*. New York: John Wiley & Sons, Inc., 1993, pp. 15–46.

Hendry, C. *Human Resource Strategies for International Growth*. London, Routledge Press, 1994, pp. 1–43.

John, R., Grimwade, N., and Cox, H. (eds.). *Global Business Strategy*. London: International Thomson Business Press, 1997.

Kinsey Gorman, C. *Managing in a Global Organization: Keys to Success in a Changing World*. Menlo Park, CA: Crisp Publications, 1994.

Luck, V. *How to Achieve Competitive Advantage in a Global Market*, London: Kogan Page Ltd., 1998.

Marquardt, M. J. *The Global Advantage: How World-Class Organizations Improve Performance Through Globalization*. Houston, TX: Gulf Publishing, 1999.

Marquardt, M. J., and Reynolds, A. *The Global Learning Organization: Gaining Competitive Advantage Through Continuous Learning*. Burr Ridge, IL: Irwin Professional Publishing, 1993.

Miza, H. *Global Competitive Strategies in the New World Economy: Multilateralism, Regionalization and the Transnational Firm*. North Hampton, MA: Edward Elgar Publications, 1999.

Moran, R. T., and Riesenberger, J. R. *The Global Challenge: Building the New Worldwide Enterprise*. New York: McGraw-Hill, 1994.

Moran, R. T., Harris, P. R. and Stripp, W. G. *Developing the Global Organization: Strategies for Human Resource Professionals*. Houston, TX: Gulf Publishing Company, 1993.

Nelson, C. A. *International Business: A Manager's Guide to Strategy in the Age of Globalization.* Stamford, CT: International Thomson Business Press, 1998.

Odenwald, S., and Matheny W. G. *Global Impact*, Chicago, IL: Irwin Professional Publishing, 1996.

Rhinesmith, S. H. *A Manager's Guide to Globalization: Six Keys to Success in a Changing World.* (2nd ed.) Alexandria, VA and New York: ASTD Press and McGraw-Hill, 1996, pp. 1–20.

Rhinesmith, S. H. "An Agenda for Globalization." *Training and Development Journal*, Feb. 1991, pp. 22–29.

Rhinesmith, S. H. "Training for Global Operations." In R. L. Craig, (ed.), *ASTD Training and Development Handbook: A Guide to Human Resource Management.* (4th ed.) New York: McGraw-Hill, 1996, pp. 124–141.

Schell, M. S., and Soloman, C. M. "Global Culture: Who's the Gatekeeper?" *Workforce*, Vol. 76, No. 11, Nov. 1997, pp. 35–39.

Schniederjams, M. J. *Operations Management in a Global Context.* Westport, CT: Quorum Books, 1998.

Cross-Border Organizational Relationship Issues

Adigan, I. "Orientations to Work: a Cross-Cultural Approach." *Journal of Cross-Cultural Psychology*, Vol. 28, No. 3, 1997, pp. 352–355.

Beard, M. J. "Developing an Effective Strategy for International Mergers and Acquisitions." *International HR Journal*, Vol. 7, No. 4, Winter 1999, pp. 22–30.

Black, S., and Gregersen, H. "Serving Two Masters: A Study in Expatriate Allegiance." *Innovations In International Compensation*, Vol. 18, No. 1, 1992, pp. 3–11.

Bleeke, J., and Ernst, D. (eds.). *Collaborating to Compete: Using Strategic Alliances and Acquisitions in the Global Marketplace.* New York: John Wiley & Sons, 1993.

Cooperrider, D. L., and Dutton J. E. (eds.). *Organizational Dimensions of Global Change: No Limits to Cooperation.* Newbury Park, CA: Sage Publications, 1997.

Cyr, C. J. *The Human Resource Challenge of International Joint Ventures.* Westport, CT: Quorum Books, 1995.

Ganitsky, J., and Watzke, G. E. "Implications of Different Time Perspectives for Human Resource Management in International Joint Ventures." *Management International Review*, Special Issue 1990, pp. 37–51.

Gemunden, H. G., Ritter, T. and Walter, A. (eds.). *Relationships and Networks in International Markets.* New York: Pergamon Press, 1998.

Geringer, J. M., and Frayne, C. A. "Human Resource Management and International Joint Venture Control." *Management International Review,* Special Issue 1990, pp. 103–120.

Gertsen, M. C., and Soderberg, A. M. (eds.). *Cultural Dimensions of International Mergers and Acquisitions.* Hawthorne, NY: Walter De Gruyter, 1998.

Harris, P. R. *The New Work Culture: HRD Strategies for Transformational Management.* Amherst, MA: HRD Press, 1998.

Hickson, D. J., and Pugh, D. S. *Management Worldwide: The Impact of Societal Culture on Organizations Around the Globe.* New York: Penguin Press, 1996.

Hofstede, G. *Cultures and Organizations: Software of the Mind.* (Rev. ed.) New York: McGraw-Hill, 1997.

Inkpen, A. *The Management of International Joint Ventures: An Organizational Learning Perspective.* New York: Van Nostrand Reinhold, 1995.

Laurent, A. "A Cultural View of Organizational Change." In P. Evans, Y. Doz, and A. Laurent (eds.), *Human Resource Management in International Firms: Change, Globalization, Innovation.* New York: St. Martin's Press, 1990, pp. 83–94.

Laurent, A. "The Cross-Cultural Puzzle of Global Human Resource Management." In V. Pucik, N. M. Tichy, and C. K Barnett (eds.), *Globalizing Management: Creating and Leading the Competitive Organization.* New York: John Wiley & Sons, Inc., 1993, pp. 174–186.

Lorange, P. "Human Resource Management in Multicultural Cooperative Ventures." In V. Pucik, N. M. Tichy, and C.K Barnett (eds.), *Globalizing Management: Creating and Leading the Competitive Organization.* New York: John Wiley & Sons, Inc., 1993, pp. 227–242.

Madhok, A. "Revisiting Multinational Firms' Tolerance for Joint Ventures: A Trust-Based Approach." *Journal of International Business Studies,* No. 26, 1995, pp. 117–137.

Morosini, P. *Managing Cultural Differences: Effective Strategy and Execution Across Cultures in Global Corporate Alliances.* Oxford, UK: Elsevier Science Ltd., 1998.

Neal, M. *The Cultural Factor: Cross-National Management and the Foreign Venture.* Hampshire, UK: Macmillan Business Publications, 1998.

Oddou, G., and Mendenhall, M. (eds.). *Cases in International Organizational Behavior.* Oxford, UK: Blackwell Publishing, 1998.

Offermann, L. R., and Hellmann, P. S. "Culture's Consequences for Leadership Behavior: National Values in Action." *Journal of Cross-Cultural Psychology*, Vol. 28, No. 3, 1997, pp. 342–351.

Pattison, J. E. "Global Joint Ventures: Secrets of Success, Reasons for Failures." *Overseas Business*, Winter 1990, pp. 25–29.

Schneider, S. C. "National vs. Corporate Culture: Implications for Human Resource Management." In M. Mendenhall and G. Oddou (eds.), *Readings and Cases in International Human Resource Management*. Boston: PWS-Kent Publishing Company, 1991, pp. 13–27.

Schuler, R. S., Jackson, S. E., Dowling, P. J., and Welch, D. E. "The Formation of an International Joint Venture." In M. Mendenhall and G. Oddou (eds.), *Readings and Cases in International Human Resource Management*. Boston: PWS-Kent Publishing Company, 1991, pp. 83–96.

Segil, L. "Managing Culture in Cross-Cultural Alliances." *Leader to Leader*, Fall 1997, pp. 12–14.

Smith, P. B., Dugan, S., and Trompenaars, F. "National Culture and the Values of Organizational Employees: A Dimensional Analysis Across 43 Nations." *Journal of Cross-Cultural Psychology*, Vol. 27, No. 2, 1996, pp. 231–266.

Solomon, C. M. "Corporate Pioneers Navigate Global Mergers." *Global Workforce*, September 1998, pp. 12–17.

Wederspahn, G. M. "Cross-Border Alliances: The HR Contribution." *International HR Journal*, Spring 1996, pp. 37–40.

Yoshino, M. Y., Ragan, U. S., and Srinivasa, U. *Strategic Alliances: An Entrepreneurial Approach to Globalization*. Cambridge, MA: Harvard Business School Press, 1995.

Intercultural Synergy

Adler, N. J. *International Dimensions of Organizational Behavior.* (3rd ed.) Cincinnati, OH: South-Western College Publishing, 1997, Chapter Four on synergy.

Buchel, B. T., Probst, G., and Ruling, C. C. *International Joint Venture Management: Learning to Cooperate and Cooperating to Learn.* New York: John Wiley & Sons, 1998.

Harris, P. R. "Team Synergy Analysis Inventory." In *Twenty Fully Reproducible Assessment Instruments for the New Work Culture.* Amherst, MA: HRD Press, 1995.

Harris, P. R., and Moran, R. T. "Leadership in Cultural Synergy." In *Managing Cultural Differences.* (5th ed.) Houston, TX: Gulf Publishing Company, 2000, pp. 94–117.

Lane, H. W., and Beamish, P. W. "Cross-Cultural Cooperative Behavior in Joint Ventures in LDCs." *Management International Review,* Special Issue 1990, pp. 103–120.

Moran, R. T., and Harris, P. R. *Managing Cultural Synergy.* Houston, TX: Gulf Publishing, 1982.

Wederspahn, G. M., and Solow, L. A. "Multicultural Teams: From Chaos to Synergy." *International Human Resources Journal,* Winter 1998, pp. 20–23.

4

Cross-Border Roles

It is now clear that global change will be a way of life in the 1990s and beyond . . . At the center of these changes, as always, will be people. Employees, managers, and leaders of organizations struggling to adapt to the new world rushing toward them—and away from them.

Stephen Rhinesmith in *A Manager's Guide to Globalization*

People, Responsibilities, and Relationships

Individual people, in countless ways, determine the success or failure of cross-border organizations. How well or how poorly they learn and perform their cross-border roles and fulfill their cross-cultural responsibilities is critically important in all types of international organizational arrangements and at all stages of globalization. The intercultural knowledge and skills of these employees are valuable assets. The quality of their worldwide relationships shapes their organization's or company's global reputation and strongly influences the performance of its international mission.

New Roles—New Requirements

Increasing integration of organizations across business and national boundaries demands that the modern manager be able to operate multiculturally.

Geert Hofstede in *Globalizing Management*

Senior management recognition of the importance of cross-border roles is a key prerequisite for gaining support for the use of intercultural services to train and develop employees to handle their transnational roles and responsibilities. A practical way you can increase senior manager's awareness is to inventory the type and number of cross-border roles that exist in your company. This exercise often results in the discovery that considerably more employees than originally thought are engaged in important cross-border activities and relationships. The surprise is because the internationalization of their jobs usually evolves gradually over time without formal planning or redefining their jobs.

The inventory will also help you verify the contributions of these roles to your company's international business and determine which employees need intercultural skills. This information is essential to you as a potential user of intercultural services. In order to select the most appropriate services and use them effectively, you must first identify the cross-cultural requirements of the cross-border roles.

Most employees who must be able to operate multiculturally are found in five groups: senior home-office executives, inter-country assignees, international business travelers, home-office staff, and host-country employees and counterparts (see Exhibit 4–1). These groups do

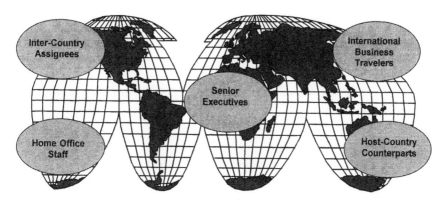

EXHIBIT 4–1. CROSS-BORDER ROLES.

not correspond either to job classifications or organizational levels. The employees may or may not live abroad. They may not even travel internationally. Their interaction with people from other cultures may be face-to-face or at long distance. The critical common denominator is that their jobs require maintaining international communications and relationships that are important to the organizatin's or company's business. These are the people most likely to benefit from intercultural services.

Senior Executives

The top-level managers in a company have ultimate responsibility for the success of the corporation's international business ventures. They must provide the global vision and apply the global thinking required to recognize and take advantage of the opportunities and to avoid the risks of doing business in the worldwide arena. The appropriateness of their decisions and the quality of their leadership depend, to a large extent, on the level of their cross-cultural awareness, knowledge, and skills.

Too often, there is little in their business school education or their domestic job experience that prepares them for the global scope of their responsibilities or the cultural issues and challenges they face. Unfortunately, this deficit of international savvy often undermines other employees' efforts to accomplish the company's international goals. The vital role of senior management includes the cognitive-based requirement of applying their minds to new intercultural realities and learning new skills for dealing with them.

Cognitive-Based
❏ Understanding the nature of culture and its impact on international business
❏ Being aware of the cultural environments in which the company's business is conducted
❏ Understanding the cross-border roles and responsibilities of the employees
❏ Comprehending the process of globalization
❏ Knowing the intercultural implications of the company's stage of globalization

❑ Acknowledging that intercultural competence is a high-priority corporate asset
❑ Recognizing their own intercultural job requirements

Skill-Based
❑ Conducting international business diplomacy with appropriate cross-cultural protocol and etiquette
❑ Establishing and maintaining good relationships with international business partners
❑ Developing their own intercultural skills
❑ Modeling intercultural effectiveness as an example to others in the company
❑ Recognizing and rewarding employees for demonstrating cross-cultural effectiveness
❑ Obtaining adequate resources for intercultural training and the development of employees who have cross-border roles and responsibilities

Intercountry Assignees

Employees and their families transferred to and from other countries form the cadre of expatriates who serve on the front line of international business. This group has grown steadily during the 1980s and 1990s. A 1998 survey of 177 companies by Windham International and the NFTC reported that 81% of the respondents expected the number of expatriates to continue to increase through the year 2000.

Probably the fastest growing segment of international corporate transferee population is nonUS employees and their families assigned to the United States. Bill Sheridan, former director of international compensation services for the NFTC, reported in 1997 that, according to two surveys, the number of expatriates inbound to the United States was expected to triple in the next 3–5 years.

Expatriates may be of different nationalities. The objectives of their international assignments vary greatly. They have different motivations for seeking and accepting international transfers. Each expatriate employee and family brings a unique set of strengths and potential weaknesses to the assignment. How well they adapt to the local culture and how effectively they meet the cross-cultural challenges of their life and work in the host country often determine the fate of the international business venture.

Local employees, customers, suppliers, business counterparts, and government officials view them as personal representatives of the sending organization. Its image and reputation is strongly influenced by their behavior. Their success or failure also has great impact on the desirability of international assignments to potential future expatriates. Intercultural requirements for effective expatriate adjustment and performance include those listed here.

Cognitive-Based

❑ Understanding culture and its impact on expatriate morale and performance

❑ Recognizing the specific cross-cultural differences faced in the host country

❑ Being aware of their own cultural values, assumptions, and expectations

❑ Understanding the process of expatriate adaptation and patterns of adjustment

❑ Learning about the host-country's geography, history, economy, and politics

❑ Understanding the corporate culture and business practices of local counterparts

❑ Planning and managing their own international career paths

❑ Applying their international knowledge and experience after their repatriation

Skill-Based

❑ Adapting to a new cultural environment

❑ Managing personal and family cross-cultural stress

❑ Creating acceptable living conditions and rewarding lifestyles in-country

❑ Gaining effective verbal and nonverbal cross-cultural communication skills

❑ Developing job-related intercultural skills

❑ Establishing and maintaining good social and job relations with local counterparts

❑ Working toward cultural synergy

❑ Readapting successfully to life and work at home upon their return

International Business Travelers

Companies at all stages of globalization rely on international business travelers to support their cross-border operations. The length of their trips may range from a few days to a few months. Their short-term involvement with international employees, customers, suppliers, and business associates may have long-term positive or negative consequences. These travelers are from various levels of the organization and have different job responsibilities.

Numerous reasons exist for international business trips. Some examples are prospecting for new business opportunities, troubleshooting, exchanging knowledge and technology, overseeing financial performance, and managing marketing and sales campaigns. Other activities include negotiating deals and commercial ventures, building and maintaining interfirm relationships, assessing international competition, and promulgating corporate values, strategies, and policies. Trips also are made merely to learn about the company's overseas operations.

Despite the variety of purposes for their visits to other countries, international business travelers have many cross-cultural challenges in common. Typically, their intercultural requirements include the following.

Cognitive-Based
❑ Understanding and accepting the company's global vision and strategy
❑ Knowing about business conditions in their assigned regions and countries
❑ Realizing how cultural differences affect international business relations
❑ Being aware of their own cultural values, assumptions, and expectations
❑ Perceiving how they are viewed by their international counterparts
❑ Recognizing the specific cross-cultural differences they face
❑ Discerning the motivations, intentions, and feelings of counterparts

Skill-Based
❑ Applying verbal and nonverbal cross-cultural communication skills
❑ Dealing effectively with local government officials and bureaucrats

❑ Adjusting to different national corporate cultures and practices
❑ Handling international business protocol and etiquette effectively
❑ Confronting and resolving cross-cultural friction and conflict
❑ Participating in and managing multicultural teams
❑ Using job-specific skills, such as cross-cultural technology transfer, training, sales, marketing, or negotiating

Home Office Staff

A group whose cross-border roles are frequently overlooked is composed of those employees who interact with people in other countries at long distance. They rarely have the opportunity to meet their international counterparts face-to-face. Nevertheless, the relationships they maintain and the impressions they create often have significant impact on the company's international business. The fact that their communication is conducted via correspondence, telephone, facsimile, e-mail, or other electronic means does not lessen the potential cross-cultural barriers to mutual understanding. On the contrary, the absence of important nonverbal cues such as gestures and facial expressions and status indicators such as age and dress can make effective communication much more difficult.

Furthermore, the parties communicating with each other have virtually no opportunity to interact with each other socially in order to build a relationship. There is no personal, much less cultural, context in which to understand each other's words. Therefore, long-distance communications tend to be relatively brief, direct, and impersonal, especially in the time-conscious US corporate environment. People in countries that place high value on personal relations may be offended by what they interpret as curt, disrespectful messages.

Likewise, if the distant counterparts consider social protocol and formality to be of great importance, attempts to be humorous, familiar, or casual could be insulting to them. Another challenge is to convey negative feedback, such as reporting late deliveries or quality problems, at a distance, to people whose cultures stress face-saving. What would be considered a mild and polite criticism in the United States could be taken as a devastating put-down. The opposite problem is that it is easy to underestimate the seriousness of their muted and subtle expressions of displeasure.

In some cases, home office staff members do get to meet their counterparts and other international business visitors. These face-to-face encounters generally occur in the corporate headquarters and in the business units. The visitors' expectations regarding hospitality, gift-giving, and social protocol may make hosting them cross-culturally challenging. The impressions these international guests carry home with them after their visit could have important business consequences. Therefore, it is important that the employees who receive them be prepared to offer them culturally appropriate hospitality. Intercultural requirements listed here are essential for home office staff involved in cross-border relations.

Cognitive-Based

❏ Understanding culture and its impact on international business communications
❏ Being aware of their own cultural values assumptions and expectations
❏ Learning about the specific cross-cultural communications differences they face
❏ Recognizing the innate limitations of long-distance communication
❏ Knowing how their communication style is likely to be interpreted by distant counterparts in different countries
❏ Appreciating the importance of their cross-border business relationships
❏ Understanding the expectations and needs of international business visitors

Skill-Based

❏ Building and maintaining good long-distance, cross-cultural relationships
❏ Tailoring their long-distance communications for cultural appropriateness
❏ Accurately interpreting international counterparts' meanings
❏ Dealing effectively with cross-cultural misunderstandings via long distance
❏ Projecting a positive image of the company via distant communications

❑ Using appropriate protocol and etiquette to host international visitors
❑ Sharing their cross-cultural insights and learning with their peers

Host-Country Employees and Counterparts

The local people who interact frequently with expatriates and international business travelers and who visit the corporate home office periodically are another group whose intercultural needs require attention. They may be employees of the company or counterparts in a local joint venture or business alliance. Although these people generally speak English and have some acquaintance with world culture, you cannot assume that they possess the awareness, knowledge, and skills they need to effectively handle their side of the cultural interface.

Their attitudes, values, and expectations naturally have been shaped by their own cultural backgrounds. Their management styles and practices reflect the national corporate cultural environments in which they were trained. Despite having a veneer of international sophistication, at a deep cultural level they often differ greatly from their colleagues from abroad. Unless these differences are confronted and dealt with constructively, they remain hidden obstacles that undermine effective transnational cooperation and teamwork.

A fundamental requirement for cultural synergy in a cross-border organization is that its coworkers understand each others' cultural backgrounds. Neglecting to recognize host-country employees' and counterparts' needs for intercultural training and development is a very common mistake. Cultural awareness and cross-cultural skills are essential on *all* sides of any interface involving two or more cultures. Among the intercultural requirements of host-country employees and counterparts are the following:

Cognitive-Based
❑ Understanding the role of their country within the company's global strategy
❑ Learning about the culture and its impact on international business relations
❑ Being aware of their own cultural values, assumptions, and expectations
❑ Perceiving how they are viewed by their colleagues from abroad

❑ Knowing what cultural differences they face in interactions with their counterparts
❑ Recognizing the cross-cultural challenges faced by expatriates and international business travelers in their country

Skill-Based
❑ Adapting to the global or parent company's culture, values, and policies
❑ Adjusting to the values and management practices of their international counterparts
❑ Guiding and assisting international colleagues in their cultural learning and adjustment
❑ Using effective verbal and nonverbal cross-cultural communication skills
❑ Participating in and managing multicultural teams
❑ Promoting and supporting cultural synergy

Cross-Border Team Membership

All of the employees in the categories described above are likely to participate in cross-border teams as members or leaders. In either case, they face new challenges and requirements as they perform their roles in intercultural teams. In order to support them with appropriate training and development, you need to be aware of the issues that must be addressed in workshops on multicultural teamwork.

The Nature of Teams

All teams are groups, but all groups are not teams. A team is an organized group with a mission. Carl Larson and Frank LaFasto write in their classic book, *Teamwork* (Sage Publishing, 1989), that "[a] team has two or more people; it has a specific performance objective or recognizable goal to be obtained; and coordination of activity is required for the attainment of the team goal or objective." For a group to become a team, it goes through several developmental stages. The following stages were described by B. Aubrey Fisher in *Small Group Decision Making* (New York: McGraw-Hill, 1980) and popularized by Ken Blanchard and other team-building trainers.

Team Developmental Stages
❏ Forming: The first phase in which the team's purpose, parameters, and membership are defined.
❏ Storming: The period when intragroup differences and task/role disagreements are confronted.
❏ Norming: The stage of developing team culture, cohesiveness, and rules.
❏ Performing: The level at which the team achieves productivity and creates solutions.

Multicultural Teamwork

It is essential for you to be aware that team members and leaders from diverse cultural backgrounds typically have very different assumptions and expectations regarding their roles and responsibilities during each of these stages. For example, westerners tend to assume that the team is being formed in order to achieve a specific outcome. Members from Asia are more likely to expect that the purpose of the team is to become an effective tool. Consequently, during the formation stage, they tend to focus more on the group process and the functioning of the team than on its end product.

In northern European cultures, "storming" is characterized by relatively frank and open confrontation. In the Far East, where face-saving is important, disagreement and divergent opinions are usually expressed indirectly or in subtle ways. Team members from countries such as the United States and Australia, where individualism is highly valued, may face some difficulty integrating themselves into the group during the "norming" phase. By contrast, Filipinos, Japanese, and Malaysians generally consider working in groups entirely natural.

The "performing" stage requires team members to give and receive feedback, recognize and confront problems, and accept individual and group accountability. How these tasks are done varies greatly in different countries. Likewise, cultural values influence how the productivity and performance of a team and its members are measured. What teams are able to accomplish depends a great deal on the quality of leadership they receive. However, the definition of a good team leader is another key area in which diverse team members are likely to disagree.

The challenges and difficulties that must be overcome by cross-border teams are apparent in the issues already identified. The potential benefits and payoffs of good intercultural teamwork are equally well worth considering. For instance, a culturally diverse team can tap a much broader range of values, viewpoints, and experiences than can a homogenous one. This asset is important when the team's task requires creative and innovative solutions. More importantly, an organization or company cannot hope to "think globally and act locally" without the contributions of effective multicultural teams (see Exhibit 4–2).

CHALLENGES	BENEFITS
Cultural value differences	Multiple perspectives
Conflicting management styles	Wide range of options/solutions
Unshared expectations	International savvy
Diverse communication patterns	Global manager incubator
Team member role ambiguity	Intercultural synergy potential

EXHIBIT 4–2. THE MULTICULTURAL TEAM.

Multicultural Team Building

Most intercultural service providers offer training workshops on multicultural team building. These programs typically include the following components:

❑ The Importance of Culture: Recognizing the impact of cultural values, perceptions, beliefs, and assumptions on teamwork.

❑ Cross-Cultural Communications: Understanding the principles of effective cross-cultural communications and gaining the required skills.

❑ Managing Cultural Differences: Learning how to identify and constructively deal with cultural difference among team members.

❑ Valuing Differences: Appreciating the richness of the members' diverse backgrounds and respecting their cultural values.

❑ Leveraging Differences: Discovering practical ways to transform differences into being assets rather than liabilities for the team.

❑ Teamwork Skill Building: Developing and practicing the skills required in order to be an effective multicultural team member.

If you determine that your employees need training in intercultural teamwork to perform their roles effectively on cross-border teams, you may use these components to assess the designs of the workshops that potential suppliers offer you for that purpose.

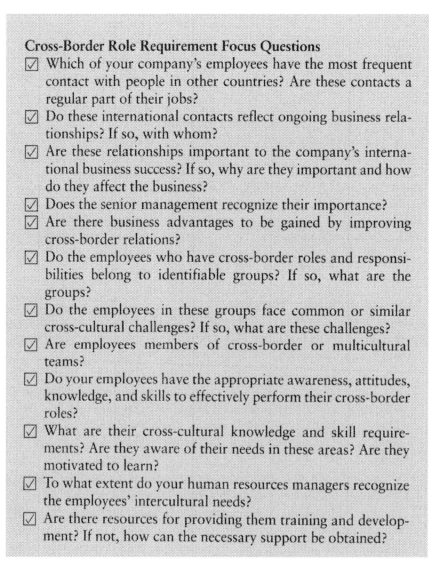

Cross-Border Role Requirement Focus Questions

☑ Which of your company's employees have the most frequent contact with people in other countries? Are these contacts a regular part of their jobs?

☑ Do these international contacts reflect ongoing business relationships? If so, with whom?

☑ Are these relationships important to the company's international business success? If so, why are they important and how do they affect the business?

☑ Does the senior management recognize their importance?

☑ Are there business advantages to be gained by improving cross-border relations?

☑ Do the employees who have cross-border roles and responsibilities belong to identifiable groups? If so, what are the groups?

☑ Do the employees in these groups face common or similar cross-cultural challenges? If so, what are these challenges?

☑ Are employees members of cross-border or multicultural teams?

☑ Do your employees have the appropriate awareness, attitudes, knowledge, and skills to effectively perform their cross-border roles?

☑ What are their cross-cultural knowledge and skill requirements? Are they aware of their needs in these areas? Are they motivated to learn?

☑ To what extent do your human resources managers recognize the employees' intercultural needs?

☑ Are there resources for providing them training and development? If not, how can the necessary support be obtained?

The Global Manager's Role

A global manager must be cosmopolitan, effective as an intercultural communicator and negotiator who creates cultural synergy . . .

Philip R. Harris and Robert T. Moran in
Managing Cultural Differences

A New Kind of Leader

Much has been written about the global manager being a new kind of leader required by the phenomenon of business globalization. The cross-border roles and responsibilities described above have mostly emerged in response to changes in the international business environment. The global manager's role transcends those roles both in scope and perspective. It requires a proactive stance that involves anticipating and exploiting new developments in the global marketplace rather than merely reacting to them. It implies having a worldwide viewpoint that has no home country bias. It means continually thinking on a global scale. It includes being responsible for marshaling, organizing, and managing corporate resources for globally maximized results.

Lawrason D. Thomas, Executive Vice President of Amoco Corporation, is an example of such a global manager. In the book, *Globalizing Management*, by Pucik, Tichy, and Barnett (see reference in Chapter 3), Thomas describes the challenge he faces:

> Globalization means doing business with a worldwide focus basis rather than doing business in an international market with the focus from a US viewpoint . . . A successful global business understands business conditions both locally and worldwide and conducts its activities (manufacturing, marketing, distribution, finance, human resources, R&D, and design and engineering) on a global optimized basis.

Senior business leaders have become aware of the need for managers who can meet this kind of challenge. A 1996 Conference Board report on the repatriation of expatriates indicated that more than two thirds of the chief executives of the world's major multinational corporations recognize that developing competent global managers is essential to their companies' success. Intercultural service providers offer consulting and training seminars on globalization, global thinking, and developing global managers. Books, videotapes, and other instructional materials are also available on these topics. To better understand these services and products, you should be aware of the competencies and attributes of the global manager.

New Competencies and Attributes

The competencies of global managers include many of those also needed by managers functioning on the international and multinational corporate levels. However, these capabilities are applied on a much broader scale and on a higher level. In addition, some requirements are unique to the role of global manager. The following lists highlight the unique ways of thinking, feeling, and acting that characterize global managers.

Ways of Thinking
Global managers are required to see the business environment differently and think about it in new ways. This "global mindset" includes developing a worldwide business perspective by

❑ Perceiving business risks and opportunities on a planetary basis
❑ Seeing the company as an entity without borders or a national identity
❑ Identifying with the global company and feeling accountable and loyal to it
❑ Representing the global viewpoint in business strategizing and planning
❑ Accessing and filtering business information from widespread international sources
❑ Keeping the global corporate mission and goals in focus amid ambiguous, dynamic, and sometimes chaotic international business conditions
❑ Being continually engaged in a global learning process

Global managers also need to exhibit new cultural perspectives in their professional life by

❑ Being aware of their own "cultural baggage" but transcending it
❑ Having keen interest in learning about other cultures
❑ Understanding the intercultural dimension of global business
❑ Recognizing opportunities for cultural synergy
❑ Discerning individual versus cultural differences
❑ Accurately interpreting cross-cultural signals of warning, threat, approval, acceptance, discomfort, agreement, displeasure, support, disagreement, and manipulation
❑ Correctly assessing the values, motivations, and agendas of international colleagues, counterparts, subordinates, and other stakeholders
❑ Thinking about business matters from different cultural viewpoints

Ways of Feeling

Global managers also have characteristic feelings about themselves, others, and the world. On a personal emotional level, they often report that their role entails

❑ Enjoying international travel and unfamiliar foods, music, and cultural events
❑ Liking the challenge of learning about other cultures and customs
❑ Being relatively uninhibited when practicing new behaviors
❑ Not feeling threatened by uncertainty or ambiguity
❑ Having self-confidence but not over-confidence
❑ Being motivated by the personal and professional rewards of a global career

On an interpersonal level, global managers find that their role requires

❑ Finding satisfaction in social interaction and personal relationships
❑ Feeling comfortable among people from other cultures
❑ Feeling empathy toward other people and their concerns and problems
❑ Accepting colleagues from other cultures as equals
❑ Enjoying mentoring and coaching colleagues from other countries

Activities and Tasks

A global manager's role requires acting in new ways and doing things differently in order to support their organization's or company's

worldwide mission and goals. These tasks and activities include dealing with the intercultural dimension by

❑ Readily adjusting to different cultural values and practices
❑ Networking with multicultural colleagues and associates on a
   worldwide basis
❑ Conducting business diplomacy at the highest corporate and gov-
   ernmental levels
❑ Balancing conflicting interests of stakeholders in different countries
❑ Promoting and supporting multicultural teamwork
❑ Learning from colleagues of all nationalities
❑ Sharing of best practices between country operations
❑ Managing cultural and ethnic diversity within the organization
❑ Facilitating cultural synergy in the company's cross-border relation-
   ships

   They also discover that effectively handling the global business dimension means

❑ Being a catalyst to move the company toward a global level of func-
   tioning
❑ Representing the global perspective in corporate strategy planning
   processes
❑ Keeping well informed about international business conditions
❑ Identifying and managing global business risks and opportunities
❑ Flexibly and quickly adapting to changes in the global business en-
   vironment
❑ Promulgating the corporate global vision, values, and strategy
❑ Protecting and enhancing the corporation's worldwide reputation
❑ Modeling global managerial attitudes and behaviors to peers and
   subordinates
❑ Encouraging and supporting the development of new global man-
   agers

   Most of the books and articles on the role of the global manager
have been written and published in the United States. The preceding
lists largely reflect the thinking of US authors. An influential report,
Redesigning Management Development Training in the New Europe,
was published in 1998 by the European Training Foundation, an

agency of the European Union. This report was written by 12 management consultants from the Torino Group who represented eight countries in western, central, and eastern Europe. In their chapter on the new challenges facing European companies, they stress the increasing need to develop the manager's capability to

- ❑ Manage in different cultures and business environments
- ❑ Manage cross-cultural management teams, project teams, and task forces
- ❑ Mobilize people across borders
- ❑ Lead global change
- ❑ Monitor business improvement globally and locally
- ❑ Develop and implement global strategies
- ❑ Be humble so as to learn, respond, respect, and be respected at any place, any time

There seems to be a lot of agreement among thinkers in the management development field worldwide regarding the general outlines of the global manager's role. Therefore, you can expect orientation and training programs on global management skills from service providers (especially in the United States and Europe) to be fairly similar in focus and content.

Global Manager Focus Questions

- ☑ Is your company, or any of its business units, currently functioning on a global scale? If not, will it be doing so in the foreseeable future?
- ☑ Are your key international managers qualified and prepared to lead global business enterprises?
- ☑ Is your international business being hampered by a shortage of global managers?
- ☑ If so, does your Human Resources department have plans to recruit, hire, train, or develop them? Are there resources available to implement these plans?
- ☑ Do your senior managers understand what is required to be an effective global manager? If not, are there plans to educate them?
- ☑ Is the global manager role clearly defined in your company? If not, why not? If so, is it a respected and valued one?

Cross-Border Role Analysis

> 'Here I am, now what do I do? Where do I start?' . . . International
> assignments are much less structured: we may not know what, who, or
> when! Once we unpack our luggage, we must figure out what to do
> next.
>
> **Gary Fontaine** in *Managing International
> Assignments*

The intercultural competencies and attributes of the various cross-border roles presented in this chapter are common requirements for anyone who may be assigned to perform those roles. They provide general definitions of the scope and content of the roles. However, much more specific and detailed requirements become apparent when employees deal with cross-border situations and relationships on an individual level where the actual cross-cultural interfaces occur. Bridging the gap between understanding one's role requirements conceptually and knowing what to do in a particular situation is essential to being interculturally effective.

Too often, however, employees are provided little or no guidance to help them take this important step. Usually, they are expected to discover on their own how to apply their cross-cultural knowledge and skills in the "real world." Giving them a technique to use to identify their individual role requirements may well make the difference between their success and failure during face-to-face interactions.

The Cross-Cultural Role Analysis Exercise

The cross-cultural role analysis exercise is a tool designed to help expatriates, international business travelers, and others with cross-border business responsibilities visualize and analyze their roles within the interpersonal and cultural context in which they are performed. The outcome of this exercise is a detailed set of attitude, skill, and knowledge requirements that pertain to their particular cross-cultural relationships. It enables them to take into account individual personalities and job definitions as well as cultural backgrounds.

To be most effective, someone who is knowledgeable about intercultural relations and well acquainted with both the employee's host culture and home culture should facilitate the exercise. Ideally, the facilitator should also be familiar with the employee's job and cross-border role. The exercise is enhanced greatly by the participation of a former expatriate or a resource person from the specific country to provide cross-cultural insights and details.

The cross-cultural role analysis exercise is based on the concepts that roles are performed in a matrix of relationships and that all relationships require two-way transactions between the people involved. Both parties must give to and receive much from each other for the relationship to work. Good relationships enable them to get what they need from each other in order to perform their respective roles. In a cross-cultural setting, understanding the expectations of one's counterpart regarding the content and the nature of these transactions is especially important. Too often, people in cross-border relationships make the mistake of assuming that their counterparts want from them what they would want under similar circumstances. This is a case where the "golden rule" is not a very good guide to behavior. It is much more effective to discover what the counterparts want and give that to them. Doing so makes it far more likely that, in turn, one will receive what is needed to perform one's own role. Using the cross-cultural role analysis exercise helps cross-border employees fine-tune those interpersonal transactions most important to their success.

Instructions for the Exercise

1. The individual cross-border employees identify the key cross-cultural counterparts with whom they must interface in order to perform their roles. As illustrated in Exhibit 4–3, on a sheet of paper, they draw a diagram consisting of a ring of four or five circles with one in the center. They place their own names in the central circle and label each of the other circles with the names of those cross-cultural counterparts most important to their success. They indicate relationships with close counterparts by positioning those circles closer to their own. They then connect each of the circles to theirs with arrows pointing in both directions to depict the two-way transactions of each relationship.

2. On another sheet of paper, they draw two boxes for each set of two-way transactions with the individual counterparts. The first box is labeled "FROM." In it, they list what they need from that counterpart in order to perform their roles in-country. In the second box,

labeled "TO," they list what they must give to the counterpart in order to receive what they need in return. Both lists are limited to only those things that are essential. The lists may include, for example, friendship, information, acceptance, openness, confidentiality, support, trust, cooperation, approval, credibility, respect, responsiveness, reliability, and confidence. This process is then repeated for each major relationship.

3. On a third piece of paper, they draw a box for each counterpart that contains three columns labeled "ATTITUDES," "KNOWLEDGE," and "SKILLS." In each box, they list the specific attitudes, knowledge, and skills they must have in order to meet the needs and expectations of that particular counterpart considering his or her cultural background, personality, and the nature of the relationship. These lists are then used to set individual development and learning goals for themselves. They also provide valuable input for custom-tailoring intercultural services to employees' needs.

An Example: Tanya's Challenge

The example illustrated in Exhibit 4–3 is based on an actual international assignment. The expatriate (we will call her Tanya) was a US employee of a major clothing manufacturer. She was located in a Central American country. As head purchaser for the company's factory in-country, she was responsible for managing supplier relations. Felipe, the owner of the local firm that supplied the textiles the company used most frequently, was Tanya's most important counterpart. Her main goal for their relationship was making Felipe feel like a "partner" rather than a mere vender.

Because Tanya's company was Felipe's largest customer, they both had much to gain from a closer relationship. However, Felipe was still resentful about how he felt her predecessor (also a US expatriate) had looked down on him and treated him "coldly." As a business leader in his community and a member of an important family, Felipe had a strong sense of pride and dignity. Tanya's role was to win him over in order to strengthen the ties between their two companies to ensure a reliable and timely supply of textiles for the factory.

When she analyzed her role, Tanya discovered that Felipe's good will was essential to the success of her assignment and that she had some relationship repairing to do. She recognized the impact of specific cultural

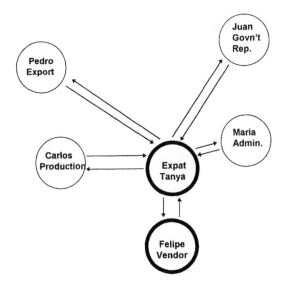

Tanya Needs from Felipe	Tanya Must Give to Felipe
Good personal relationship	Respect due his status
Healed hurt feelings	Latin-style "personableness"
Credibility as a manager	Evidence of professional competence
Commitment to "partnership"	Vision of win-win "partnership"
Supplier reliability	Credible sincerity
Accurate, timely production data	Stable customer assurance

EXHIBIT 4–3. CROSS-CULTURAL ROLE ANALYSIS EXERCISE: TANYA'S ROLE DIAGRAM.

values such as social status consciousness, the high value placed on personal warmth (being "simpático"), the precedence of relationship over task, the importance of cordial formality in communications, and Felipe's traditional Latino attitudes towards women in the workplace. She

Tanya's key cross-cultural role requirements for relating to Felipe

Attitudes	Knowledge	Skills
Interpersonal interest	History of Felipe's relationship	Building relationships
Cultural curiosity	Identification of cultural issues	Managing cultural differences
Respect	Latin emphasis on pride and dignity	Showing respect appropriately
Sociability	Importance of being "simpático"	Demonstrating personal warmth
Desire for good communication	Latin American communication style	Communicating across cultures
Professional self-confidence	Latin American gender roles	Projecting competence and professionalism

became aware of the attitudes, knowledge, and skills she required to be able to give Felipe what he needed from their relationship. She then applied herself to demonstrating these attitudes, gaining the knowledge, and practicing the skills. Eventually, she won his trust and friendship.

Visualizing and understanding cross-border roles at the individual level generates useful input for assessing employees' needs for orientation, training, or development. It also gives them stronger motivation for learning because it vividly demonstrates the connection between their performance cross-culturally and their success or failure. In addition, having a clear picture of your employees' role requirements in such detail enables you to help providers custom-tailor the objectives of their programs to the learners.

Cross-Cultural Role Analysis Questions
☑ How could a role analysis be helpful to Tanya and Filipe?

☑ Do your cross-border employees have a clear picture of their roles in relation to their key international counterparts?

_____

☑ Do they understand the importance of each of these personal relationships? _____

☑ Are they aware of the individual as well as cultural factors involved in these relationships? _____

☑ Have they considered the attitudes, knowledge, and skills they require?

_____

☑ How well do they understand what they need to give and what they must receive in their interpersonal transactions in order to successfully perform their cross-border roles? _____

_____

☑ Have they been prepared to handle these transactions effectively? _____ If not, would they welcome a role clarification exercise? _____

☑ Do you have qualified in-house facilitators or cultural resource people to conduct cross-cultural role analysis exercises? _____ If not, do you have access to external assistance? _____

☑ How could expatriate role analysis exercises be useful to your training and expatriate support staff? _____

_____

Summary and Suggested Action Steps

This chapter is an overview of the cross-border roles, relationships, and responsibilities of the people who actually implement the global business mission of a company. Senior executives, expatriates, international business travelers, and many home office staff have important roles to play. The cultural settings in which they must function are described in Chapters 2 and 3. The cross-cultural competencies of these employees contribute directly to tangible international business results.

The new role of global manager as a "driver" and facilitator of a company's globalization process is also an increasingly essential corporate asset. Knowing the intercultural challenges these people face is the first step toward enabling you to help prepare them for their cross-border roles.

Here are some ways you can use the content of this chapter:

1. Inventory the cross-border roles in your company or business unit by reviewing the international activities of the members of the four groups presented (senior home office executives, inter-country assignees, international business travelers, home office staff engaged in distant communications, and host-country employees and counterparts).
2. Share the appropriate list of competencies from this chapter with each group and discuss it with them to determine its relevance and importance to them.
3. Contact the video producers and publishers on the recommended resources list to identify videos and business guides about your company's specific host-countries. Provide these resources to the appropriate employees in the groups listed to start orienting them to the cultures with which they interface.
4. Determine which employees are members of cross-border or multi-cultural teams. Assess their need for the kind of intercultural team building workshop described in this chapter.
5. Identity actual or potential global managers, if any. Share and discuss the section on the global manager's role with them. Ask them to consider possible professional development goals that may come to mind. Suggest that they read appropriate books or articles on the resource list.
6. Conduct a Cross-Cultural Role Analysis of the cross-border relationships and transactions of several representative employees. Decide on the feasibility and desirability of using it with others. Use the information generated as input for setting objectives of learning activities.
7. Ask internationally experienced colleagues the focus questions and document their answers. Share this information with key human resource managers and senior executives.
8. Announce new expatriate assignments and repatriations, important cross-border business trips, and visits from international counterparts in your company newsletter or intranet to increase their visibility and to highlight the importance of their roles.

9. Consult with potential intercultural service providers and share your lists of cross-border employee requirements with them. Get their recommendations for appropriate products or services.

Resources

Cross-Border Role Requirements

Acuff, F. L. *How to Negotiate Anything with Anyone, Anywhere Around the World.* New York: AMACOM Press, 1997.

Adler, N. J., and Izraeli, D. N. (eds.). *Competitive Frontiers: Women Managers in a Global Economy.* Oxford, UK: Blackwell Publishing, 1994.

Aguilar, L., and Stokes, L. *Multicultural Customer Service: Providing Outstanding Service Across Cultures.* New York: McGraw-Hill, 1995.

Axtell, R. E. *Do's and Taboos of Hosting International Visitors.* New York: John Wiley & Sons, 1990.

Bartlett, C. A., and Ghoshal, S. *Cross-Border Management: Text, Cases, and Readings in Cross-Cultural Management.* Homewood, IL: Business One Irwin, 1992.

Bartlett, C. A., and Ghoshal, S. *Managing Across Borders: The Transnational Solution.* (2nd ed.) Cambridge, MA: Harvard Business School Press, 1998.

Brake, T., Walker, D. M., and Walker, T. *Doing Business Internationally: The Guide to Cross-Cultural Success.* Burr Ridge, IL: Irwin Publishing, 1995.

Briggs, T., and Corcoran, M., with Axtell, R. E. (ed.). *Do's and Taboos around the World for Women in Business.* New York: John Wiley & Sons, Inc., 1997.

Buckley, P. J., Campos, J. and Mirza, H. (eds.). *International Technology Transfer by Small- and Medium-Sized Enterprises.* New York: St. Martins Press, 1997.

Cullen, J. B. *Multinational Management: A Strategic Approach.* Cincinnati, OH: South-Western College Publishing, 1998.

DeKieffer, D. E. *The International Business Traveler's Companion,* Yarmouth, ME: Intercultural Press, 1992.

Dersky, H. *International Management: Managing Across Borders.* Reading, MA: Addison-Wesley Longman Publishing Company, 1997.

"Doing Business Internationally: The Cross-Cultural Challenges," 43-minute videotape (includes leader's guide, participant workbook, and audio cassette), MultiMedia Inc., 15 North Summit Street, Tenafly, NJ 07670, tel: (800) 682–1992 and Princeton Training Press, 247 Nassau Street, Princeton, NJ 08542, tel: (609) 497–0645,1994.

Dowling, P., Welch, D. E., and Schuler, R. S. *International Human Resource Management: Managing People in a Multinational Context.* Cincinnati, OH: South-Western College Publishing, 1998.

Dresser, N. *Multicultural Manners.* New York: John Wiley & Sons, 1996.

Earley, C., and Erez, M. *The Transplanted Executive: Why You Need To Understand How Workers in Other Countries See the World Differently.* Oxford, UK: Oxford University Press, 1997.

Elashmawi, F. *Competing Globally: Mastering Cross-Cultural Negotiation.* Houston, TX: Gulf Publishing Company, 2000.

Fatehi, K. *International Management: A Cross-Cultural and Functional Perspective.* Englewood Cliffs, NJ: Prentice Hall, 1997.

Ferraro, G. P. *The Cultural Dimension of International Business.* (2nd ed.) Englewood Cliffs, NJ: Prentice Hall, 1994, pp. 86–111.

Fisher, G. *Mindsets: The Role of Culture and Perception in International Relations.* (2nd ed.) Yarmouth, ME: Intercultural Press, 1997.

Foster, D. A. *Bargaining Across Borders: How To Negotiate Business Successfully Anywhere in the World.* New York: McGraw-Hill, 1992.

Frazee, V. "Send Your Expats Prepared for Success." *Workforce,* Vol. 78, No. 3, 1999, pp. 6–11.

Gesteland, R. R. *Cross-Cultural Business Behavior: Marketing, Sourcing, Negotiating and Managing across Cultures.* (2nd ed.) Copenhagen, Denmark: Copenhagen Business School Press, 1999.

Ghauri, P. N., and Usunier, J. C. (eds.). *International Business Negotiations.* New York, Pergamon Press, 1996.

Gudykunst, W. B., Ting-Toomey, S., and Nishida, T. *Communication in Personal Relationships Across Cultures.* Thousand Oaks, CA: Sage Publications, 1996.

Guy, V., and Mattocks, J. *The International Business Book: All the Tools, Tactics, and Tips You Need for Doing Business Across Cultures.* Lincolnwood, IL: NTC Business Books, 1995.

Ioannou, L. "Stateless Executives." *International Business.* Feb. 1995, pp. 48–52.

Hailey, J. *The Essence of Cross-Cultural Management.* Englewood Cliffs, NJ: Prentice Hall, 2000.

Jackson, T. *Cross-Cultural Management*. Oxford, UK: Butterworth-Heinemann, Linacre House, 1993.

Korzenney, F., and Ting-Toomey, S. *Cross-Cultural Interpersonal Communication*. Newbury Park, CA: Sage Publications, 1991.

Koslow, L. E. *Business Abroad: A 10-Step Guide to International Business Transactions*. Houston, TX: Gulf Publishing Company, 1996.

Kubin, M. *International Negotiating: A Primer for American Business Professionals*. Binghamton, NY: Haworth Press, 1995.

Lewis, R. D. *When Cultures Collide: Managing Across Cultures*. Sonoma, CA: Nicholas Brealey Publishing, 1996.

Mead, R. *International Management: Cross-Cultural Dimensions*. (2nd ed.) Oxford, UK: Blackwell Publishing, 1998.

Mendenhall, M., and Oddou, G. (eds.). *Readings and Cases in International Human Resource Management*. (2nd ed.) Cincinnati, OH: South-Western College Publishing, 1995.

Mockler, R. J., and Dologite, D. G. *Multinational Cross-Cultural Management*. Westport, CT: Greenwood Publishing Group, 1997.

Moran, R. T. (ed.). *Global Business Management in the 1990s*. Washington, DC: Beachman Publishing, 1990.

Moran, R. T., Braaten, D., and Walsh, J. (eds.). *International Business Case Studies for the Multicultural Marketplace*. Houston, TX: Gulf Publishing Company, 1993.

Moran, R. T., and Stripp, W. *Dynamics of Successful International Business Negotiations*. Houston, TX: Gulf Publishing Company, 1991.

Morrison, T., Conaway, W. A., and Douress, J. J. *Dunn & Bradstreet's Guide to Doing Business Around the World*. Englewood Cliffs, New Jersey: Prentice Hall, 1997.

Nelson, C. A. *Protocol for Profit: A Manager's Guide to Competing Worldwide*. Stamford, CT: International Thomson Business Press, 1998.

Oddou, G. R., and Derr C. B. *Managing Internationally: A Personal Journey*. Orlando, FL: Harcourt Brace College Publishers, 1998.

O'Hara-Devereaux, M., and Johansen, R. *Globalwork: Bridging Distance, Culture, and Time*. San Francisco, CA: Jossey-Bass Publishers, 1994.

Osland, J. S. *The Adventure of Working Abroad—Hero Tales from the Global Frontier*. San Francisco, CA: Jossey-Bass, 1995.

Puffer, S. M. (ed.). *Management Across Cultures*. Malden, MA: Blackwell Publishers, Inc., 1996.

Rosen, R., Digh, P., Singer, M., and Phillips, C. *Global Literacies: Lessons on Business Leadership and National Cultures.* New York: Simon & Schuster, 2000.

Solomon, C. M. "Short-Term Assignments and Other Solutions." *Workforce,* Vol. 78, No. 3, Mar. 1999, pp. 38–42.

Ting-Toomey, S. *The Challenge of Facework: Cross-Cultural and Interpersonal Issues.* Albany, NY: State University of New York Press, 1994.

Torrington, D. *International Human Resource Management: Think Globally, Act Locally.* Englewood Cliffs, NJ: Prentice Hall, 1994.

Varner, I., and Beamer, L. *Intercultural Communication in the Global Workplace.* Chicago, IL: Irwin Professional Publishers, 1995.

Wilson, M. S., Hoppe, M. H., and Sayles, L. R. *Managing Across Cultures: A Learning Framework.* Greensboro, NC: Center for Creative Leadership, 1996.

Country-Specific Business Cultures

Country Business Guides, brief guide books on 11 countries, are available from Meridian Resources Associates, 1741 Buchanan Street, San Francisco, CA 94115, tel: (800) 626–2047 and (415) 749–2920, fax: (415) 749–0124, e-mail: contact@mera.com.

Culturegrams, four-page country briefing pamphlets on 167 countries, are available from Kennedy Center Publications, Brigham Young University, 280 Herald R. Clark Building, PO Box 24538, Provo, UT 84602–4538, tel: (800) 528–6279 and (801) 378–6528, fax: (801) 378–5882, Web site: http://www.edu/culturegrams.

Culture Shock! Country Guides, a series of brief books on cultural practices in 36 different countries, are available from Graphic Arts Publishing Company, 3019 N. W. Yeon, Portland, OR 97210, tel: (503) 226–2402, fax: (503) 223–1410, e-mail: sales@gacpc.com.

Doing Business Internationally: Business Reports, a series of 84 brief country-specific books, can be obtained from Craighead Publications, Inc., PO Box 1006 Darien, CT 06820–1006, tel: (203) 655–1007, fax: (203) 655–0018, e-mail: info@craighead.com.

Do's and Don'ts around the World, is a series of books on cultural and social taboos and etiquette in Africa, Asia, Europe, the Middle East, South America, the Caribbean, Oceania, the United States, and Canada by Gladson S. Nwanna, published by World Travel Institute Press, 1997–1998. These books are available from Open Communications, Inc., 10640 North 28th Drive, Suite A200,

Phoenix, AZ 85029, fax: (602) 530–3569, e-mail: open.media@pobox.com.

Dunung, S. P. *Doing Business in Asia: The Complete Guide*. (2nd ed.) San Francisco, CA: Jossey-Bass, 1998.

E.I.U. Country Profiles & Reports, brief overviews and reports on 83 countries, are available from the Economist Intelligence Unit, 111 West 57th Street, New York, NY 10019, tel: (800) 938–4685 and (212) 554–0600, fax: (212) 586-1181/2, e-mail: newyork@eiu.com.

The Hunter Country Review series, *Africa Review; 53 Countries, Asia and Pacific Review; 58 Countries*, and *Americas Review; 50 Countries* was produced in 1997 by Hunter Publishing. It is available from Open Communications, Inc. online bookstore at http://www.opengroup.com/cgi-bin/search/find on the Internet.

Interact Country Guides, a series of in-depth overviews of the cultures of 15 countries, edited by George Renwick, is available from Intercultural Press, PO Box 700, Yarmouth, ME 04096, tel: (800) 370–2665 and (207) 846–5168, fax: (207) 846–5168, e-mail: books@interculturalpress.com.

International Business Interact series is a set of booklets on more than 45 countries. They are available from Shersen International, Inc., 29 Arden Road, Mountain Lakes, NJ 07046, tel: (973) 625–5916, fax: (973) 625–1035, e-mail: sst@att.net.

International Business Videos, a series of videotapes on 14 countries in Latin America and Asia, can be ordered from Big World Inc., 4204 Tamarack Court, Suite 100, Boulder, CO 80304, tel: (800) 682–1261 and (303) 444–6179, fax: (303) 444–6190, e-mail: bigworld@aol.com.

International Straight Talk, a series of video tapes on human resource management issues in 14 different countries, is available from William Drake & Associates, PO Box 2838, Waxahachie, TX 75165, tel/fax: (972) 938–2927, e-mail: bdrake@onramp.net.

ITRI Videos, a series of multi-part videos on working in Japan, China, and the United States (for Asians), is available from Meridian Resources Associates, Inc., 1741 Buchanan Street, San Francisco, CA 94115, tel: (800) 626–2047 and (415) 749–2920, fax: (415) 749–0124, e-mail: contact@mera.com.

Living Abroad Country Profiles, profiles of 84 countries, are available from Living Abroad Business Association, 32 Nassau Street, Princeton, NJ 08542, tel: (6069) 924–9302, fax: (609) 924–7844, e-mail: laba@livingabroad.com.

Morrison, T., and Conaway, W. A. *The International Traveler's Guide to Doing Business in Latin America.* New York: Macmillan Spectrum Press, 1997, is a book with overviews of 18 countries.

Morrison, T., Conaway, W. A., and Border, G. A. *Kiss, Bow, or Shake Hands: How To Do Business in Sixty Countries.* Holbrook, MA: Bob Adams Media Corporation, 1994.

Passport to the World Books is a series of booklets on 22 countries published between 1994–1996. They are available from World Trade Press, 1450 Grant Avenue, Suite 204, Novato, CA 94901, tel: (800) 833–8586 and (415) 898–1124, fax: (415) 898–1080, e-mail: world press@aol.com.

Peregrine Audio Guides, business-oriented audiotapes produced in 1992 on China, Mexico, Japan, and Germany, are available from Peregrine Media Group, PO Box 6721, Yorkville Finance Station, New York, NY 10128.

Price Waterhouse Information Guidebooks is a series of business-oriented booklets on 119 different countries from Price Waterhouse Coopers, 1251 Avenue of the Americas, New York, NY 10020–1104, tel: (212) 596–7000, fax: (212) 6620, Web site: http://www.132.174.112/infosrc/pw/.

Put Your Best Foot Forward is a series of guide books on doing business in Europe, Asia, Mexico, Canada, Russia, and South America and business-oriented audiotapes on China, Japan, Mexico, Germany, Morocco, France, and Brazil. They are available from Terra Cognita, 300 West 40th Street 314, New York, NY 10019, tel: (212) 262–4529, fax: 92120 262–5789, e-mail: info@terracognita.com.

Sabath, A. M. *International Business Etiquette: Asia & the Pacific Rim*, Franklin Lakes, NJ: Career Press, 1998.

Seldon, P. *Business Travelers' World Guide*, New York: McGraw-Hill, Inc., 1998.

Williams, J. *Don't They Know It's Friday? Cross-Cultural Considerations for Business and Life in the Arabian Gulf.* Dubai, United Arab Emirates: Motivate Publishing, 1998.

Worldwide Business Briefings is a series of briefing booklets on 52 countries (in print and online), and *International Business Audio Guides*, is a series of audio tapes with booklets on 22 countries. They are available from International Cultural Enterprises, Inc., 1241 Dartmouth Lane, Deerfield, IL 60015, tel: (800) 626–2772 and (708) 945–9516, fax: (708) 945–9614, e-mail: ice@mcs.com.

Cross-Border Team Membership

Bataglia, B. "Multicultural Team Building: Avoiding Mistakes." in *Cultural Diversity at Work*, Vol. 5, No. 4, March 1993, pp. 4.

Bataglia, B. "Skills for Managing Multinational Teams." In *Cultural Diversity at Work*, Vol. 4, No. 3, January 1992, pp. 5.

Berger, M. (ed.). *Cross-Cultural Team Building: Guidelines for More Effective Communication and Negotiation*, London: McGraw-Hill, 1996.

Building the Transnational Team is a training videotape available from the American Society for Training and Development, 1640 King Street, Box 1443, Alexandria, VA 223313–2943, tel: (800) 628–2788 and (703) 683–3100, fax: (703) 693–1523, e-mail: csc4@astd.org.

Global Team Process Questionnaire is an intercultural diagnostic instrument available from ITAP International, 268 Wall Street, Princeton, NJ 08540, tel: (609) 921–1446, fax: (609) 924–7946, e-mail: itap@itapintl.com.

Halverson, C. "Managing Differences on Multicultural Teams." In *Cultural Diversity at Work*, Vol. 4, No. 5, May 1992, pp. 10–15.

Harris, P. R. *Twenty Fully Reproducible Assessment Instruments for the New Work Culture*, Amherst, MA: HRD Press, 1995. See "Team Performance Survey."

Hatch, E. K. "Cross-Cultural Team Building and Training," *Journal for Quality & Participation*, No. 18, 1995 , pp. 44–49.

Larson, C., and LaFasto, F. *Teamwork: What Must Go Right, What Can Go Wrong*. Newbury Park, CA: Sage Publications, 1989.

Moran, R. T., Harris, P. R. and Stripp, W. G. *Developing the Global Organization*. Houston, TX: Gulf Publishing, 1993. See "Cross-Cultural Team Development," pp. 59–89.

Leslie, J. B., and Van Valsor, E. *A Cross-Cultural Comparison of Effective Leadership and Teamwork: Toward a Global Workforce*. Greensboro, NC: Center for Creative Leadership, 1998.

Myers, S. G. *Teambuilding for Diverse Work Groups: A Practical Guide to Gaining and Sustaining Performance in Diverse Teams*. Irvine, CA: Richard Chang Associates, Inc. and Jossey-Bass, 1996.

Phillips, N. *Managing International Teams*. London: Pitman Publishing, 1992.

RHR International "Making Teams Work Across Distances and Differences." *Executive Insights*, Vol.13, No. 4, 1996.

Werner, J. M. "Managing a Multinational Team." *Business & Economic Review*, Vol. 41, 1995, pp. 15–18.

The Global Manager's Role

Adler, N. J., and Bartholomew, S. "Managing Globally Competent People." In S. M. Puffer (ed.), *Management Across Cultures: Insights from Fiction and Practice.* Cambridge, MA: Blackwell Publishers, Inc., 1996, pp. 408–429.

Alkhafaji, A. F. *Competitive Global Management: Principles and Strategies.* Delray Beach, FL: St. Lucie Press, 1995.

Bartlett, C. A., and Ghoshal, S. "What Is a Global Manager?" *Harvard Business Review*, September/October, 1992, pp. 131.

Black S. J., Gregersen, H. B., Mendenhall, M. E., and Stroh, L. *Globalizing People through International Assignments.* Reading, MA: Addison-Wesley Longman Publishing Company, 1999.

Brake, T. *The Global Leader: Critical Factors for Creating the World Class Organization.* Burr Ridge, IL: Irwin Professional Publishers, 1996.

Elashmawi, F., and Harris, P. R. *Multicultural Management 2000: Essential Cultural Insights for Global Business Success.* Houston, TX: Gulf Publishing Company, 1998.

Funakawa, A. *Transcultural Management: A New Approach for Global Organizations.* San Francisco, CA: Jossey-Bass Publishers, 1997.

Harris, P. R. *The New Work Culture: HRD Strategies for Transformational Management.* Amherst, MA: HRD Press, 1997.

Hofstede, G. "Think Locally, Act Globally: Cultural Constraints in Personnel Management." Management International Review, Vol. 38, No. 2, 1998, pp. 7–26.

Javis, J. "Training Global Managers for Cultural Dexterity." *Cultural Diversity at Work*, Vol. 9, No. 4, March 1997, pp. 12–17.

Kets de Vries, M.F.R., and Mead C. "The Development of the Global Leader within the Multinational Corporation." In V. Pucik, N. M. Tichy, and C. K. Barnett (eds.), *Globalizing Management: Creating and Leading the Competitive Organization*, New York: John Wiley & Sons, Inc., 1993, pp. 187–205.

Kinsey Goman, C. *Managing in a Global Organization: Keys to Success in a Changing World.* Menlo Park, CA: Crisp Publications, 1994.

Lobel, S. "Global Leadership Competencies : Managing to a Different Drumbeat." *Human Resources Management*, No. 26, 1990, pp. 39–47.

Moynihan, M. *The Economist Intelligence Unit Global Manager: Recruiting, Developing, and Keeping World Class Executives.* New York: McGraw-Hill, Inc., 1993, pp. 99–117.

"New Skills for Global Management." A 39-minute videotape with a booklet produced in 1993 by MultiMedia Inc., 15 North Summit Street, Tenafly, NJ 07670, tel: (800) 682–1992.

Rhinesmith, S. H. *A Manager's Guide to Globalization: Six Keys to Success in a Changing World.* (2nd ed.) Alexandria, VA and New York: ASTD Press and McGraw-Hill, 1996.

Rhinesmith, S. H. "Global Mindsets for Global Managers." *Training and Development*, October 1992, pp. 63–68.

Saner, R., Yiu, L. and Sondergaard, M. "Business Diplomacy Management: A Core Competency for Global Companies," *Academy of Management Executive*, Vol. 14, No. 1, February 2000, pp. 1–13

Simons, G. F., Vasquez, C., and Harris, P. R. *Transcultural Leadership.* Houston, TX: Gulf Publishing Company, 1993.

Stewart, T. A. "How To Manage in the Global Era." *Fortune*, January 15, 1990, pp. 58–72.

The Torino Group, *Redesigning Management Development Training in the New Europe.* Torino, Italy: European Training Foundation, 1998.

Wolniansky, N. "International Training for Global Leadership." *Management Review*, May 1990, pp. 27–28.

5

Foundations of Intercultural Learning

If you don't know to what harbor you are sailing, no wind is sufficient to take you there.

Seneca

What, Why, Who, and How
The diverse and complex ways in which people and organizations act and interact in cross-cultural settings generate a multitude of challenges and opportunities often masked as complaints, obstacles, and problems. Sorting through these issues to identify tangible, high-priority needs and then transforming them into on-target learning objectives are critical tasks. By setting the objectives, the client maintains control over the direction and content of the learning and development process. What are the most important needs? Why are they important to the organization? Who has these needs? How can the needs best be fulfilled? These are the essential questions that must be answered in order to ensure that intercultural services and products are used to maximum advantage.

Assessing Intercultural Needs

> Assessment is objective perception of the actual situation. It is of the first order.
>
> From the prologue of *Secret Art of War: The 36 Stratagems*, an ancient Chinese military text

Why Assess Needs?

Prior to deciding to use any intercultural program or product, you must determine the need for it. Needs should be described in clear and compelling terms to help justify the investment of your organization's or company's resources in meeting them. But more importantly, well-defined needs are the foundation of the entire intercultural service cycle, which includes objective-setting, delivery of services, measurement of outcomes, evaluation, and quality improvement. Exhibit 5–1 depicts this cycle and highlights the importance of starting with well-defined needs statements and then using them to set specific objectives.

Needs assessment is a process used to

❑ Identify gaps between current results and desired ones
❑ Prioritize the gaps (expressed as needs)
❑ Select the most important needs to be addressed

Effective needs assessment enables you to establish learning objectives that are more likely to be on-target, to select relevant, results-oriented services, and to achieve measurable outcomes. Having a clear understanding of the needs will give you assurance that you are heading in the right direction and enable you to explain and justify your choice of services and providers. It also strengthens your role when planning learning activities in conjunction with service providers and makes your discussions with them more productive. In addition, the exercise of examining needs, in itself, contributes to raising cultural awareness within your organization.

Lack of thorough needs assessment often leads to inappropriate buying decisions, ambiguous learning objectives, faulty program

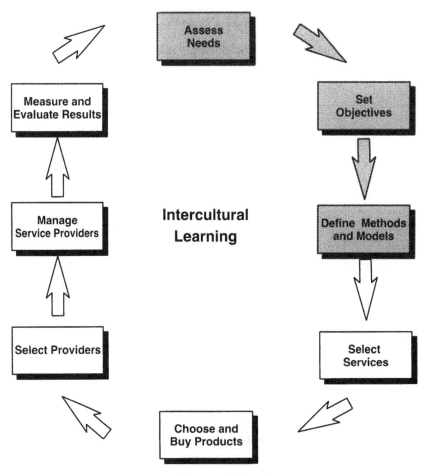

EXHIBIT 5–1. INTERCULTURAL SERVICES CYCLE.

implementation, a waste of time and resources, and learner dissatisfaction. Such false starts not only cause "buyer's remorse," but they also undermine in-house support for intercultural services. These high-potential payoffs and possible negative outcomes make it well worth your time and effort to do a careful job of needs definition "up front."

In-House Needs Assessment Clients

When you design and conduct intercultural needs assessments, you should keep two key constituencies in mind: those who have the needs and those in a position to enable them to fulfill their needs. The support and cooperation of both sets of in-house "clients" are essential to your efforts to gather thorough and accurate information on needs. Also, they are potential allies who can support your initiatives to acquire and introduce services aimed at fulfilling the needs you have discovered. In addition, the prospective learners are more motivated to participate in training and development activities if they clearly understand their needs. Therefore, their requirements and interests must be considered when deciding what kind of information to collect.

Needs Assessment Target Groups
- ❑ Senior executives concerned with the global mission of the company and responsible for its international business strategies
- ❑ Managers of business units that have significant cross-border operations
- ❑ Directors of particular international business ventures and projects
- ❑ Trainers and human resource managers responsible for international personnel
- ❑ International business travelers
- ❑ Expatriates and their families (including non-US expatriates)
- ❑ Repatriating employees and their families
- ❑ Home office staff who have long-distance, cross-cultural roles and relationships
- ❑ Members of multicultural work groups
- ❑ International negotiation team members

The Concept of Needs

Effective definition of needs depends on a clear understanding of the concept of "need." Simply put, a need is a gap between current results and outcomes and those desired. Recognizing the existence and size of the gap and wanting the improved results provide motivation for seeking fulfillment of the need. Therefore, two major aspects of need definition must be considered:

❑ Visualization of attractive and attainable potential results
❑ Analysis of the nature and extent of the gap between current and desired results

Exhibit 5–2 illustrates the gap concept of need. The process of visualization and gap analysis described here applies equally to individuals, work groups, functional categories, business units, and entire organizations. Any method selected for assessing needs should incorporate these two elements and address both of them.

The Visualization Stage

The first step in need identification is to picture more rewarding alternatives than the present results of one's efforts. However, intercultural needs may be difficult to identify because the desirable payoffs are often beyond the awareness of the individual. An international buyer, for example, may have a vague feeling that a relationship with a certain Mexican supplier could be more satisfying and less stressful. But, not knowing what a good business relationship is from a Mexican viewpoint, the purchaser cannot picture it or use it as a model. Likewise,

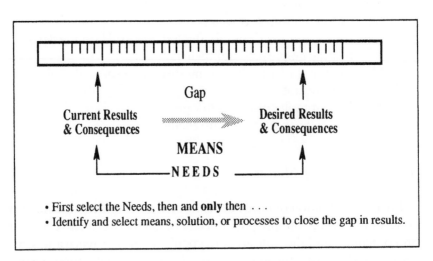

EXHIBIT 5–2. THE GAP CONCEPT OF NEED. (Source: Roger Kaufman, Alicia Rojas and Hanna Mayer, Needs Assessment: A User's Guide. Educational Technologies Publications, 1993. Used with permission.)

those who have no idea that their jokes may be offensive to Japanese associates are unable to perceive the benefit of changing their behavior. On the surface, Japanese counterparts generally continue to be polite and accommodating whether they are offended or not, so there is no feedback to help one visualize a better approach. Also, many international employees are simply working at such a fast pace that they have not paused to reflect on ways in which their intercultural relationships might be improved.

These are cases of the potential learners not knowing what they don't know. Being unable to see that there are better options available to them, they are unaware of their needs. Awareness-building activities and constructive feedback are very helpful in this kind of situation. At a minimum, these interventions help employees discover that they have something useful to learn and that what they don't know may, in fact, be hurting them. Ideally, they will form clearly focused mental pictures of desirable results they want to achieve.

Gap Analysis

The goal of gap analysis is to recognize where you are presently compared to where you want to be. This process is quite straightforward. In the book *Effective Training Strategies*, Ricardo Rezende, a Brazilian human resources director, was quoted as saying "It's fairly simple. There is a job to do. The guy has this, but the guy needs that (to do the job). In between there's a gap. Our job is to find and describe the gap. Then we design programs to help people bridge the gap."

This process enables you to determine the direction of required change and to estimate the time and effort it will take to achieve the desired results you have visualized. However, judging the distance between current and desired intercultural outcomes is hampered by the "invisibility" of culture. Comparison of your intangible beliefs, attitudes, and values with those of someone from a different culture is intrinsically difficult.

The lack of candor that characterizes communications in many cultures also increases the challenge of discovering gaps. Even when feedback is available, it may be in the form of nonverbal messages that are difficult to decipher. Furthermore, people who have been limited to their home cultural backgrounds rarely have sufficient self-awareness to determine their own cultural starting points. Not having a basis for comparison prevents them from gauging the distance between their current and optimal levels of intercultural performance and from recognizing the kind of changes required to bridge the gap.

These factors also favor the use of awareness-building activities during the needs assessment process. Bicultural employees often can play an important role in these activities. They should be credible representatives of their cultures who have overcome the inhibitions they may have had about giving direct feedback. Usually they require encouragement, support, and preparation to effectively play this culturally challenging role. Alternatively, outside consultants and resource people may be used to give feedback and analyze intercultural need gaps. Questionnaires may also be designed for analyzing gaps and planning training program content. Typically they use rating scales to measure the learners' own estimates of the size of the gaps they face. Exhibit 5–3 shows samples of questions that might be used with potential expatriates.

Writing Needs Statements

Needs assessments typically produce a set of written statements of particular needs. Their usefulness for setting learning and development objectives depends on their clarity and precision. The following criteria are helpful when writing needs statements:

❑ Single focus: Each need identified should focus on only one topic.
❑ Brevity: The statements should be no more than one or two sentences in length.
❑ Results-orientation: The desired results to be achieved should be clear.
❑ Gap description: The gap between current and desired results should be described.

An example of a poorly written needs statement is "I need information on Japanese business etiquette to be more effective during my next business trip to Japan." This statement is too broad. "Business etiquette" could include gift exchange, table manners, introductions, greeting protocol, and much more. It does not describe either the desired result (being "more effective" is too general), and it does not indicate the nature or size of the gap ("needing information" is only a hint of the gap). A well-written statement would be "I want to show Mr. Nakajima I appreciate the extra work he did for me during my last visit. But I don't know what kind of gift to take him, how it should be

Please *check* the number that describes your current level of *knowledge* about your host-country and *circle* the number that best indicates the level required for you to be successful in your international assignment:

❑ The culture (major values, beliefs and attitudes) of the host—country people
Very little   1   2   3   4   5   A great deal

❑ The history of the country (key events, leaders, and influences of the past)
Very little   1   2   3   4   5   A great deal

❑ Current events (contemporary happenings, trends, issues, and news topics)
Very little   1   2   3   4   5   A great deal

Please *check* the number which describes your current level of intercultural *skill* and *circle* the number that best indicates your required level:

❑ Establishing new business relationships with local clients
Little skill   1   2   3   4   5   Highly skilled

❑ Managing a household in your country of assignment
Little skill   1   2   3   4   5   Highly skilled

❑ Entertaining host-country friends, counterparts, and business associates
Little skill   1   2   3   4   5   Highly skilled

EXHIBIT 5–3. SAMPLE GAP ANALYSIS QUESTIONS.

wrapped, or when and how to give it to him." In this statement, the desired outcome (Nakajima's awareness of being appreciated) and the gap (lack of knowledge and skill in appropriate gift-giving) are both clearly identified. The statement is brief and focused on a single topic. The different approaches to needs assessment described in the following section should produce well-written needs statements that lend themselves to setting objectives.

Approaches to Needs Assessment

You can use different methods and techniques to assess the intercultural needs of individuals, groups, and organizations. The selection of a particular one depends on the time and resources available, the nature, depth and thoroughness of the information being sought, the type of assessment practices accepted within the corporate culture, and the preference of the person(s) conducting the assessment. The methods commonly used include

Questionnaire-Based Surveys

Custom-tailored questionnaires aimed at specific potential learners can be effective and flexible tools for gathering information on intercultural needs. These questionnaires typically are 2–4 pages in length and include

❑ Explanation of the purpose and importance of the survey
❑ Request for background information on the learners' intercultural roles, responsibilities, and experience
❑ Instructions for completing and returning the questionnaire
❑ A list of preselected potential needs with a five- or seven-point rating scale to indicate the perceived importance of each one. The intercultural challenges and cross-border requirements described in Chapters 2, 3, and 4 offer many possible needs from which to select in creating such a list.
❑ Several blank items for adding needs not included on the preselected list
❑ Space for open-ended suggestions and comments

The questionnaires may be designed to focus on expatriates, international business travelers, global managers, multicultural teams, or any other group whose intercultural needs you may want to assess. This method produces quantitative and qualitative data useful for prioritizing needs and for setting learning objectives. It also helps raise cultural awareness by requiring the respondents to consider their intercultural needs in a structured way. Questionnaires may be sent and received via mail, fax, or e-mail. Better response rates are obtained if senior management stresses the importance of the survey. The completed questionnaires are relatively easy to summarize into reports for the respondents and the managers who must approve the use of intercultural services. If feasible, combine the questionnaire-based survey with other methods.

Assessment Interviews

Face-to-face interviewing of employees who represent groups that have cross-cultural roles and responsibilities is another technique for gathering information on intercultural needs. This approach has the benefit of allowing a deeper exploration of issues and feelings in a highly personal context. Follow-up questions during the interview and feedback from the interviewees may lead to productive discussions of unanticipated topics and areas of need. The interviews typically are one to two hours long. The subjective descriptions of needs obtained in interviews often contain anecdotes and concrete examples that are highly credible and compelling when used to promote the use of intercultural services.

Interviews are also used to diagnose the intercultural needs of employees and their spouses who are bound for overseas assignments. In this application, the interview results are usually shared with appropriate human resource and training managers. The data is used to customize cross-cultural training programs for them and to determine other development resources or support they require to be successful in their assignments. In some case, the results are shared only with the interviewees themselves as feedback to be used for gaining self-awareness and setting self-development goals.

Compared to the questionnaire–based survey approach, interviews are somewhat more demanding because of the scheduling challenges involved, the time needed to conduct the interviews, the interviewer skills required, and the difficulty of analyzing, interpreting, and reporting the relatively open-ended (and sometimes emotional) information gathered. These factors necessitate more time investment and expertise on the part of the staff responsible for managing the interviews and make this approach more costly than most other methods of needs assessment.

Considerations for planning and conducting interviews include

❑ Positioning the interviews: The employees should consider the interviews a high-priority activity in which it is an honor to participate. Having them announced by a senior international figure in the company, for example, will enhance the perceived importance of the interviews and increase the motivation of the interviewees.

❑ Defining the sample: If not everyone in a category is to be interviewed, a sample must be selected. The sample should include people who face the most obvious and high-priority, cross-cultural challenges. They should be seen by their peers to be representative. People of different cultural backgrounds should be included. Expatriate spouses and non-US employees and counterparts should not be overlooked.

❑ Focusing the interviews: Determine in advance if the focus is on the needs of the individuals being interviewed, the needs of the groups they represent, or some combination of the two. In any case, the interviewer should have a structured set of questions based on specific potential intercultural needs, which permits the gathering of comparable data from the different interviews. Open-ended questions should also be used. These questions should be broad enough in scope to elicit unrestrained responses but narrow enough to keep the focus on intercultural topics generally.

❑ Selecting the interviewers: The interviewers must have had successful, in-depth cross-cultural experience themselves to be effective intercultural needs gatherers. In addition, they should possess good listening, interviewing, and note-taking skills.

❑ Preparing the interviewees: The interviews are more productive if their purpose and focus is shared with the interviewees in advance. Also providing them with an appropriate reading or video (from the resources listed in Chapters 2 and 4) before the interview will stimulate their thinking process and help them focus on the topics to be discussed.

❑ Structuring the setting: The interviews are best conducted in a comfortable non-office environment away from business distractions and interruptions. Having some sort of international or ethnic decoration in the room symbolically sets a pleasant intercultural tone for the interview.

❑ Preparing the interviewers: They should receive detailed information on the interviewees' cultural backgrounds and cross-cultural experience. If a written survey or an assessment instrument has been administered, information pertaining to the interviewees should be read in advance. Interviewers also must have clear guidelines regarding the amount and type of data desired in the reports they are to write.

❑ Analyzing the data: Compiling, interpreting, and organizing the relatively subjective and unstructured data that may be generated by interviews requires a higher level of skill than does processing a questionnaire-based survey. A qualified person should be responsible for collecting and synthesizing the information contained in the interviewers' reports.

❏ Writing the report: The interviewees need to know that their views were accurately heard, and the decision-makers considering the possible use of intercultural services must be given an overall summary of the findings and recommendations. The report has to satisfy both types of readers. This dual requirement often makes the writing of the report a challenge.

Focus Groups

Another common method of intercultural needs assessment is the use of focus groups. These groups are formed to gather input from a number of stakeholders simultaneously. They might be focused on any issue or topic. The composition of the group depends on its task. For a broad focus on the general intercultural challenges of an organization, a cross-section of international employees and nonemployees such as expatriate family members, consultants, suppliers, subcontractors, clients, and joint venture counterparts may be included. A narrower topic, improving expatriate morale, for example, typically involves only a representative sample of expatriates, their international human resource managers, and a specialist consultant. Depending on its scope and the number of participants, a focus group meeting may take from several hours to a full day to conduct.

This approach to needs assessment often produces a greater number of ideas because participants stimulate each other's thinking, and the group exercises generate creativity. It is also an excellent occasion for conducting cultural awareness building activities, which increase the quality of the group's output. In addition, using a focus group permits some on-the-spot compromise and synthesis of diverse viewpoints and allows for an initial prioritization of needs.

The participants tend to develop a sense of group solidarity as they discover they have similar needs and concerns. This group spirit helps build support for meeting the needs identified. The focus group participants also may become the nucleus of a network through which to promote interest in the intercultural services you ultimately decide to use. Often, an on-going task force is organized at the end of the meeting.

Some particular challenges are involved in using this method. The quality of a focus group's output depends, to a large extent, on the skill of the group facilitator(s). Effective management of the discussions and group exercises such as icebreakers, problem identification, brain-storming, consensus-building, and needs prioritization is essential to the success of the event. Therefore, well-qualified facilitators must be found. The groups tend to produce a wide variety of unstructured ideas at a rapid pace, which makes the data difficult to record, summarize, and quantify. Writing a report suitable for planning and decision-making purposes is often challenging. Another consideration is the time, effort, and cost required to organize and manage the event and to bring the participants together.

It is important to report the results of the focus group session(s) to the participants. Their expectations probably will have been raised. Their motivation for continuing to support your initiatives to introduce inter-cultural services largely depends on receiving credible evidence that they have been listened to and that something tangible will be done to meet their needs. At a minimum, your report should include a summary of the major findings, the priority of the needs identified, what the next planning steps are, and when they will be taken. A more comprehensive and detailed version of the report may be necessary for key decision-makers if you need their approval before exploring possible solutions.

Assessment Instruments

There are a variety of multipurpose instruments available for screening, assessing, selecting, and recruiting international personnel (which will be described in Chapter 6). Some of these tools are very useful for diagnosing individuals' needs for intercultural training and development. Each instrument is based on its own theories, research methods, and results. Some of them are products of in-depth statistical studies or surveys of expatriates or international business people, whereas others are based on the insights of well-recognized interculturalists. Still others are linked to standard psychological tests. They may be "stand-alone" self-scored questionnaires or require analysis and interpretation by assessment specialists.

When considering the selection of a particular instrument, several criteria are worth keeping in mind:

❏ Appropriateness: Some instruments are more suitable than others for identifying needs for training and development. Those specifically aimed at screening and selection for international assignments, for example, may be less useful in this case than those designed to measure general cultural awareness or knowledge.

❑ Employee acceptance: Psychological testing and instrument-based assessments are well accepted by employees in some companies. In other corporate environments, these methods are distrusted and resisted. It is essential that the employees with whom the instruments are to be used have positive attitudes toward them.

❑ Credibility: The instruments vary greatly in their face validity. The potential learners, your human resource management colleagues, and you must have confidence in the validity of the instrument and the quality and relevance of the data upon which it is based. Looking beyond a vendor's claims to examine the product's technical underpinnings should greatly increase your own confidence and comfort level.

❑ User-friendliness: Some instruments are short, simple to complete, and self-scored. Others are more complicated and involve having a specialist administer them or require sending the completed questionnaires to a central facility for analysis and scoring. Avoid instruments that are so superficial and transparent that they are unlikely to be taken seriously. Likewise beware of those that are too complex or theoretical to provide clear and practical feedback. Tradeoffs generally have to be made to obtain the best combination of ease of use and value of product. The main consideration should be the quality, amount, and usefulness of the information produced for the interviewees and the planners of their intercultural learning and development activities.

❑ Cost/Benefit: Prices of instruments range from about $5 to nearly $300 US each. This expense has to be justified by its contribution to the cost-effectiveness of training and development or to gains in productivity on the job. Because actual financial data on the benefits of intercultural competence is rarely available, most purchasers must rely on estimates of savings and productivity gains to decide whether the price of an instrument is reasonable.

Direct Observation

Intercultural specialists may be used to monitor the interaction of employees and their counterparts in cross-cultural settings. For example, observations may be done during business meetings, sales presentations, face-to-face or long-distance customer relations, negotiation sessions, technical training classes, multicultural teamwork, and during interviews of culturally diverse employees or job applicants. The direct observation approach requires selecting appropriate settings, designing instruments for recording observation notes, advising employees that they will be monitored and explaining why, conducting the observations, and compiling, analyzing, and reporting the data.

This method has the advantage of gathering data on problems and issues within the actual context in which they occur. The information obtained is objective and highly credible. It provides useful input for the analysis of gaps between current and desired results. If done unobtrusively, this approach causes minimal interruption of work flow and group activities. The quality of the information produced is highly dependent on the skill of the observers, the extent of their knowledge of the process and content of the work being performed, and the appropriateness of the observation categories being used. In addition, a high level of trust is required on the part of the employees to allow them to behave normally while under observation.

Critical Case Analysis

Outstanding cases of success or failure of cross-cultural business transactions may be examined for evidence of intercultural needs. This approach entails reviewing project plans, reports, evaluations, and communications between the parties involved. It also requires interviewing the principal players individually and conducting group sessions to debrief the major incidents and events leading to the success or failure. The aim is to determine what went right and what went wrong and why. Then the conclusions are analyzed to assess the impact and importance of intercultural factors.

This method is intrinsically complex, open-ended, and unstructured. However, if it is done effectively, it can be a powerful stimulus for change. This method requires an intercultural assessor who has a high level of business knowledge and professionalism plus strong analytical and consulting capabilities. Obtaining accurate information on failed projects is especially difficult because of the understandable embarrassment and defensiveness typically shown by those involved. Overcoming this obstacle is possible only through the application of exceptional relationship and trust-building skills. The data obtained is generally of great interest to high-level management and to all employees familiar with the case. Reporting the findings requires a finely tuned sense of balance between constructive criticism and discretion. It is unlikely that a person with such a unique combination of business and intercultural qualifications can be found in-house. Therefore, this approach generally necessitates contracting for the services of a consultant. Furthermore, an outsider may be viewed as being more objective and neutral.

Cross-Cultural Role Analysis Exercise

Another tool for assessing the intercultural needs of individual expatriates and international business travelers is the cross-cultural role analysis exercise. It was described in Chapter 4 as a method of raising awareness of the implications of cross-border roles and responsibilities. This exercise is also helpful for determining individuals' needs for training and development. It is particularly useful in cases where the employees understand their cross-border roles well enough to permit a productive analysis. Because it does not involve the purchase of a product and does not require a high level of expertise to facilitate, it is a relatively simple and inexpensive alternative. Nevertheless, a qualified intercultural specialist should be used to obtain the maximum benefits of this method.

Prioritizing Needs

Intercultural needs must be ranked by importance so that your organization's or company's resources can be used most wisely. The key to effectively prioritizing needs is to carefully define the criteria upon which they are to be based. The criteria must be consistent with your organization's values, directions, and goals. Therefore, selecting criteria involves considering where your company or organization is going, why it is moving in that direction, and how it plans to get there. Intercultural needs prioritization focuses on the global dimension of these considerations. Commonly used criteria include the following:

❏ Payoffs: What are the tangible benefits of closing the gaps between current and desired results? The benefits may be qualitatively and quantitatively measured and compared. Those with the most certain and biggest payoffs usually are considered the most critical ones.
❏ Urgency: Which needs should be addressed first and in what order? If a deadline or potential crisis is looming, fulfilling those needs required to meet the deadline or avoid the crisis is most important.

❑ Potential damage: What kind of harm might be done or costs incurred if the needs are not met? This criterion relates to matters such as failed expatriate assignments, conflicts with off-shore joint venture partners, ethnic discrimination lawsuits, attrition of internationally experienced employees, cross-cultural business ethics problems, and other incidents that could cause negative publicity.

❑ Employees affected: How broad is the impact of the needs? The larger the number of people who would be helped by the fulfillment of the needs, the more important the needs may be.

❑ Organizational values: Is meeting of the need(s) considered the right thing to do regardless of the tangible benefits of doing so? Some needs may have high priority simply because certain strongly held organizational values require that they be met.

A scale may be designed to rate the priority of the needs according to the preceding criteria or others you may want to consider. Then they can be compared and ordered by rank. This exercise does not replace the use of professional judgment during the process. But it does help surface those needs that merit priority attention and improves the effectiveness of discussions about them.

The Role of Service Providers

Ideally, intercultural needs assessment is a team effort involving the people in-house who have the needs, those responsible for fulfilling them, and service providers, who have tools and skills with which to help. Determining the needs of your employees ultimately is the responsibility of the appropriate in-house managers and should not be delegated to a supplier. The role of service providers is to contribute the expertise and resources that you lack in-house so you can fulfill that responsibility. Some ways in which vendors may offer valuable assistance with intercultural needs assessments include

❑ Sharing (nonconfidential) information on the kinds of needs their other clients face

❑ Providing data from studies and surveys of intercultural needs

❑ Benchmarking the practices of other companies

❑ Advising on assessment strategies and approaches

❑ Designing survey questionnaires and conducting surveys
❑ Interviewing employees
❑ Administering assessment instruments
❑ Organizing and facilitating focus groups
❑ Monitoring employees' intercultural performance
❑ Reviewing critical intercultural cases and events
❑ Analyzing assessment data and preparing reports
❑ Presenting intercultural needs awareness activities

Many providers are willing to offer some help identifying your company's needs, free of charge, in the hope of selling their services to you. Some suppliers include a certain amount of needs assessment in the planning and preparation of the services they deliver. Others prefer to perform assessments as separate services not necessarily linked to particular programs or products. In any case, the cost of gathering the information will be paid for directly or indirectly. Therefore, initial expense should not be the predominant factor when deciding how to finance the assessment.

If you already have done a thorough assessment in-house and are confident that you understand your employees' needs, you may want the supplier to gather only sufficient information to tailor a specific program or apply a product to those specific needs and concerns. However, if you are unsure of the nature and extent of your company's needs, you are well advised to contract with a consultant to help you assess them before considering the purchase of services.

You should be sure that your providers conduct assessments objectively and free from bias in favor of their own services. Avoidance of such conflicts of interest is an indication of a provider's integrity and trustworthiness. It pays to be skeptical of suppliers that try to convince you that they know your needs better than you do and those that claim needs assessment is unnecessary because their generic services meet the needs of all learners. Choosing the right consultant at the needs assessment stage can save you much time, money, and effort later.

Needs Assessment Focus Questions
☑ Are there any intercultural needs that affect your entire company or organization? If so, what are they?

☑ Which business units or work groups confront significant cross-cultural difficulties and challenges? What needs underlie these challenges?

☑ Are there particular individuals who have critical intercultural needs? Do they recognize them?

☑ How well do the key decision-makers understand the intercultural needs of the company and the groups and people in it?

☑ Have the needs been assessed systematically? If not, what has stood in the way?

☑ Which types of assessment methods are most compatible with your organizational culture? Which are most feasible?

☑ Are there in-house people qualified to conduct needs assessments? Do they have the necessary time and resources?

☑ Would cultural awareness activities help employees recognize their needs?

☑ Would the assistance of service providers be helpful for conducting awareness-building activities or implementing assessments? Do you have support for obtaining outside assistance?

Intercultural Learning Objectives

> Objectives are not fate; they are direction. They are not commands; they are commitments. They do not determine the future: they are the means to mobilize the resources and energies . . . for the making of the future.
>
> **Peter F. Drucker** in *People and Performance*

Having clear-cut, explicit objectives is essential for employees to effectively use the services made available to them and to know when they have gained their desired results. Service providers need well-defined learner objectives in order to tailor programs or apply products appropriately to the learners' needs. In-house managers and overseers of intercultural services require well-defined objectives to evaluate the performance of learners and providers. You need to ensure that providers are not only doing things right but doing the right things. By actively establishing objectives, a client determines the content and direction of the learning. For all these reasons, you should familiarize yourself with some of the basics of objective setting.

Selecting Learning Areas

Before setting objectives, you need to select the areas on which the learning or development activities should be focused. An assessment produces a wide variety of needs statements. Each one has implications for the kinds of objectives that would be most relevant. Therefore, you must consider which of the following learning categories apply to them:

❑ Awareness: Are the employees unaware of cultural realities that prevent them from reaching their desired results?
❑ Knowledge: Do the learners lack specific information required to meet their cross-border responsibilities?
❑ Skills: Are critical abilities missing that hinder employees' cross-cultural performance?
❑ Feelings: Are there emotional obstacles they need to overcome to be effective?
❑ Attitudes: Are their attitudes suitable for establishing and maintaining successful intercultural relations?

These learning areas are listed previously according to the difficulty of making changes in the learners. It is relatively easy to promote awareness but difficult to change attitudes. The length, depth, and rigor of intercultural training programs should take these factors into account. Short-cuts and superficial learning activities often fail to meet the learners' needs. Likewise, excessively detailed, lengthy, or comprehensive programs may be more than is required to achieve acceptable outcomes. Both of these design flaws cause the waste of resources. By setting feasible, on-target learning objectives, you can safeguard resources and establish an appropriate scope of work for your provider.

Setting Learning Objectives

The Oxford dictionary defines an objective as an aim, goal, or end of an action. When employees or work groups have clearly identified the goals they aim to achieve by bridging the intercultural need gaps that confront them, they are well on their way toward being able to set objectives. The assessment process produces needs statements that determine the starting points and directions for change. Objectives describe the desired destinations. They are the "targets" that the different approaches, methods, and models of instruction are designed to hit.

The following concepts and recommendations are aimed at enabling you to participate as an active and informed partner with your service providers when setting program objectives. You do not need to become an expert in writing objectives, nor do all your objectives have to be absolutely measurable. However, applying the principles of effective objective writing, to the extent feasible in your circumstances, will help your providers better help you.

Behavioral Objectives

Robert F. Mager, perhaps the most widely recognized expert on instructional objectives, strongly recommends that behavioral objectives be used for planning training and development activities. Characteristics of a well-written behavioral objective include

❑ Behavioral focus: It describes an observable action or behavior.
❑ Measurability: It can be measured in quantitative or qualitative terms.
❑ Performance-standard: It sets a standard for demonstrating an acceptable level of competency.
❑ Conditions specified: It defines the resources available to the learner and the context in which the learning will be demonstrated.

Behavioral objectives use action words (verbs) that are unambiguous and open to few interpretations. They describe what learners will be able to do upon completion of a training program. Using precise action words in objectives for training and development activities will help sharpen the focus of the learning and make the outcomes more measurable. Exhibit 5–4 provides examples of action words that are preferable in well-worded objectives, as well as some that should be avoided.

Despite the strong emphasis that behavioral objective setting guidelines put on measurable outcomes, it is wise to recognize that nonmeasurable objectives also have their place. The learners' more subjective, subtle, and intangible needs do not have to be forced to conform strictly to a predetermined objective setting technique. Remember Albert Einstein's saying, "Everything that can be counted doesn't necessarily count, and everything that counts can't necessarily be counted." Employees' feelings, attitudes, and self-concepts tend to fall within this realm.

LESS PRECISE	MORE PRECISE
Know	Demonstrate
Understand	Define
Be aware	Identify
Learn	List
Develop	Perform
Appreciate	Explain
Value	Prioritize
Comprehend	Describe
Recognize	Compare
Apply	Utilize
Perceive	Contrast
Analyze	Differentiate
Review	Write
Accept	Articulate

EXHIBIT 5–4. SAMPLE ACTION WORDS.

Help from Providers

Ideally, setting objectives should be a team effort including those who desire the improved results, the in-house people responsible for helping them achieve the results, and the service providers. Reputable providers are well versed in the art and science of objective setting. If you are conversant with the basic concepts and principles, your collaboration with them can greatly enhance the relevance and effectiveness of their services.

Providers can help in many ways, including

❑ Sharing samples of objectives from other programs
❑ Providing instructions and informative materials on objective writing
❑ Instructing or coaching employees or training managers in objective writing skills

❑ Editing and sharpening the focus of objectives
❑ Writing objectives for proposed learning and development activities

Objective Setting Focus Questions
☑ Are employees' and groups' definitions of their desired results clear and precise enough to be converted into practical learning objectives?
☑ If not, do they need help in writing objectives? Would a workshop or coaching be useful?
☑ Have their objectives been classified according to Learning Target Areas?
☑ Are in-house trainers and program designers competent in writing behavioral objectives? If not, would the assistance of providers be useful? Would other resources help?
☑ Will the objectives help determine realistic decisions regarding the required length, depth, and rigor of learning and development activities?
☑ Who is responsible for setting and approving the objectives?
☑ Should this responsibility be shared? If so, with whom and how?
☑ Is it appropriate to delegate objective setting to service providers? Why or why not?

Paths to Intercultural Learning

> World-class companies are . . . *learning-oriented*, searching for ideas and experience through informal inquisitiveness as well as formal education, . . . and investing in their people's knowledge and skills.
>
> **Rosabeth Moss Kanter** in *World Class*

Nearly all intercultural services are based on some form of learning. The wide range of services available is due, in part, to different assumptions and beliefs on the part of program designers regarding how people best learn. Therefore, before considering the purchase of a particular kind of program or product, it is important for you to become familiar with the various approaches, methods, and models that are typically used. None of them is either better or worse than the others, and each of them has unique advantages and drawbacks depending upon the circumstances in which it is used. Understanding the tradeoffs among them will help you distinguish between diverse services and assess which ones are most likely to enable your employees to meet their needs and achieve their learning objectives.

Basic Approaches

Broadly speaking, three general approaches commonly are used by providers of intercultural orientation and training. Each approach is characterized by its assumptions regarding the roles of the instructor and learner, by the methods it uses, and by the outcomes it expects. The approaches can be viewed as points along a spectrum representing the amount of active involvement required on the part of the learner. The didactic approach requires the least involvement, the participative approach is about mid-point, and the experiential approach is the most demanding. A particular program may combine elements of more than one of these approaches.

The Didactic Approach

The didactic approach, also referred to as the academic approach, is the traditional way in which instruction has been delivered. It is the approach most commonly used for orientation programs or briefings. The teacher is viewed as possessing knowledge the student lacks and needs. The teacher's role is to manage the instruction and transmit the knowledge to the student. The student's role is to be attentive and receptive. The outcomes expected are that the student will gain awareness and acquire a specific body of information. Teaching methods commonly used by this approach include

❏ Readings
❏ Lists of tips and "do's and don'ts"
❏ Written assignments
❏ Presentations and lectures
❏ Videotape viewing
❏ Demonstrations
❏ Student reports
❏ Guest interviews
❏ "Read-only" computer-assisted instruction

The Participative Approach

The participative approach emphasizes the active participation of the learner in the learning process. This approach is commonly used in training programs. The instructor or trainer is responsible for managing training sessions and involving the learners. The trainee's role is to participate and interact with the instructor(s) and the other trainees. This role demands more personal engagement and risk-taking on the part of the student than does the didactic approach. The expected learning outcomes include awareness, knowledge, and skills. The trainer and trainees share responsibility for achieving these outcomes. Methods generally used are

- ❑ Questions and answers
- ❑ Guided group discussions
- ❑ Panels and roundtables
- ❑ Case study analysis
- ❑ Brainstorming
- ❑ Debates
- ❑ Colloquia
- ❑ Board games
- ❑ Interactive computer-assisted instruction

The Experiential Approach

The experiential approach is based on the idea that learning occurs most effectively when the learner has had an experience that is later processed and analyzed. The learning discovered is then generalized and applied to a new experience. The role of the instructor is to guide and facilitate this discovery process. The learner's role is to have the experiences, to analyze them for lessons learned, and then apply those lessons to new situations. This approach gives the major responsibility to the learner, who uses the instructor as a resource. It demands more initiative, emotional involvement, and risk-taking on the part of the learner than do the other two approaches. Expected outcomes of the experiential approach include awareness, knowledge, skills, attitude changes, and increased capacity for self-directed learning. Methods commonly used include

- ❑ Role-plays
- ❑ Simulations

❑ Skill practice sessions and feedback
❑ Trust-building activities
❑ Actual problem-solving tasks
❑ Assessment profiles and feedback
❑ Field trips
❑ Host-culture home stays and visits
❑ Outdoor teambuilding and adventure techniques
❑ Self-disclosure exercises

Instructional Models

The preceding approaches are applied to different instructional models commonly used for employee development. Whereas philosophies and methods define approaches, models are characterized by their goals and the way they organize, structure, and deliver instruction. The major models used in cross-cultural instruction are orientation, training, and education. Orientation, sometimes referred to as "briefing," is based on information transfer and awareness-building. It usually is a relatively brief learning event. Training goes beyond orientation to teach the learners new skills and requires more time than orientation. Training often encompasses a series of seminars or workshops. Education focuses on giving the learners a broader and deeper understanding of the intellectual principles involved and the context in which their knowledge and skills may be applied. It also aims to enable the students to "learn how to learn" and to pursue further learning on their own. It is a fairly long-term process involving multiple interventions over time.

A specific program design may include features of different models. However, you can distinguish between learning models by comparing their goals, approaches, techniques, and methodologies. Exhibit 5–5 illustrates these differences.

Two-Axis Chart of Cross-Cultural Training Techniques and Methodologies
By Alexander Patico
Used with permission.

1. Description: Selected techniques are arranged according to two dimensions: a continuum between two types of *goals* (for training), from *cognitive* (related to thought, the abstract, the

(continued on page 163)

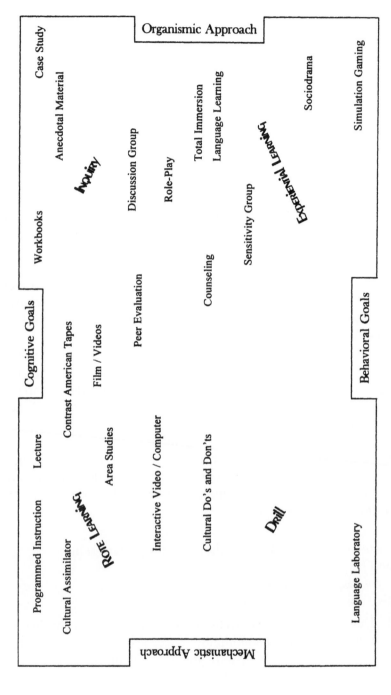

EXHIBIT 5-5. CROSS-CULTURAL TRAINING TECHNIQUES AND METHODOLOGIES. (Chart© 1984 by Alexander Patico. Permission has been obtained.)

(continued from page 161)

rational) to *behavioral* (related to action, the concrete, the functional). A second axis defined by the polar opposites *mechanistic* and *organismic* is used here to describe different *approaches* to training in which the learner is seen either as a "learning machine" or as a "person" in a holistic sense.

2. Placement: The arrangement of items is illustrative, not definitive. Each technique *seems to fit* in a particular *region* of the universe represented by the chart. For example, a simulation game is *involving* and *engaging* of a person at many levels; whereas computer instruction may be merely *interactive*, with the only requirement being perception of the contents of a monitor screen and emission of a very limited set of responses (mouse clicks, keystrokes, and so on.)

3. Uses of the Chart: Different learners are best served by different techniques; the chart may help to identify appropriate tools to use. However, the most effective program, unless a very simple one, will make use of varying sorts of methods, in order to reach the widest population in the most effective way.

4. Caution: Each technique taken together with its *specific content*, the overall *training context*, the *skills* of the trainers, and other circumstances must be analyzed to determine the real anticipated impact on the learner.

Selecting Approaches, Methods, and Models

The appropriateness of a particular approach, method, or model depends upon the needs, objectives, and interests of the organizations and individuals with whom it is to be used. In assessing the suitability of these different alternatives, keep in mind the following considerations:

❑ Outcomes required: What kind of results must the program or learning activity produce in order to meet the learners' needs and fulfill their objectives? Do these outcomes fall within the scope of awareness, knowledge, skills, feelings, or attitude changes? Which approach, method, or model is most likely to produce those results?

❑ Appropriateness of model: Is the instruction to be based on orientation, training, or education? Which model is most appropriate considering the needs, objectives, resources, and time horizons of your organization and employees? Is a combination of models advisable?

❑ Intensity of methods: How intense should the learning be? The teaching methods used by the different approaches vary greatly in their rigor and the intensity of what they demand from the learner. The more intense a method is, the higher level of skill is required on the part of the trainer or facilitator. Intense methods also tend to be relatively expensive and need more time for preparation and delivery. Exhibit 5–6 compares the intensity level of the most common methods.

❑ Learning styles: Within the context of your organizational culture, how are employees accustomed to learning? What level of emotional involvement and risk-taking would be most suitable for them? How open are they to new ways of learning?

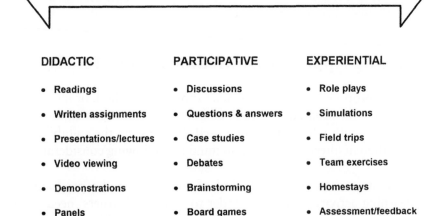

DIDACTIC	PARTICIPATIVE	EXPERIENTIAL
• Readings	• Discussions	• Role plays
• Written assignments	• Questions & answers	• Simulations
• Presentations/lectures	• Case studies	• Field trips
• Video viewing	• Debates	• Team exercises
• Demonstrations	• Brainstorming	• Homestays
• Panels	• Board games	• Assessment/feedback
• Guest interviews	• Colloquia	• Outdoor adventure techniques

EXHIBIT 5–6. INTENSITY OF TEACHING METHODS.

❑ Cultural backgrounds: What are the cultural backgrounds of the learners? Which approaches, methods, or models are most compatible with the ways they are comfortable learning? Many Asians, for example, find it difficult to participate in role-plays, brainstorming sessions, and learning games due to their aversion to embarrassment or loss of face. Germans tend to prefer methodologies such as case studies that are systematic and analytical. The French often enjoy lively, witty exchanges in activities like debates and brainstorming. If the learners have mixed cultural backgrounds, what combination of approaches is most appropriate?

❑ Organizational commitment: How committed is your organization to investing the resources required by the different models? A simple orientation program, for example, is less expensive than a more in-depth training program aimed at building skills. Do you understand the different learning models' time requirements for effective follow-through? For example, education of employees is a much longer process than orientation or training. Is your company willing and able to make that commitment?

Systematic Training and Development

Considered individually, the wide variety of approaches, methods, and models can be confusing and daunting for a layperson outside of the field of education. The appropriateness of any of them depends on many factors such as your organization's needs, interests, values, circumstances, constraints, and goals. Much of their effectiveness is lost if they are applied piece-meal. For these reasons, it is important for you to have a *systematic* overall approach to training and development. It will help you to make sense of the different alternatives and to integrate them into a coherent process for increasing the intercultural competence of your employees. Qualified intercultural program designers can help you plan such a systematic approach. Exhibit 5–7 illustrates a model containing the basic components.

Approaches, Methods, and Models Focus Questions

☑ What is your own learning philosophy? Do other key training and human resource managers share it?

☑ If there are different and conflicting learning philosophies within your company, do you need to build a consensus or majority opinion? If so, how do you plan to do so?

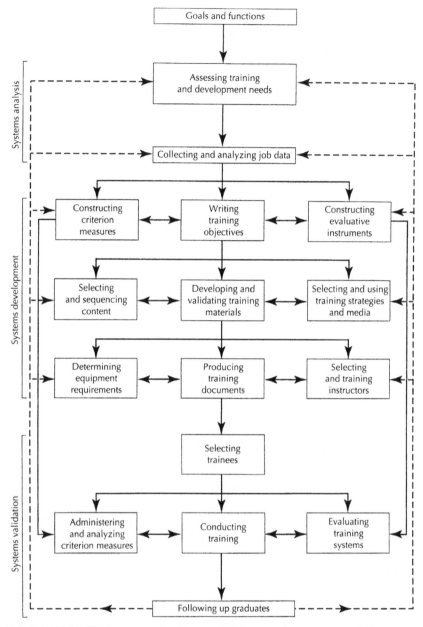

EXHIBIT 5–7. TRAINING AND DEVELOPMENT SYSTEMS APPROACH.
(Source: The Intercultural Sourcebook: Cross-Cultural Training Methods, Vol. 1, by Sandra
M. Fowler and Monica G. Mumford (eds.), Intercultural Press, Yarmouth, ME, 1995. Used
with Permission.)

☑ Are you familiar with the learning styles and preferences of the employees to whom intercultural services would be provided? If not, how will you select the most appropriate learning approaches, methods, and models for them?

☑ Which ones are most consistent with your employees' needs, concerns, and interests?

☑ Are there cultural differences among your employees that may have an impact on how they learn? Are these differences recognized by them and by your human resource and training managers?

☑ Does your senior management understand the level of commitment of time and financial resources required by the different approaches, methods, and models? If not, how do you plan to make them aware?

☑ Does your organization have a systematic approach to intercultural training and development? Does it need one?

☑ Would the assistance of an intercultural training design consultant be useful?

Summary and Suggested Action Steps

The needs and objectives of employees and groups within an organization are the most important input into the selection of learning and development approaches, methods, and models. These, in turn, determine the relevance and effectiveness of services or products you may purchase. The investment of time, care, and effort to ensure that this process is done thoroughly and systematically is very worthwhile. The selection of services and products, the design of programs, the measurement of outcomes, and evaluation of results are all much easier if you establish a solid conceptual and methodological foundation in advance and use a systematic approach to intercultural training and development.

Here are some ways you can use the content of this chapter:

1. Review the issues, obstacles, and challenges identified by employees and groups that have cross-cultural relationships and responsibilities and consider what needs they may reveal.

2. Discuss different options for conducting needs assessments with human resource managers, trainers, and potential providers. Share the appropriate sections of this chapter with them.

3. Determine the necessity of conducting intercultural awareness activities to enhance the effectiveness of needs assessments. Discuss these with potential providers.

4. Familiarize potential learners and in-house training program designers with the concept of needs gap analysis. Orient them to the guidelines for writing focused needs statements and objectives.

5. Use objective setting as leverage to establish the content and direction of intercultural services.

6. Host in-house discussion sessions on learning philosophies and theories. Try to develop agreement regarding instructional approaches, methods, and models.

7. Evaluate proposed programs and products in terms of the relevance and clarity of their objectives and the appropriateness of their instructional approaches, methods, and models.

8. Explore ways that providers may help in the process of needs assessment, objective setting, and the selection of instructional approaches, methods, and models. Refer to the list of suggestions in this chapter.

9. Consider using the services of an intercultural program design consultant to help you build a systematic approach to training and development.

10. Check the recommended resources list for additional ideas and information.

11. Refer providers to resources you feel might enhance their services to your organization or company.

Resources

Needs Assessment and Objective Setting

Brethower, D., and Smalley, K. *Performance-Based Instruction: Linking Training to Business Results*. San Francisco: Jossey-Bass/ Pfeiffer and Company, 1998.

Davis, R. D., and Davis A. B. *Effective Training Strategies: A Comprehensive Guide to Maximizing Learning in Organizations*. San Francisco: Berrett-Koehler Publishers, Inc., 1998, pp. 105–115.

Dean, P. J., and Ripley, D. E. (eds.). *Performance Improvement Interventions: Instructional Design and Training.* Washington, DC: ISPI Publications, 1998.

Honey, P. "Preferred Learning Styles." In J. Prior (ed.), *Gower Handbook of Training and Development.* (2nd ed.) Brookfield, VT: Gower Publishing Company Limited, 1994, pp. 259–273.

Kaufman, R., Rojas, A. M., and Mayer, H. *Needs Assessment: A User's Guide.* Englewood Cliffs, NJ: Educational Technology Publications, 1993.

Kohls, R. L., with Brussow H. L. *Training Know-How for Cross-Cultural and Diversity Trainers.* Duncanville, TX: Adult Learning Systems, Inc., 1995, pp. 77–87 and 90–98.

Mager, R. F. *Analyzing Performance Problems or "You Really Oughta Wanna."* (3rd ed.) Atlanta, GA: Center for Effective Performance Press, 1997.

Mager, R. F. *Preparing Instructional Objectives: A Self-Programmed Workbook.* (3rd ed.) Atlanta, GA: Center for Effective Performance Press, 1997.

Odenwald S. B. *Global Training: How To Design a Program for the Multinational Corporation.* Homewood, IL: ASTD/Business One Irwin, 1993, pp. 1–17.

Silberman, M. *Active Training: A Handbook of Techniques, Case Examples, and Tips.* (2nd ed.) San Francisco, CA: Jossey-Bass Pfeiffer, 1998. See "Assessing the Need for Training and the Participants," pp. 37–48.

Sims, R. R. *Reinventing Training and Development.* Westport, CT: Quorum Books, 1998. See "Analyzing Training and Development Needs," pp. 13–34.

Williams, L. A. "Measurement Made Simple." In J. H. Woods and J. W. Cortada (eds.), *1997 ASTD Training and Performance Yearbook.* New York: McGraw-Hill, 1997, pp. 360–366.

Intercultural Needs Assessment Instruments

The following list contains sources of instruments especially suited for assessing needs for intercultural learning. Some of them also may be used for screening potential international assignees as described in Chapter 6.

Cross-Cultural Adaptability Inventory (CCAI): A Training and Consulting Tool, developed by Colleen Kelley and Judith Meyers, and GAPtest, *Global Awareness Profile*, developed by J. Nathan Corbitt, are available from Intercultural Press, Inc., PO Box 700, Yarmouth, ME 04096, tel: (800) 370–2665 and (207) 846–5168, fax: (207) 846–5181, e-mail: interculturalpress@internetmci.com.

Cultural Orientations Indicator (COI), a cross-cultural self-assessment tool, is available from Training Management Corporation, 600 Alexander Road, Princeton, NJ 08540–6011, tel: (609) 951–0525, fax: (609) 951–0395, e-mail: info@tmcorp.com and Web site: http://www.tmcorp.com.

Harris, P. R. *Twenty Reproducible Assessment Instruments for the New Work Culture* is available from HRD Press Inc., 22 Amherst Road, Amherst, MA 01002, tel: (800) 822–2801, fax: (413) 253–3490, e-mail: info@hrdpress.com and Web site: http://www.hrdpress.com.

Hutcheson, C. *The Learning Style Questionnaire*, Amherst, MA: HRD Press, 1999.

Individual Global Competency Assessment, developed by Robert T. Moran and John R. Riesenberger, is available from Robert T. Moran, 5000 N. Wilkinson Road, Scottsdale, AZ 85253, tel: (602) 946–8046, fax: (602) 949–8716, e-mail: bmoran@aztec.asu.edu.

Intercultural Development Inventory, developed by Milton Bennett and Mitchell Hammer, is available to users qualified by the Intercultural Communication Institute, 8835 SW Canyon Lane, Suite 238 Portland, OR 97225; tel: (503) 297–4622, fax: (503) 297–4695, e-mail: ici@intercultural.org and Web site: http://www.intercultural.org.

The Questions of Diversity: Assessment Tools for Organizations and Individuals, developed by George F. Simons and Bob Abramms, is available from HRD Press, Inc., 22 Amherst Road, Amherst, MA 10002, tel (800) 822–2801, fax (413) 253–3490, e-mail: hrdpress@aol and Web site: http://www.hrdpress.com/.

Self-Assessment for Global Endeavors (SAGE), developed by Paula Caligiuri, is available from FGI, 10 Commerce Valley Drive East, Suite 200, Thornhill, Ontario, Canada L3T 7N7, tel: (905) 886–2157.

Training Needs Assessment Test, a general instrument available from Talico, Inc., 2320 South 3rd Street #5, Jacksonville, FL 32250, tel: (904) 241–1721, fax: (904) 241–4388, e-mail: talico@bellshouth.net.

Approaches, Methods, and Models

Black, S. J., and Mendenhall M. "Practical but Theory-Based Framework for Selecting Cross-Cultural Training Methods." In M. Mendenhall and G. Oddou (eds.), *Readings and Cases in International Human Resource Management*. Boston: PWS-Kent Publishing Company, 1991, pp. 177–204.

Brislin, R. W., and Yoshida, T. *Intercultural Communications Training: An Introduction*, Thousand Oaks, CA: Sage Publications, 1994.

Cohen, S. L. "The Case for Custom Training." *Training & Development*, August 1998, pp. 37–41.

Gochenour, T. (ed.). *Beyond Experience: The Experiential Approach to Cross-Cultural Education*. (2nd ed.) Yarmouth, MA: Intercultural Press, Inc., 1993.

Gudykunst, W. B., Guzley, R. M., and Hammer, R. M. "Designing Intercultural Training." In D. Landis and S. Bhagat (eds.), *Handbook of Intercultural Training*. (2nd ed.) Thousand Oaks, CA: Sage Publications, 1996, pp. 61–80.

Kohls, R. L. with Brussow H. L. *Training Know-How for Cross-Cultural and Diversity Trainers*. Duncanville, TX: Adult Learning Systems, Inc., 1995. See "Four Traditional Approaches To Developing Cross-Cultural Preparedness in Adults," pp. 31–56.

Lawrie, J. "Differentiate Between Training, Education, and Development." *Personnel*, October 1990, pp. 44–45.

Levy, J. "Intercultural Training Design." In M. G. Fowler and S. M. Fowler (eds.), *Intercultural Sourcebook: Cross-Cultural Training Methods*, Vol. 1, Yarmouth, MA: Intercultural Press, Inc., 1995.

Mager, R. F. *What Every Manager Should Know About Training*. Atlanta, GA: Center for Effective Performance Press, 1997.

Marquardt, M. J. *Action Learning in Action: Transforming Problems and People for World-Class Organizational Learning*, Alexandria, VA: ASTD Press, 1999.

Pruegger, V. J., and Rogers, T. B. "Cross-Cultural Sensitivity Training: Methods and Assessment." *International Journal of Intercultural Relations*, No. 18, 1994, pp. 369–387.

Nadler, L., and Nadler, Z. *Designing Training Programs: The Critical Events Model*. (2nd ed.) Houston, TX: Gulf Publishing Company, 1994.

Reid, M. A. "Approaches and Strategies." In J. Prior (ed.), *Gower Handbook of Training and Development*. (2nd ed.) Brookfield, VT: Gower Publishing Company Limited, 1994, pp. 100–112.

Silberman, M. *Active Training: A Handbook of Techniques, Case Examples, and Tips*. (2nd ed.) San Francisco, CA: Jossey-Bass Pfeiffer, 1998. See "Using Experiential Learning Approaches," pp. 119–152.

Silberman, M., with Lawson, K. *101 Ways to Make Training Active*, San Francisco: Jossey-Bass Pfeiffer, 1995.

Sloman, M. *A Handbook for Training Strategy*, Brookfield, VT: Gower Publishing Ltd., 1994. See "Models for Training," pp. 21–44.

Training Magazine. *Designing Training for Results*. Minneapolis, MN: Lakewood Publications, 1996.

Training Magazine. *The Training Mix: Choosing and Using Media and Methods*, Minneapolis, MN: Lakewood Publications, 1996.

Wight, A. R. "Contrasting Roles of Traditional and Experimental Trainer." In R. L. Kohls with H. L. Brussow (eds.), *Training Know-How for Cross-Cultural and Diversity Trainers*. Duncanville, TX: Adult Learning Systems, Inc., 1995, pp. 5–6.

6

Intercultural Services

The time has come, the walrus said, to talk of many things; Of shoes and ships and sealing wax, of cabbages and kings; And why the sea is boiling hot and whether pigs have wings.

Lewis Carroll in *Through the Looking-Glass*

Offerings, Approaches, and Options
The intercultural marketplace is filled with an abundant, creative, and diverse array of organizations and consultants, each of which offers a set of services and programs. The already wide variety of options available is rapidly expanding as new techniques and technologies are introduced. Inexperienced purchasers of these services face the daunting challenge of differentiating among the many alternatives and understanding their unique features and applications. By being discriminating and knowledgeable consumers, buyers can contribute significantly to the intercultural learning and development of their companies' personnel.

Overview of Services

There are no "quick fixes," "magic wands" or simple solutions. Success is directly proportional to the investment of time, energy and . . . resources devoted to the development of a truly multicultural organization.

D. W. Sue in "A Model for Diversity Training" from the *Journal of Counseling and Development*

During its 50-year history, the intercultural field has steadily grown
in both sophistication and practicality. The good intentions of the practitioners, so evident in the early years, have survived. But now an emphasis also is placed on good results. Much creativity and experimen-
tation has gone into the design and development of cross-cultural
training programs and learning activities. Consequently, the number
and types of services have proliferated greatly. During recent years, the
application of research findings has begun to provide a more solid
foundation for these services.

The field has matured to the point where most of the services are
generally accepted as reliable tools for international management. Still,
dynamic changes are under way that will add even more to the complexity of the marketplace. For example, recent intellectual cross-
fertilization with other disciplines, such as comparative management
and instructional design, has contributed new substance and methodologies. And today, modern technologies are opening doors to new innovative approaches to intercultural learning.

As a purchaser of intercultural services, you might feel a bit overwhelmed by the growing cornucopia of alternatives being offered to
you. It is helpful to have some familiarity with the purposes and features of the various services so that you can sort through them and focus on those that may be most useful to your company or organization.
The most common ways in which they are structured and delivered are
as programs and professional services, in addition to a new mode, online learning. The summaries that follow will give you an introductory-
level acquaintance with what each type of service contains, how it is
designed, and what it aims to accomplish.

A key to making the best use of intercultural services is to integrate
them into a coherent *system* of training and development (see Exhibit
6–1). This advice especially applies to the deployment and management of international personnel. A systemic approach typically includes four major components: assessment, orientation, on-site
support, and repatriation assistance. For details of such an approach,
see "Components of a Deployment System" in *Managing Cultural Differences*, 5th edition, Houston, TX: Gulf Publishing Company, 2000.

Training and orientation programs or briefings are the most common modes of delivery of intercultural services. They may be custom-
tailored or generic. They may be designed for individuals, couples,
small groups, or large groups. Target trainee populations typically include expatriates, international business travelers, global executives,

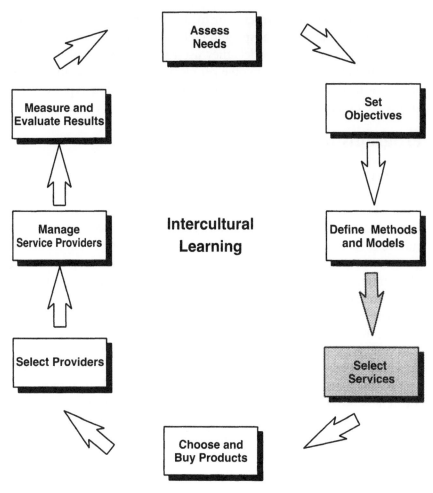

EXHIBIT 6–1. INTERCULTURAL SERVICES CYCLE.

home office employees who have cross-cultural relationships and re-sponsibilities, and multicultural team members. Programs may be a few hours to several days in length.

They can be delivered on your premises or at service providers' lo-cations. In some cases, programs are located in the host-countries. Gen-erally they are scheduled at your convenience, but open enrollment programs on specified dates are also sometimes available. They may be conducted by a single instructor or by a training team that includes a lead trainer, content specialists, and cultural resource people. The approaches, methods, and models they use vary greatly. What they have in common is that they all involve people attending a structured learning event held at a specific location. The most familiar types of programs are described here:

Programs for International Transferees

Cultural Awareness Orientations

These programs may be called "Global Awareness," "Culture Matters," "Life and Work Overseas," or another similarly broad title. They are aimed at helping the learners recognize the presence and power of culture in cross-cultural settings. They typically include explanations of general intercultural concepts and exercises to make the learners aware of their own cultural values. Generally, they are not country-specific. However, examples and illustrations from particular countries and cultures can be used to adapt the programs to your organization's or company's interests.

Although these kinds of programs usually are aimed at potential expatriates, participants may be drawn from any group of employees whose effectiveness is hampered by lack of cultural awareness. An awareness program often is the first in a series of workshops and is designed to motivate employees to participate in follow-on training. By itself, a general awareness program should not be considered sufficient preparation for handling complex cross-cultural situations effectively or for living and working abroad.

Expatriate Training Programs

These programs provide your potential expatriates (including transferees bound for the United States or those moving between other countries) the awareness, knowledge, attitudes, and skills they will need during their international assignments. Therefore, they should be country-specific. Usually they include the entire expatriate family, with separate training tracks for the adults, teenagers, and children. In cases where several families are relocating simultaneously to the same country, multifamily programs may be designed. The needs, interests, and concerns of the learners are usually ascertained by means of a preprogram questionnaire or telephone interviews.

Program content typically includes a host-country overview, key intercultural concepts, cultural self-awareness exercises, everyday life information, cross-cultural value contrasts, patterns of expatriate adjustment, cultural adaptation and stress management techniques, business and social protocol, and cross-cultural communication skills. A program may also involve counseling if critical issues such as marital or family discord or the learning problems of a child, for example, are detected in the preprogram needs assessment or if they surface during the program.

The programs may be conducted prior to departure for the international assignment, after arrival in the host-country, or partially before departure and then completed after arrival in the country. The rationale for deciding the optimal time and place for the programs depends largely on the availability of qualified training staff in each location and the relative costs of the different options.

Repatriation Programs

Repatriation or re-entry programs are designed for expatriates returning to their home countries after an international assignment. These programs should include the entire family and are best conducted within 90 days of the date of return home while the issues and challenges are still fresh. The programs most often are conducted for one family at a time. However, multifamily programs are feasible if several families are returning home close to the same time. A survey of 114 companies in 1998 by Prudential Relocation found that 75% of the expatriates surveyed felt that "an effective repatriation program is critical."

The purpose of these programs is to help your returning expatriates readjust to their former cultural environments by making them aware of how they personally have changed during their international assignments and how life and work at home have changed during their absence. They are encouraged to apply the adaptation skills they gained abroad to their cultural readjustment challenges at home. The program content also generally includes tips for appropriately sharing their international experiences with friends, family members, and colleagues. The participants usually are given suggestions regarding how to apply their international expertise to their companies' needs and to their own career advancement.

Programs for International Business People

Intercultural Business Workshops

These programs are aimed at your international business travelers and are designed to provide them with the awareness, attitudes, knowledge, and skills they need to be effective in their cross-border roles, relationships, and responsibilities. The titles of the programs may be something like "Doing Business Abroad," or "Working in Country X." Normally the programs are adapted to the participants' job requirements. For example, they may focus on relations with host-country governments, customers, suppliers, joint venture partners, or employees. They also may be designed for cross-functional groups. Typically they are country-specific, but they may cover several countries in a region.

The content of these programs often includes a country or regional business overview, key intercultural concepts, cultural self-awareness, business and social protocol, cross-cultural value differences in the workplace, verbal and nonverbal communication skills, international business ethics, and the concept of cultural synergy. The value of this kind of program (and the global business and negotiations programs that follow) is significantly enhanced if the case studies and examples used are based on actual events and situations in your organization or company. At the end of these programs, participants frequently are asked to identify and prioritize their cross-cultural skill requirements and to establish personal learning action plans.

Global Management Seminars

These programs are aimed at the senior executives who are responsible for important aspects of your worldwide business ventures. They may be called "Doing Business Globally," "Managing in a Global Marketplace," or something similar. The content usually focuses on the stages of corporate globalization, international trends in your company's industry, the business environment in key countries or regions, and the impact of globalization on your company and its implications for corporate vision, strategy, policies, and human resource development.

Other topics typically include key intercultural concepts, cultural self-awareness, national differences in management values and practices, cultural synergy, and the competencies and skills needed by the global manager. Program participants are often asked to assess their own global management capabilities and to set relevant professional development goals. Some programs are designed to teach the skills required by global managers.

Technology Transfer Training

This type of program is for your employees who are responsible for transferring technology or providing technical training to counterparts from other cultures. The recipients of the technology may be host-country employees, customers, or counterparts in local joint ventures. Therefore, these programs usually are country-specific. The program participants are normally expected to gain awareness and knowledge, reflect on the suitability of their attitudes and teaching styles, and learn culturally appropriate instructional methods and skills.

The content typically includes an overview of the counterparts' technical backgrounds, key intercultural concepts, cultural self-awareness, and verbal and nonverbal cross-cultural technical communication skills. These programs usually provide contrasts of differences pertaining to local values and attitudes about technology, learning, the role of student and teacher, learning style preferences, criticism and feedback, and motivation and reward of trainees. There is also generally a description of the local education system and the traditional teaching methods used in the host country.

Intercultural Negotiations Workshops

Intercultural negotiations training workshops are for your employees who negotiate, formally or informally, with international vendors, clients, joint venture or business alliance partners, labor union representatives, and government officials. These programs focus on the learners' cultural awareness, attitudes, knowledge, and skills and usually are country-specific. Follow-up observation and debriefing activities after actual or simulated intercultural negotiation sessions are very helpful to consolidate and deepen the participants' learning.

The programs often include an overview of the host-country or regional business environment, key intercultural concepts, cultural self-knowledge, cross-cultural verbal and nonverbal communication skills, and cultural synergy. The content also generally includes contrasts of cultural differences pertaining to communication styles, inter-firm business relations, organizational structure, corporate ethics, trust and confidence-building, decision-making, business agreements and legal contracts, negotiating styles, and tactics and timeframes.

Multicultural Team-Building Programs

These programs focus on the needs of teams and workgroups at home or abroad that are composed of employees from different cultural backgrounds. Intercultural team-building requires considerable practice and a series of coaching or training interventions over a period of time. It is not something that can be achieved by a single program. Therefore, the programs are generally designed to initiate an ongoing learning process.

These programs typically focus on basic teamwork principles and skills applied to a multicultural setting. Sessions usually cover key intercultural concepts, the cultural backgrounds of the team members, cultural self-awareness, and verbal and nonverbal communication styles. Other common topics are the stages of team development, roles and responsibilities of team members, and the concept of cultural synergy. These programs also generally include cross-cultural contrasts of values and attitudes regarding individualism, group identity, leadership, decision-making, cooperation and competition, conflict resolution, and teamwork.

Program participants are often required to engage in experiential team-building exercises focused on problem-solving, learning to trust each other, and becoming effective team members. Therefore, it is essential that the design and delivery of these programs take into account the individual and national learning styles of the trainees. This kind of program is best led by co-trainers from different cultural backgrounds.

Programs for Home Office Personnel

Orientations to Hosting International Visitors

These programs are designed for your home office staff who are responsible for receiving and hosting visitors from other countries. Their visitors may be employees, clients, suppliers, government officials, or representatives of cross-border joint ventures and business alliances. The dual purposes of this type of program are to help the trainees feel comfortable and confident when dealing with international visitors and to ensure that the visits themselves are pleasant and productive for the visitors.

Topics usually included are the importance of international visitors, the role of corporate hosts, key cross-cultural concepts, cultural self-awareness, national differences in host/guest obligations, formality and informality, gender roles, social status, and hierarchy. There is instruction on business protocol regarding greetings, introductions, use of titles, entertaining, and giving/receiving gifts. The programs can be general in scope or might focus on the visitors' home countries. The program participants are often encouraged to learn more about the countries and cultures of the visitors they host and are provided with resources for doing so.

Distance Communications Workshops

This kind of program is for your home office employees whose cross-border roles and responsibilities require communicating internationally via correspondence, telephone, e-mail, fax, and video conferencing. The programs usually focus on key intercultural concepts, cultural self-awareness, differences in communication styles, common pitfalls in cross-cultural communications, dealing with problems and misunderstandings, relationship building, and the special challenges of communicating without the benefit of face-to-face interaction.

If feasible, the programs provide country-specific information on the communication styles of the international counterparts with whom the employees most frequently interact. Role-plays and simulations often are used in addition to presentations and group discussions and exercises. The program participants are expected to gain cultural awareness, obtain practical information, develop cross-cultural communication skills, and become motivated to learn more about other cultures.

Workplace Diversity Programs

Diversity issues usually are concerns to be addressed in the domestic work environment. The field of diversity training and consulting has a well-developed set of providers, practitioners, services, methods, and materials of its own. Nevertheless, in some situations international intercultural and domestic diversity problems coincide.

Examples of such "hybrid" situations include

❏ Male employees from countries where sexual inequality is the norm may inadvertently cause sexual harassment complaints or lawsuits due to their mannerisms and ways of relating to female coworkers in the United States.

❑ Employees from countries with little ethnic or racial diversity may be ill-prepared, uncomfortable, and inept in dealing with the practical aspects and legal requirements of diversity in the US workforce.

❑ Gay employees or same-sex couples may be assigned to locations overseas where they would likely encounter exceptionally strong prejudice from host-country colleagues and counterparts.

❑ Female or minority employees may feel that they are not receiving their fair share of international assignments.

❑ Domestic sales and marketing personnel may attempt to find it difficult to relate effectively to ethnically diverse customers who reflect the cultural preferences of their home countries with regard to products and style of service.

❑ Expatriates may face strong prejudice against women and some racial groups in certain countries.

❑ A corporation may implement its domestic diversity policies and programs at its international locations without understanding the cross-cultural implications and obstacles involved.

❑ Trainees from different countries, ethnic groups, and cultures may be mixed in company-wide training programs without regard for their diverse learning styles and expectations.

In these kinds of situations, the best approach to effectively confront the challenges may be for you to select a combination of techniques and service providers from both the domestic diversity and international intercultural fields. The cross-fertilization and synergy between them can result in the creation of unique and innovative programs.

Professional Services

In contrast to structured programs, professional intercultural services are usually delivered by a single consultant or a small team. These services tend to be relatively open-ended and custom-tailored. Most providers would welcome the opportunity to demonstrate their creativity and resourcefulness by working with you on this basis. The most common intercultural professional services are assessment/selection and counseling/coaching of potential expatriates and international business travelers. Also, research and consulting on specific intercultural challenges are widely available. These categories are not entirely mutually exclusive, but they are useful for distinguishing between various alternatives that you are likely to be offered. The following descriptions summarize the most typical kinds of services in each of the categories.

Assessment/Selection Services

Many intercultural firms offer assessment and selection services for international assignees. The 1998 Prudential Relocation survey reported that 43% of the responding companies used a "specific selection process for international assignments." This process may be provided separately or in combination with training programs or counseling. Most use a selection or assessment instrument such as those referenced in the resources list at the end of this chapter. There is no consensus in the intercultural field regarding exactly which traits and attributes contribute to successful cross-cultural performance. Therefore, the instruments and the assessors emphasize different factors. For advice on how to compare these instruments, review the section on needs assessment tools in Chapter 5.

Assessment and selection involve evaluating personal and psychological characteristics of employees and, frequently, their spouses. During the process, sensitive emotional issues are often raised that may have an impact on employees' careers. Therefore, a high level of counseling and interpersonal relations skill is required on the part of the assessor.

Common Applications of Assessment Services
- ❑ Screening candidates for international assignments
- ❑ Promoting cultural self-awareness in expatriates and business travelers
- ❑ Assessing employees' individual needs for intercultural training and self-development
- ❑ Identifying employees' personal and professional problems dealing with diversity in the workplace
- ❑ Obtaining input for the planning and design of training programs and development processes

Coaching/Counseling

Virtually all the issues and topics addressed by structured training programs also can be dealt with via individual coaching or counseling. Coaching generally refers to job performance-related matters, and counseling focuses on psychological or attitudinal concerns. In cases where flexibility, convenience, and confidentiality are critical, most intercultural service providers are prepared to work one-on-one with your employees. This approach has the benefit of tailoring the service entirely to the individuals' needs, concerns, and interests. In addition, this approach generally reinforces learning through multiple interventions over a period of time.

Compared to training programs, this alternative requires a higher level of expertise on the part of the coach or counselor; therefore, it is relatively expensive. Nevertheless, in situations where much is at stake for the employee or the company (for example, when a senior executive must be brought "up to speed" quickly on a complex intercultural business challenge), it is worthwhile for you to consider using coaching and counseling services.

Research

Cross-border organizations and corporations often lack information critical to the effectiveness of their intercultural management and the success of their international ventures. Given the elusiveness and subtly of cultural factors, detecting and analyzing them is difficult. Therefore, some intercultural service providers have developed the capability to conduct custom-tailored research for their clients.

Usually this work is based on the use of surveys, interviews, focus groups, and a review of their clients' records. The quality and utility of the research results depend to a large extent on the specialized knowledge and expertise of the researchers. The types of research projects and the kind of data they gather are as broad as the clients' needs and interests. Typical research projects include

❑ Organizational culture and climate audits to identify intercultural challenges and opportunities
❑ Scans of international operations to identify country-specific, cross-cultural issues
❑ Assessment of employees' intercultural learning needs
❑ Surveys of expatriate satisfaction, morale, and performance

❑ Diagnosis of multicultural teamwork problems
❑ Critique of international human resource strategies, policies, and procedures
❑ Opinion and attitude surveys of host-country employees or customers
❑ Evaluation of the effectiveness of intercultural training
❑ Identification of workforce diversity issues

Consulting

Intercultural business consulting often includes and builds upon research. But it goes beyond gathering information and identifying and examining problems to making recommendations for concrete solutions, directions, and strategies. Therefore, consultants are likely to have a direct impact on your company's or organization's international success or failure.

In addition to having exceptional expertise in their own fields, intercultural business consultants need to be well-versed in business and management principles and be adept at using the management consultant's analytical and modeling tools and techniques. Likewise, they must be versatile enough to play a variety of roles such as planner, expert, advisor, problem-solver, advocate, and facilitator. Consequently, only the most highly qualified and experienced practitioners are suitable as consultants.

A successful consultant-client relationship is based on confidence and trust. You and other key in-house stakeholders need to assure yourselves that the consultant's reputation, credentials, and capabilities meet the highest standards. Intercultural business consultants may bill their time on a daily rate, retainer, or project basis. Only the client's needs and priorities limit the range of potential consulting assignments. The following examples are only a few of the possibilities:

❑ Helping develop strategies and plans to exploit intercultural opportunities created by globalization
❑ Advising on international human resource policy issues including expatriate deployment, retention, and career path planning
❑ Supporting cross-border business organizational relationship-building

❑ Facilitating cross-cultural conflict resolution
❑ Accompanying and supporting cross-border negotiating teams
❑ Assisting with the recruitment and retention of talented host-country managers
❑ Designing specialized intercultural training programs and systems
❑ Ensuring the cultural appropriateness of marketing strategies and materials
❑ Confronting domestic and international diversity issues
❑ Advising on cross-cultural business ethics issues
❑ Reviewing and revising corporate guidelines for international business conduct

Online Services

Web-based learning is a new field. Some providers are combining technologies such as electronic databases, intranets, and the global Internet to make intercultural services available online. Most of the information and assistance offered is similar to what can be obtained by other means. However, the capacity to access services at any time, any place, and in highly individualized ways, makes this delivery option very attractive to computer-literate and technically savvy users. Also, the amount and variety of information available is vast, and the potential for interactivity is great. Other features that makes online programs of interest that they can be updated easily and that it is technically feasible to design them to measure, record, and report the users' learning performance automatically.

Online providers have gathered and organized the kinds of resources they feel their clients need and have developed ways for users to electronically access them. The services described here may be entirely Internet-based with users working at designated Web sites, or they may be provided via links to a company's or organization's intranet. They also may make use of fax and e-mail correspondence, chat rooms, individual telephone consultations, and teleconferences or videoconferences.

Although the online mode of delivery is relatively new and unproven, it is rapidly growing in capability, sophistication, and user-friendliness. According to a 1998 survey of 177 companies by Windham International and the NFTC, 34% of them use dedicated Web sites to communicate globally within their human resources departments and 23% use the same technology to support their expatriates. Virtual services cannot provide the level of personal interaction that face-to-face training programs offer, and they are unlikely to replace them. However, they already have added an exciting new dimension to the marketplace.

Country Profiles

Both commercial and free country overviews and profiles are available online. The commercial ones include detailed information on the geography, climate, history, politics, economics, business environment, and culture of the countries. These services also generally include contact lists for finding key commercial and governmental agencies and organizations and tips regarding social and business protocol. They often contain articles and documents that may be downloaded and copied. Most of them also have links to other sources of related information on the World Wide Web. Some providers offer custom-tailored content such as industry or trade-specific news and information. These services usually are fee-based systems in which the subscribers are provided user codes and passwords in order to access the data.

The free sources of country information are mostly from government organizations such as the US Department of State, Department of Commerce, and Central Intelligence Agency. Other sources include the Web sites of the countries themselves and their tourist, investment, and trade promotion organizations. Travel information providers, such as guidebook publishers and travel agencies, may also post country data on the World Wide Web.

Most of these overviews are composed of statistics and brief descriptions on the same topics covered by the commercial profiles, although they tend to be less thorough. Also, it is time-consuming to locate them on the Internet, and they may not be as user-friendly as the commercial online services custom-designed for busy employees. Nevertheless, they are useful sources of general information for those with the skills and time to search for them.

Expatriation/Repatriation Orientations

A few providers offer country-specific orientations and training programs online for out-bound and returning expatriates. These have the same general content that face-to-face programs would provide. By means of "homework" assignments, quizzes, e-mail follow-up communications and, in some cases, telephone consultations and conferences, the providers strive to make the learning as interactive as possible given the electronic medium through which the programs are conducted.

These Web-based courses have only recently been developed and are still somewhat experimental and unproven. You should test them cautiously before relying on them routinely. Nevertheless, they have much potential for helping the many international assignees who are unable to attend conventional predeparture programs learn the essentials of successful expatriate life and work and for easing repatriation adjustment.

Support for Expatriates

A variety of fee-based and free expatriate support services are available on the World Wide Web. These services are generally offered through electronic bulletin boards or chat rooms aimed at expatriates with similar needs, interests, and concerns. For example, some services are designed for expatriate couples, spouses, teenagers, and children. The free services make use of networking between peers for giving and receiving emotional support and advice. They also provide links and referrals to sources of information and assistance. Most of them are related to membership-based organizations. These services are very useful for helping expatriates deal with routine issues and challenges. However, the commercial services are better-equipped to handle more serious concerns and problems.

Some providers offer expatriate support via online guidance and counseling sessions. Ideally, experienced professional counselors who have been expatriates themselves conduct these services. Arrangements can be made with providers to maintain confidentiality or to bring crisis or emergency situations to the attention of your appropriate human resources or employee assistance staff. The online sessions may be combined with counseling via telephone, face-to-face sessions with local host-country counselors, or visits to the counselor during home leave. A client may contract for a specific number of sessions or for ongoing support as needed.

Online counseling is a very new concept, and its effectiveness has not yet been fully proven. Given its newness and considering the highly personal and sensitive issues likely to be involved, you should use extra caution and discrimination when contracting for this type of counseling. "High-tech" must be integrated with "high-touch" for this new service to be viable.

Intercultural Business Orientations

A few intercultural service providers offer general cross-cultural or country-specific business orientations online. These programs contain much of the country background information already mentioned in the description of the online country profiles. However, they stress business protocol and entertaining, current economic and political conditions, international business travel advice, cultural differences, important business and governmental contacts, and tips for networking and making connections. They may also include specialized topics such as intercultural corporate ethics, the Foreign Corrupt Practices Act, cross-cultural negotiating, sales and marketing, technology transfer, and guidelines for using interpreters and translators.

Many of these online services are based directly on the providers' training programs or products. Some are standardized, but others may be custom-tailored. A few providers offer interactive online coaching for individual users. In general, however, the Web-based orientations are best suited for conveying information. Therefore, they are probably not the best choice in situations in which the learner's success depends on gaining high-level intercultural communications and relationship-building skills.

Customized Online Programs

The flexibility of online learning makes it a potential delivery system for instruction on nearly any topic. Some service providers are prepared to design online distance learning programs according to their clients' requirements and specifications. These programs may be used simultaneously by a group of employees in different locations or by individual employees at any time or place convenient to them. Theoretically, all the programs described in this chapter could be delivered as online courses. In addition, highly specific topics such as managing vendor relations in Mexico, recruiting Indian software developers, or orienting new employees to your company's standards of international business conduct might be feasible for custom-tailored distance learning programs online.

Selecting Online Services

As a purchaser of online services, you should take into account a number of factors in order to make wise buying decisions. Some of these considerations pertain to the medium itself. Others have to do with the nature of the services, backgrounds of the intended users, and the qualifications of the service providers. A few things to keep in mind are:

❑ Availability of technology: Fairly modern and powerful computers, fast modems, sophisticated software, and good telecommunications services are required to use online services effectively. Are these resources available to your intended users in different locations worldwide?

❑ Users' technical sophistication: The level of technical sophistication varies greatly from country to country. Are all of the intended users computer literate and comfortable using the Internet or your company's intranet? If not, do they have access to technical support from your in-house help desk or from the service provider?

❑ Provider's experience: Online services are relatively new and unproven ways of delivering intercultural learning. How experienced are your potential providers with this new technology? Are they able to give you references from clients who have successfully used their online services?

❑ Level of interactivity: Some "services" may be little more than online readings. Others truly engage the users in two-way interaction by using online exercises, tests, feedback and communications with instructors, cultural "informants" and other learners. More interaction generally leads to more learning. What is the level of interactivity built into the providers' services?

❑ User friendliness: The ease with which the user can navigate within the subject matter, access information, understand instructions, and use online forms and exercises is an important consideration. The response speed of the program is also a key factor. How user-friendly is the service in these terms?

❑ Users' cultural backgrounds: People from cultures that focus on the context in which communications occur and those that place high value on face-to-face personal relations tend to find Web-based programs uncomfortable and difficult to use. Are online services culturally appropriate for all your intended users?

❑ Users' language skills: Nearly all services online currently on the market are in English. To what extent are the intended users able to understand and use English? What is the minimum English proficiency level required? Are the online materials, explanations, and instructions suitable for non-native speakers of English?

❑ Results recording/reporting: Do the services have mechanisms for measuring and recording what the users have learned? Are there electronic forms for the learners to evaluate the services? If so, how will this information be shared with you?

Intercultural Services Focus Questions

☑ Based on your organization or company's decisions regarding which learning approaches, methods, and models it wants to use, which services are most appropriate and feasible?

☑ Which services seem most compatible with the learning styles and preferences of your employees? Which will best meet their needs and fulfill their objectives?

☑ Are your key human resource managers and training staff familiar with the features of the different options? If not, how do you plan to familiarize them?

☑ Are the providers' marketing materials and other descriptive information on the services detailed and clear regarding the approaches, methods, and models upon which they are based? If not, how will you obtain this information?

☑ Do you understand the tradeoff between various programs and professional and online services?

☑ If budgetary or other constraints limit your options, which of the services are most feasible under current conditions? Which ones will best help build support and lay a foundation for more comprehensive and effective solutions in the future?

Summary and Suggested Action Steps

A very wide range of intercultural services is available to international organizations and corporations today. The number and complexity of the options is growing rapidly. The services are unique and should not be considered interchangeable commodities. In order to choose wisely from among so many alternatives, you must have an independent basis of comparison. To gain this perspective, you must become familiar with the purposes, features, and applications of the various choices. This investment of time and attention will produce excellent payoffs in the quality of the buying decisions you make.

Here are some ways you can use the content of this chapter:

1. Copy appropriate sections of this chapter and distribute them to your key human resources, training, and diversity managers. Follow up with discussions aimed at familiarizing them with the different options for services.
2. Focus these discussions on the implications of your organizational culture and structure and your financial constraints for purchasing services.
3. Use these discussions to build consensus and support for buying those services that will best meet your company's needs and goals both in the near-term and the long-term.
4. Share portions of this chapter with potential providers. That will support your inquiries for more details than what they may have included in their marketing materials and generic proposals.
5. Discuss the topics in this chapter with providers' training managers and curriculum developers. Do the same with in-house training program designers and diversity managers.
6. Incorporate concepts from this chapter in your criteria for assessing potential providers' marketing materials, proposals, and sales presentations.
7. Make use of the resources listed at the end of this chapter to deepen your knowledge of those topics you feel are most important to your role as purchaser.

Resources

Training Program Content and Design

Bhawuk, D.P.S. "The Role of Cultural Theory in Cross-Cultural Training: A Multi-Method Study of Culture-Specific, Culture-General, and Culture Theory-Based Assimilators." *Journal of Cross-Cultural Psychology*, Vol. 29, No. 5. 1998, pp. 630–655.

Brislin, R. W. and Yoshida T. *Improving Intercultural Interactions: Modules for Cross-Cultural Training Programs.* Thousand Oaks, CA: Sage Publications, Inc., 1997.

Cohen, S. L. "The Case for Custom Training." *Training & Development*, Aug., 1998, pp. 37–41.

Fontaine, G. *Successfully Meeting the Three Challenges of All International Assignments.* Online book at http://www2.hawaii.edu/~fontaine/garyspage.html posted on the Internet in 1998 by Gary Fontaine, University of Hawaii, Honolulu, HI, 96822, (808) 956–3335. See Chapter 9.

Gudykunst, W. B., Guzley, R. M., and Hammer M. R. "Designing Intercultural Training." In D. Landis and R. S. Bhagat (eds.), *Handbook of Intercultural Training.* (2nd ed.) Thousand Oaks, CA: Sage Publications, Inc., 1996, pp. 61–80.

Hutchinson, C. S. "How To Assess and Compare Off-the-Shelf Training Packages." In M. Silberman (ed.), *The 1999 Training and Performance Sourcebook.* New York: McGraw-Hill, 1998.

Kohls, R. L. with Brussow H. L. *Training Know-How for Cross-Cultural and Diversity Trainers.* Duncanville, TX: Adult Learning Systems, Inc., 1995, pp. 21–28.

Martin, J. N., and Harrell, T. "Reentry Training for Intercultural Sojourners." In D. Landis and R. S. Bhagat (eds.), *Handbook of Intercultural Training.* (2nd ed.) Thousand Oaks, CA: Sage Publications, Inc., 1996, pp. 307–326.

Moricol, K., and Tsai, B. "Adapting Training for Other Cultures." *Training & Development Magazine*, Apr. 1992, pp. 65–68.

Moynihan, M. *The Economist Intelligence Unit Global Manager: Recruiting, Developing, and Keeping World Class Executives.* New York: McGraw-Hill, Inc., 1993, pp. 52–66.

Odenwald, S. B. *Global Training: How To Design a Program for the Multinational Corporation.* Homewood, IL: Business One Irwin, 1993, pp. 69–104.

Phillips N., *Managing International Teams.* London: Pitman Publishing, 1992, pp. 181–188.

Ptak, C., Cooper, J., and Brislin, R. "Cross-Cultural Training Programs: Advice and Insights from Experienced Trainers." *International Journal of Intercultural Relations*, No. 19, 1995, pp. 425–453.

Stoltz-Loike, M. "Ensuring Successful Repatriation: Solutions." *International HR Journal*, Vol. 7, No. 4, Winter 1999, pp. 11–16.

Assessment/Selection Services

Arthur, W., and Bennet, W. "The International Assignee: The Relative Importance of Factors Perceived To Contribute to Success." *Personnel Psychology*, No. 48, 1995, pp. 99–114.

Grove, C., and Hallowell, W. "The Ideal Expatriate." *Benefits & Compensation Solutions*, May 1998, pp. 40–42.

Jenkins, L. "Overseas Assignments: Sending the Right People." *International HR Journal*, Summer 1995, pp. 41–43.

International Sourcing and Selection Practices 1995 Survey Report. New York: National Foreign Trade Council and Selection Research International, Sep. 1995.

Kealy, D. J. "The Challenge of International Personnel Selection." In D. Landis and R. S. Bhagat (eds.), *Handbook of Intercultural Training.* (2nd ed.) Thousand Oaks, CA: Sage Publications, Inc., 1996, pp. 81–104.

Porter, G., and Tansky, J. W. "Expatriate Success May Depend on a 'Learning Orientation': Considerations for Selection and Training." *Human Resource Management*, Vol. 38, No. 1, Spring 1999, pp. 47–60.

Solomon, C. M. "How Does Your Global Talent Measure Up? International Personnel Performance Measures." *Personnel Journal*, Vol. 73, Oct. 1994, pp. 96–97.

Teagarden, M. B., and Gordon, G. D. "Corporate Selection Strategies and Expatriate Manager Success." In J. Selmer (ed.), *Expatriate Management: New Ideas for International Business.* Westport, CT: Quorum Books, 1995.

Wilson, M. S., and Dalton, M. A. *International Success: Selecting, Developing, and Supporting Expatriate Managers*, Greensboro, NC: Center for Creative Leadership, 1998.

Research Services

Adler, N. J. "Cross-Cultural Management Research: The Ostrich and the Trend." *Academy of Management Review*, Vol. 8, No. 2, 1983, pp. 226–232.

Dinges, N. G., and Baldwin K. D. "Intercultural Competence: A Research Perspective." In D. Landis and R. S. Bhagat (eds.), *Handbook of Intercultural Training.* (2nd ed.) Thousand Oaks, CA: Sage Publications, Inc., 1996, pp. 106–123.

Ember, C. R. "Improvements in Cross-Cultural Research Methods." *Cross-Cultural Research*, Vol. 28, No, 4, Nov. 1994, pp. 360–370.

Ember, C. R., and Ember, M. "Cross-Cultural Research." In H. R. Bernard (ed.), *Handbook of Methods in Cultural Anthropology.* Thousand Oaks, CA: Sage Publications, Inc., 1998, pp. 647–687.

Hansen, C. D., and Brooks, A. K. "A Review of Cross-Cultural Research on Human Resource Development." *Human Resource Development Quarterly*, Vol. 5, No. 1, Spring 1994, pp. 55–74.

Limaye, M. R., and Victor, D. A. "Cross-Cultural Business Communication Research: State of the Art and Hypotheses for the 1990s." *Journal of Business Communication*, Vol. 28, 1991, pp. 277–299.

Van de Vijver, F., and Kwok, L. *Methods and Data Analysis for Cross-Cultural Research*. Thousand Oaks, CA: Sage Publications, Inc., 1997.

Counseling Services

Eleftheriadou, Z. *Transcultural Counselling*. London: Central Publishing House, 1994.

Moorby, E. "Mentoring and Coaching." In J. Prior (ed.), *Gower Handbook of Training and Development*. (2nd ed.) Brookfield, VT: Gower Publishing Company Limited, 1994, pp. 359–372.

Pederson, P. B. *Cultural-Centered Counseling Interventions: Striving for Accuracy.* Thousand Oaks, CA: Sage Publications, Inc., 1997.

Pederson, P. B., Draguns, J., Lonner, W. J., and Trimble, J. E. *Counseling Across Cultures.* (4th ed.) Thousand Oaks, CA: Sage Publications, Inc., 1996.

Ponterrotto, J. G., Casas, M., Suzuki, L., and Alexander, A. (eds.) *Handbook of Multicultural Counseling*. Thousand Oaks, CA: Sage Publications, Inc., 1995.

Sue, D. W. *Counseling the Culturally Different: Theory and Practice.* (2nd ed.) New York: John Wiley & Sons, 1990.

Consulting Services

Felkins, P. K., Chakiris, B. J., and Charkisis, K. N. "Global Consultation." In *Change Consultation*, White Plains, NY: Quality Resources, 1993.

Gormley, W. "International Training and Human Resource Development Practices: Consulting More Effectively in Other Cultures." *International HRD Annual,* Vol. 3, American Society for Training and Development, Alexandria, VA: ASTD Press, 1987, pp. 108–115.

Harris P. R. "Cross-Cultural Consulting Effectiveness." *Consultation,* Vol. 1.2, Spring 1983, pp. 4–10.

Harrison, R. *Consultant's Journey: A Dance of Work and Spirit.* San Francisco, CA: Jossey-Bass Publishers, 1995, pp. 53–77.

Lynton, R. P. "Cross-Cultural Perspectives." In R. T. Golembiewski (ed.), *Handbook of Organizational Consultation.* New York: Marcel Dekker, Inc., 1993, pp. 549–554.

Marquardt, M. J., and Engel, D. W. *Global Human Resource Development.* Englewood Cliffs, NJ: Prentice-Hall, Inc., 1993, pp. 60–71.

Odenwald, S. B. *Global Training: How To Design a Program for the Multinational Corporation.* Homewood, IL: Business One Irwin, 1993. See "Selecting Global Consultants," pp. 167–168.

Reynolds, A., and Nadler, L. *The Global HRD Consultant's and Practitioner's Handbook.* Amherst, MA: HRD Press, 1993.

Workplace Diversity

Abramms, B., and Simons, G. F. *Cultural Diversity Sourcebook.* Amherst, MA: HRD Press, 1996.

Anand, R. *Teaching Skills and Cultural Competency: A Guide for Trainers.* (3rd ed.) Washington, DC: National Multicultural Institute, 1999.

Anand, R., and Shipler, L. K. *Multicultural Case Studies: Tools for Training.* Washington, DC: National Multicultural Institute, 1998.

Applebaum, E., and Batt, R. *The New American Workplace.* Ithaca, NY: IRL Press/Cornell University, 1994.

Banks, G. *The Human Diversity Workshop.* Amherst, MA: HRD Press, 1994.

Chang, R. Y. *Capitalizing on Workplace Diversity.* Irvine, CA, Richard Chang Associates, Inc. and Jossey-Bass, 1996.

Cornell, S., and Hartmann, D. *Ethnicity and Race: Making Identities in a Changing World.* Thousand Oaks, CA: Pine Forge Press, 1998.

Dass, P., and Parker, B. "Strategies for Managing Human Resource Diversity: From Resistance to Learning." *Academy of Management Executive,* Vol. 13, No. 2, May 1999, pp. 68–80.

Dickerson-Jones, T. *50 Activities for Managing Cultural Diversity.* Fredonia, NY: HR Press, 1999.

Fernandez, J. P., and Davis, J. *Race, Gender, and Rhetoric: the True State of Race and Gender Relations in Corporate America.* New York: McGraw-Hill, Inc., 1998.

Fyock, C. D. *Bridging the Age Gap.* Burr Ridge, IL: Irwin Professional Publishing, 1994.

Fyock, C. D. *Cultural Diversity: Challenges and Opportunities.* Burr Ridge, IL: Irwin Professional Publishing, 1994.

Fyock, C. D. *Women in the Workplace: Eliminating Sexual Harassment and Improving Cross-Gender Communication.* Burr Ridge, IL: Irwin Professional Publishing, 1994.

Gardenswartz, L., and Rowe, A. *Diverse Teams at Work.* Burr Ridge, IL: Irwin Professional Publishing, 1994.

Gardenswartz, L., and Rowe, A. *The Diversity Tool Kit*, Burr Ridge, IL: Irwin Professional Publishing, 1994.

Gardenswartz, L., and Rowe, A. *Managing Diversity: A Complete Reference and Planning Guide.* (Rev. ed.) New York: McGraw-Hill, Inc., 1998.

Gardenswartz, L., and Rowe, A. *The Managing Diversity Survival Guide: A Complete Collection of Checklists, Activities and Tips.* Burr Ridge, IL: Irwin Professional Publishing, 1994.

Harris, A. W., and Myers, S. G. *Tools for Valuing Diversity: Techniques to Capitalize on Diversity.* Irvine, CA, Richard Chang Associates, Inc. and Jossey-Bass, 1996.

Harris, P. R. *The New Work Culture: HRD Strategies for Transformational Management.* Amherst, MA: HRD Press, 1997.

Hart, L. B., and Dalke, D. J. *The Sexes at Work: Workshops Designs and Activities for Improving Gender Relations in the Workplace.* Amherst, MA: HRD Press, 1995.

Hudson Institute, *Workforce 2000*, Indianapolis, IN: Hudson Institute Publications, 1988.

Ipsaro, A. J. *White Men, Women, and Minorities*, Denver, CO: Meridian Associates, 1997.

Jackson, S. E., and Ruderman, M. N. (eds.). *Work Team Diversity: Paradigms and Perspectives.* Washington, DC: American Psychological Association, 1996.

Jamieson, D., and O'Mara, J. *Managing Workforce 2000: Gaining the Diversity Advantage.* San Francisco, CA: Jossey-Bass Publishers, 1991.

Judy, R. W., Domico, C., D'Amico, C. and Geipel, G. L. *Workforce 2020: Work and Workers in the 21st Century.* Indianapolis, IN: Hudson Institute Publications, 1997.

Kuga, L. A. *Communicating in a Diverse Workplace.* Irvine, CA, Richard Chang Associates, Inc. and Jossey-Bass, 1996.

Lambert, J., and Myers, S. G. *50 Activities for Diversity Training.* Amherst, MA: HRD Press, 1994.

Loden, M. *Implementing Diversity: Best Practices for Making Diversity Work in Your Organization.* Burr Ridge, IL: Irwin Professional Publishing, 1995.

Morrison A. M., et al. *Leadership Diversity: Women and People of Color in Management.* San Francisco, CA: Jossey-Bass, 1992.

Morrison, A. M. *The New Leaders: Guidelines on Leadership Diversity in America.* San Francisco, CA: Jossey-Bass, 1992.

Myers, S. G. *Teambuilding for Diverse Work Groups: A Practical Guide to Gaining and Sustaining Performance in Diverse Teams.* Irvine, CA, Richard Chang Associates, Inc. and Jossey-Bass, 1996.

Nile, L. N. *Developing Diversity Training for the Workplace: A Guide for Trainers.* (6th ed.) Washington, DC: National Multicultural Institute, 1999.

O'Mara, J. *Diversity: Activities and Training Designs.* Toronto, Canada: Pfeiffer & Company, 1994.

Orlov, D., and Roumell, M. T. *What Every Manager Needs to Know About Sexual Harassment.* New York: AMACOM Press, 1999.

Ricci, L., with Wilkerson, G. *12 Views from Women's Eyes: Managing the New Majority.* Austin, TX: R3 Publication, 1997.

Salett, E. P., and Koslow, D. R. (eds.). *Race, Ethnicity, and Self: Identity in Multicultural Perspective.* Washington, DC: National Multicultural Institute, 1994.

Shusta, R. M., Levine, D. R., Harris, P. R., and Wong, H. Z. *Multicultural Law Enforcement—Strategies for Peacekeeping in a Diverse Society.* Englewood Cliffs, NJ: Prentice Hall, 1995.

Simon, G. M., Vasques-Colin, C., and Harris P. R. *Transformational Leadership-Strategies for Empowering the Multicultural Workforce and Capitalizing on People Diversity.* Houston, TX: Gulf Publishing Company, 1993.

Simons, G. F., Abramms, R., Hopkins, L. A. and Johnson, O. J. (eds.). *Cultural Diversity Fieldbook,* Princeton, NJ: Peterson/Pacesetter Books, 1996.

Simons, G. F., Allen, S., and De Raaff, C. *Gender Dynamics in the Workplace*, Amherst, MA: ODT, 1997.

Swiss, D. J. *Women Breaking Through: Overcoming the Final 10 Obstacles at Work*. Princeton, NJ: Peterson's Guides, 1996.

Thomas, R. R. *Redefining Diversity*. New York: AMACOM Press, 1996.

Thomas, R. R. *Differences Do Make a Difference*. Atlanta, GA: American Institute for Managing Diversity, 1992.

Williams, J. P., and Capole, D. *Unfinished Business: The Diversity Promise*. Rockville, MD: BNA Communications, 1999.

Zuckerman, A., and Simons, G. F. *Sexual Orientation in the Workplace*. Santa Cruz: CA: International Partners Press, 1994.

Online Services

The following resources include sources of online services and references to books and articles that will help you make the best use of them.

Abernathy, D. J. "http://www.Online.Learning." *Training & Development*, Vol. 53, No. 9, September 1999, pp. 36–41.

American Citizens Abroad (ACA), 5 B rue Liotard, CH – 1202, Geneva, Switzerland, tel: (41–22) 340–0233, e-mail: acage@aca.ch and Web site: http://www.aca.ch/. This is a nonprofit association dedicated to serving and defending the interests of US citizens worldwide. It is useful for networking and exchanging practical information about issues affecting expatriates.

Barron, T. "Harnessing Online Learning." *Training & Development*, Vol. 53, No. 9, September 1999, pp. 28–33.

Carlinger, S., and Gery, G. *An Overview of On-line Learning*, Amherst, MA: HRD Press, 1999.

Country Business Guides on 13 countries available online from Meridian Resources Associates, Inc., 1741 Buchanan Street, San Francisco, CA 94115, tel: (800) 626–2047 and (415) 749–2920, fax: (415) 749–0124, e-mail: contact@mera.com and Web site: http://www.mera.com.

Country/City Travel Guides, a Web site with free country-specific information for international travelers available at Web site: http://www.travel.yahoo.com/.

The Country Library, a Web site with free economic and trade data on most countries, is located at http://www.tradeport.org/ts/countries on the Internet.

CountryNet, a series of 84 country-specific overviews produced by Arthur Andersen, Craighead Publications, Inc., and the Economist Intelligence Unit, is available online from Craighead Publications, Inc., PO Box 1006 Darien, CT 06820–1006, tel: (203) 655–1007, fax: (203) 655–0018, e-mail: countrynetinfo@countrynetcom: or Web site: http://eiu.com.

Cross Cultures Distance Learning Courses, Web-based courses on 48 countries conducted via e-mail and teleconferencing, available from Integrated Resources Group, Bank One Building, Suite 505, 3444 North First Street, Abilene, TX 79603, tel: (915) 676–2290, fax: (915) 676–1383, e-mail: irg@expat-repat.com and Web site: http://www.expat-repat.com/xculture.html.

CultureBank, an online cultural information reporting service, is available from William Drake & Associates, PO Box 2838, Waxahachie, TX 75165, tel/fax: (972) 938–2927, e-mail: bdrake@onramp.net, Web site: http://www.culturebank.com.

Deans, C. with Dakin, S. *Thunderbird Guide to International Business Resources on the World Wide Web*, New York: John Wiley and Sons, Inc., 1996.

Diversity Database, an online list of resources, is located at http://www.inform.umd.edu/edres/topic/diversity/general/internet/.

DiversityInc.Com, an online newsletter focused on workplace diversity issues, is located at http://www.diversityinc.com.

Diversity Resources on the WWW is a Web site with links to services and products for managing cultural diversity in the workplace. It is located at http://www.sine.edu/~jandris/htmldocuments?andris/diversity.html.

Doing Business Internationally is an online cross-cultural business awareness and communications course from Asia Pacific International University and Training Management Corporation, and *R-BASE* is a database with cross-cultural business information on over 90 countries. They are available from Training Management Corporation, 600 Alexander Road, Princeton, NJ 08540, tel: (609) 951–0525, fax: (609) 951–0395, e-mail: info@tmcorp.com and Web site: http://www.tmcorp.com.

Easy Access Country Profiles, online profiles on 76 countries, are available from Living Abroad Publishing, Inc., 32 Nassau Street, Princeton, NJ 08542, tel: (609) 924–9302, fax: (609) 924–7844, e-mail: info@livingabroad.com and Web site: http://www.livingabroad.com.

Ellram, L. M., and Easton, L. "Purchasing Education on the Internet." *The Journal of Supply Chain Management,* Vol. 35, No. 1, Winter 1999, pp. 11–19.

The Embassy Page is a Web site with free information on visa requirements, travel advice, and country–specific overviews at http://embpage.org/ on the Internet.

Expat Exchange is an information center that offers a free online expatriate chat room and e-mail networking among international assignees in many countries. It is located at 174 West 89th Street, Suite 4C, New York, NY 10024, tel: (212) 875–1103, e-mail: betsy@expatexchange.com and at http://www.expatexchange.com/ on the Internet.

ExpatSpouse.Com is the Web page for a fee-based online support service available from Windham International, ECA International, and Global Relocation Partnership. It is available from Windham International, 55 Fifth Avenue, New York, NY 10003, tel: (212) 647–0555, fax: (212) 647–0494), e-mail: expat@windhamint.com and Web site: http://www.expatspouse.com.

Expatriate Online is a free membership Web site sponsored by John Pollard Publishers. It offers a variety of services and resources for expatriates and visitors in Belgium. It can be found at http://www.epatriate-online.com on the Internet or reached via e-mail at johnpollard@expatriate-online.com.

FAWCO, the Federation of American Women's Clubs Overseas, a not-for-profit organization with clubs in 34 countries. It is based at FAWCO USA, PO Box 448, Marfa, TX 79843, e-mail: arconinn@iglobal.net and Web site: http://wwwfawco.org/. This organization informally assists expatriate spouses with cultural orientation and adjustment.

Gulliver: Performing Successfully Across Cultures is an intercultural business training program that may be delivered either online or via CD-ROM. It was produced in 1999 by PricewaterhouseCoopers and Richard D. Lewis. It is available from Richard Lewis Communications, 3c New York Inc., 450 West 15th Street, Suite 305, New York, NY 10011, tel: (212) 328–0710, fax: (212) 271–6372, e-mail: ternsing@3cny.com.

Guodo Liu, L. *Internet Resources and Services for International Business: A Global Guide.* Phoenix, AZ: Oryx Press, 1998.

Hall, B. *Web-Based Training Cookbook.* Amherst, MA: HRD Press, 1997.

Hart, W. "Intercultural Computer-Mediated Communication" is an article in *The Edge*, an online journal of intercultural relations. It is located at http://www.swcp.com/biz/theedge/fall98.htm on the Internet.

Hays, S. "Reach Out to Expats Via the Web." *Workforce*, Vol. 79, No. 3, Mar. 1999, pp. 44–46.

Intercultural Business Solutions is a Web site with access to articles on intercultural topics and links to sites on the World Wide Web that are useful to international business travelers. It is located at http://www.omn.com/wederspahn on the Internet and at 4838 West Moorhead Circle, Boulder, CO, 80303, tel: (303) 494–5403 and e-mail: wederspn@worf.omn.com.

The Living Abroad E-mail Help Desk is a fee-based service for expatriates offered by Living Abroad Business Association, 32 Nassau Street, Princeton, NJ, 08542, tel: (609) 924–9302, fax: (609) 924–7844, e-mail: laba@livingabroad.com, Web site: http://www.livingabroad.com.

Ravet, S., and Layte, M. *Technology-Based Training: A Comprehensive Guide to Choosing, Implementing, Managing and Developing New Technologies in Training.* Houston, TX: Gulf Publishing Company, 1997. See "Locating Resources for Learning on the Internet," pp. 271–280.

The *International Trade Administration* Web site is a free source of trade statistics, business information, and economic data at http://www.ita.gov/ on the Internet.

Learning Styles ID, an online self-administered learning preferences inventory, is available from Outside Software, Ltd. at http://www.outsider.co-uk.com.

Multicultural Pavilion is an online resource with links to numerous diversity-related Web sites, located at http://www.curry.edschool.virginia.edu/go/multicultural/sites1.html on the Internet.

Terra Cognita offers online training focused on living and working abroad and business oriented topics on China, Japan, Mexico, Germany, Morocco, France, and Brazil. It is available from Terra Cognita, 300 West 40th Street 314, New York, NY 10019, tel: (212) 262–4529, fax: (212) 262–5789, e-mail info@terracognita.com and Web site: http://www.terracognita.com.

The World Factbook, the Web site of the Central Intelligence Agency, has free profiles on virtually every country in the world. It is located http://www.odcia.gov/cia/publications/factbook/index.html on the World Wide Web.

Webb, W. *A Trainer's Guide to the World Wide Web and Intranets: Using On-Line Technology to Create Powerful, Cost-Effective Learning in Your Organization.* Amherst MA: HRD Press, 1999.

Worldwide Business Briefings, a series reports on doing business in 52 countries, is available online from International Cultural Enterprises, Inc., 1241 Dartmouth Lane, Deerfield, IL 60015, tel: (708) 945–9516, fax: (708) 945–9614, e-mail: ice@mcs.com and Web site: http://www.businessculture.com/.

Yahoo: Society and Culture Web Page has links to country-specific information on more than 300 countries. It is located at http://search.yahoo.com/bin/search?p=society%Bculture on the World Wide Web.

7

Intercultural Products

A good thing sells itself.

Twi proverb from Ghana

A Proliferation of Products

A rapidly increasing selection of products is available to organizations and companies seeking resources in the intercultural marketplace. Vendors usually promote their products as tools for enhancing programs and other learning activities. In some cases, products are being sold as substitutes for training programs. Buyers need a good grasp of the benefits and drawbacks of the various products and the tradeoffs among them. Likewise, they must understand the appropriateness of using products versus face-to-face services. Choosing and buying suitable products are important parts of the Intercultural Services Cycle (see Exhibit 7–1).

Overview of Products

Nothing can have value without being an object of utility.

Karl Marx in *Das Kapital*

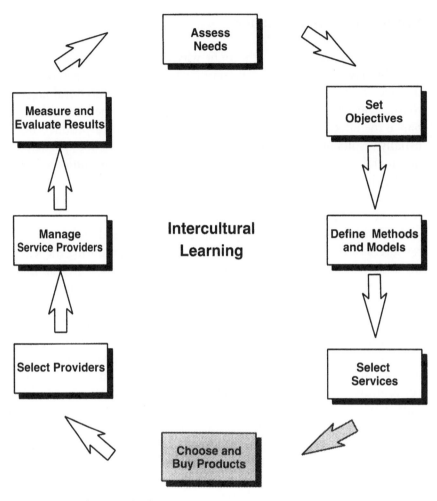

EXHIBIT 7–1. INTERCULTURAL SERVICES CYCLE.

A broad selection of products is available for intercultural training and development. These products include books, films, videos and audiotapes, self-study guides and workbooks, country profiles, games and simulations, assessment instruments, and CD-ROMs. Many books are listed in the resources at the end of each chapter of this book. The other types of products are discussed in the following sections.

General Considerations

The proper tool used in the right way on an appropriate task is a valuable asset for promoting intercultural learning. These products are designed to be used alone or in conjunction with structured training activities. Generally, the best use of the products described here is to enhance the effectiveness of face-to-face services. Using a product alone usually results in a more passive form of learning than does participating in an interactive program. As the German proverb cautions, "One teacher is worth more than many books."

Nevertheless, appropriate tools can greatly increase the impact and relevance of orientations, briefings, and training programs. Your service providers should be aware of the most recent and highest quality resources of this type. In addition to their application during the learning activities, they can be used ahead of time to promote interest. Likewise, you can use them for follow up and reinforcement after programs.

Budget or time constraints and the difficulty of gathering participants for programs may incline you to consider using products in a "Stand alone" fashion. In these cases, products can provide employees with a fair amount of useful information and help raise their level of cultural awareness. Use of the products may also create demand for more participative kinds of learning. An obvious benefit of products is that their cost is lower than most instructor–delivered services. With some products, you can gain additional utility from the expense of their purchase by making them available to multiple users over time. Others, such as workbooks and a few simulations, are designed as consumables and can be used only once.

Keep in mind the limitations of products. By themselves, they usually do not teach skills. Nor can they have much impact on the attitudes of the users compared to "live" forms of intercultural training that can engage learners on an emotional level. Furthermore, they are difficult to customize to the individual needs of employees. Another disadvantage is that the rapidly changing realities of global business, politics, and economics tend to reduce the effective "shelf life" of most products.

From a cost-effectiveness viewpoint, you should consider if a product is likely to produce the outcomes desired for your employees. If their needs are for general cultural awareness or factual information about specific countries, books, videos, and CD-ROMs, for example, might be good investments. However, if their needs are more individual, subtle, or complex, relying on these kinds of tools may not be advisable. Likewise, these products must be well-targeted to the users' needs and be up-to-date in order to be optimally useful. As a general rule, such products are effective only with highly motivated self-directed learners. Self-study materials are more effective when they require active involvement on the part of the users rather than merely allowing them to take in information passively.

ADVANTAGES	DISADVANTAGES
Useful for gaining information	Short "shelf life"
Convenient for users	Relatively generic
Relatively inexpensive	Ineffective for learning most skills
Repeat usage possible	Require high level of self-motivation
May support training activities	
May stimulate desire for more learning	May give users overconfidence in their knowledge levels
	May be misused as substitutes for more appropriate training

EXHIBIT 7–2. USING INTERCULTURAL PRODUCTS.

"Stand Alone" Products

Some kinds of products are mostly used outside of group programs. The learners are free to use them in their own way and at their own pace. In some cases, however, trainers may assign these products as supplemental study materials for training programs.

Country Profiles and Guide Books

Many written materials are aimed at international business travelers and expatriates. They range from substantial booklets containing several chapters to pamphlets a few pages in length. Most of them are country-specific and contain information on the country's geography, climate, history, politics, economy, culture, business practices and protocol, living conditions, travel and health information, and frequently some local language phrases. They also may provide maps, lists of local contacts, and social tips and taboos.

Although such booklets are quite helpful and reassuring for people entering a country with which they are completely unfamiliar, they cannot be expected to give them the depth of insight and understanding required to handle sensitive or complex cross-cultural challenges. Another shortcoming is that they tend to get dated very quickly in today's rapidly changing world.

Self-Help Workbooks

Several workbooks are available to help learners study intercultural topics on their own. These materials include readings, written exercises, self-tests, and bibliographies containing sources of additional information. Different workbooks are aimed at expatriates, international business travelers, and transcultural negotiators. They are not culture-specific. However, they do contain examples and illustrations from various cultures. They would be used best in conjunction with a country-specific guide book.

CD-ROMS

Several intercultural service providers have put CD-ROMs on the market recently. The topics covered include cultural awareness, cross-cultural communications, the expatriate adaptation process, differences in cultural values, multicultural management, and how to do business in specific countries. Most contain the same type of information provided by orientation and training programs. Many are directly based on the providers' other products such as guide books and videos.

A few vendors claim that their CD-ROMs are fully interactive learning tools. However, the degree of interactivity is limited, in most cases, to simple page-clicking, note-taking, and free navigation within the subject matter. It appears that the full potential of this new technology has not been exploited yet. Nevertheless, the multimedia content (text, sound, photographs, video clips, animations, and still graphics) does engage the user on several levels, which tends to enhance learning. Also, there is the advantage that the learners are able to move through the program components in any order they wish and at their own speed.

Compared to workshops, some studies suggest that computer-based training can transmit the same amount of information in 40–60 % of the time. However, currently the content of the learning is best limited to factual, cognitive knowledge. In addition, the learner must be highly motivated to apply the discipline necessary to effectively use computer-based instruction. The price of "off-the shelf" CD-ROMs ranges from under $100 to around $1,000, which makes them more costly than print-based products but less expensive than most training programs on a per-learner basis. Of course, their cost-effectiveness increases if multiple users can share them. Future generations of CD-ROMs will become more interactive, engaging, and user-friendly. It is worthwhile for you to keep abreast of new developments in this area.

Videos and Audiotapes

A great variety of intercultural videos and audiotapes is available for purchase. These products cover topics ranging from doing business in specific countries to cross-cultural communications, expatriate cultural adaptation, global management issues, and cultural diversity in the workplace. These tools are useful for helping learners to get a feel for other cultures in a way that written materials cannot convey. However, the amount of information they provide is often less than is typically contained in booklets or country guides.

Country-specific videos and audiotapes become dated fairly rapidly because the relatively high media production costs make frequent updating expensive and impractical. However, those that focus on deep cultural values, patterns of cultural adjustment, and general cross-cultural communications have a longer shelf life. Videos are best used as instructional aids in orientation and training programs where they can be discussed and explained. Audiotapes are basically self-study tools.

Facilitated Products

Some products are designed to be used by a professional instructor, counselor, or trainer. Selection/assessment instruments and games and simulations are common examples of this type of instructional tool.

Selection and Assessment Instruments

Different kinds of instruments and "tests" are being sold by intercultural service providers. Some are designed to determine the suitability of potential expatriates for international assignments and are used to generate input for in-depth interviews and counseling sessions. Many are meant to be used for cultural self-awareness and self-development purposes. Others are aimed at assessing the intercultural learning needs of program participants. (See Chapter 5 for a description and discussion of this type of instrument.) A few providers claim their instruments are multipurpose.

According to the *1997 Survey of Human Resource Trends* published by Aon Consulting, only 11% of the 1,700 US international organizations surveyed used a psychological profile in their expatriate selection process. Fifteen percent of them were considering using one in the future. These tools generally are self-response questionnaires, some of which have to be sent to the provider for scoring and interpretation. Others are self-scored by the respondents.

The cost of these products may range from under $10 to more than $300 per person. The scientific validity of the different instruments also varies greatly. They may be based on rigorous original research, on secondary sources, or on adaptations of instruments developed for other purposes. In general, the better the research, the more effective the instrument.

Games and Simulations

Various learning games and simulations are available for purchase. They are generally designed for use within the context of an orientation, training program, or other learning activity. These products may consist of board games, playing cards, and other artifacts. Use of them often involves structured interaction between simulated cultural groups. Usually an intercultural trainer or facilitator is required to conduct these sessions most of them. They are seldom country-specific. Their main purposes are to help learners gain cultural awareness, recognize cultural differences, and feel some of the stress of cross-cultural communications and relations. These products are particularly useful for enlivening training programs and for reaching the learners on an emotional as well as intellectual level.

Intercultural Products Focus Questions

☑ What are your reasons for buying products? Cost savings? Flexibility of use? Enhancement of other services?

☑ How do the products support your organization's or company's overall plans for gaining intercultural competence?

☑ Is a product the right tool for the job?

☑ Is the purchase of products a temporary response to an immediate need or part of a long-term strategy? Are they the most cost-effective use of your training budget?

☑ Who are the intended users? Are they sufficiently well motivated to make effective use of the products?

☑ Are the products current? When were they produced? Are revised versions pending? If so, is it feasible or worthwhile to wait for the updated versions?

☑ To what extent can the products be adapted to the needs of your employees?

☑ Does the vendor provide product support? If so, is it included in the price of purchase?

☑ Are the products available from distributors and the producers? Are there convenience and price tradeoffs in purchasing from one or the other?

☑ What criteria will you use to make your selection among similar products?

Summary and Suggested Action Steps

Intercultural learning can be achieved and enhanced through effective use of products such as books, videos, audiotapes, CD-ROMs, instruments, games, and simulations. As a buyer, you should be aware of the limitations of these products and their usefulness relative to face-to-face learning services. In cases where they are the best options, they can be flexible and relatively inexpensive resources to the global organization or corporation. The availability and sophistication of intercultural products are constantly growing. Judiciously assessing the numerous products on the market is an important responsibility for international training managers.

Here are some ways you can use the content of this chapter:

1. Develop a written rationale and criteria for purchasing intercultural products.
2. Search for appropriate products by using the resource lists.
3. Assess the various products, taking into account the considerations presented in this chapter.
4. Relate the purchase of products to your overall strategies and plans for the intercultural training and development of your employees.
5. Identify the most suitable users of the products and solicit their input prior to purchasing these tools.
6. Consider ways to motivate the users to make the best use of the products.
7. Integrate the use of products with any other intercultural learning activities your organization or company may have in progress.
8. Copy and share appropriate sections of this chapter with vendors to raise issues for discussion prior to purchasing their products.

Resources

The following lists contain contact information for obtaining various products and references for books and articles, which should help you locate and make good use of them.

Country Profiles and Self-Help Workbooks

Black, S. J., and Gregersen, H. B. *So You're Going Overseas: A Handbook for Personal & Professional Success* includes workbooks for spouses, teenagers, and children. It is available from Global Business Publishers, 2907 Shelter Island Drive, Suite 105–272, San Diego, CA 92106, 1998.

Brake, T., and Walker Medina, D. *Doing Business Internationally: The Workbook to Cross-Cultural Success*. Available from Princeton Training Press, 247 Nassau Street, Princeton, NJ 08542, 1995, tel: (609) 497–0645, fax: (609) 497–1295, e-mail: info@tmcorp.com.

The Business Guide Series, a set of books on China, Hong Kong, Philippines, Thailand, and Taiwan published between 1997–1998 by Butterworth-Heinemann, 255 Wildwood Avenue, Woburn, MA 01801, tel: (800) 366–2665 and (718) 904–2500, fax: (781) 933–6333, e-mail: orders@bhusa.com.

Country Business Guides, brief guide books on 11 countries, are available from Meridian Resources Associates, 1741 Buchanan Street,

San Francisco, CA 94115, tel: (800) 626–2047 and (415) 749–2920, fax: (415) 749–0124, e-mail contact@mera.com.

Culture Shock: Country Guides, a series of brief books on cultural issues in 36 countries, is available from Graphic Arts Publishing company, 3019 N. W. Yeon, Portland, OR 97210, tel: (503) 226–2402, fax: (503) 223–1410, e-mail: sales@gacpc.com.

Culturegrams, four-page country briefing pamphlets on 167 countries available from Kennedy Center Publications, Brigham Young University, 280 Herald R. Clark Building, PO Box 24538, Provo, UT 84602–4538, tel: (800) 528–6279 and (801) 378–6528, fax: (801) 378–5882, Web site: http://www.edu.culturegrams.

Doing Business Globally Series is a set of 48 books published in 1999 by Training Management Corporation, 600 Alexander Road, Princeton, NJ, 08540, tel: (609) 0525, fax: (609) 951–0395, e-mail: info@tmcorp.com.

Doing Business Internationally: Business Reports, a series of 84 brief country-specific books, is available from Craighead Publications, Inc., PO Box 1006 Darien, CT 06820–1006, tel: (203) 655–1007, fax: (203) 655–0018, e-mail: info@craighead.com Web site: http://www. craighead.com/index.html.

Do's and Don'ts Around the World is a series of books on cultural and social taboos and etiquette in Africa, Asia, Europe, the Middle East, South America, the Caribbean, Oceania, the United States and Canada, by Gladson S. Nwanna, published by World Travel Institute Press, 1997–1998. These books are available from Open Communications, Inc., 10640 North 28th Drive, Suite A200, Phoenix, AZ 85029, tel: (800) 437–6736, fax: (602) 530–3569, e-mail: open.media@ pobox.com.

Dunung, S. P. *Doing Business in Asia: The Complete Guide*, 2nd ed. San Francisco, CA: Jossey-Bass, 1998.

ECA Country Profiles, basic expatriate-oriented information on 77 countries, available from ECA International, Anchor House, 15 Britten Street, London SW3 3TY, England, tel: 44 (0) 171–5000, fax: 44 (0) 171 351–9396, e-mail: eca@ecaltd.com.

E.I.U. Country Profiles & Reports, brief overviews and reports on 83 countries available from the Economist Intelligence Unit, 111 West 57th Street, New York, NY 10019, tel: (800) 938–4685 and (212) 554–0600, fax: (212) 586-1181/2 , e-mail: newyork@eiu.com.

Hunter Country Review series: *Africa Review; 53 Countries, Asia and Pacific Review; 58 Countries, Americas Review; 50 Countries,* produced in 1997 by Hunter Publishing available from Open Communications, Inc. at its online book store http://www.opengroup. com/cgi-bin/search/find and via e-mail at open.com@pobox.com.

Interact Country Guides, a series of in-depth overviews of the cultures of 15 countries, edited by George Renwick, available from Intercultural Press, PO Box 700, Yarmouth, ME 04096, tel: (800) 370–2665 and (207) 846–5168, fax: (207) 846–5168, e-mail: inter culturalpress@internetmci.com.

International Business Interact series is a set of booklets on more than 45 countries. They are available in printed form or in HTML format from Shersen International, Inc., 29 Arden Road, Mountain Lakes, NJ 07046, tel: (973) 625–5916, fax: (973) 625–1035, e-mail: sse@att.net.

Kogan Doing Business in . . . Series, is a set of books on Ukraine, Uzbekistan, China, Croatia, France, Romania, South Africa, and Saudi Arabia published between 1997 and 2000 by Kogan Page Ltd., 120 Pentonville Road, London, UK, N1 9JN, tel: 44–171–278–0433, fax: 44–171–837–6348, e-mail: kpinfo@kogan-page.co.uk.

Living Abroad Country Profiles, profiles of 84 countries, are available from Living Abroad Business Association, 32 Nassau Street, Princeton, NJ 08542, tel: (609) 924–9302, fax: (609) 924–7844, e-mail: laba@livingabroad.com.

Morrison, T., and Conaway, W. A. *The International Traveler's Guide to Doing Business in Latin America.* Foster City, CA: IDG Books Worldwide, 1997.

Morrison, T., and Conaway, W. A. *The International Traveler's Guide to Doing Business in the European Union.* Foster City, CA: IDG Books Worldwide, 1997.

Morrison, T., Conaway, W. A., and Border, G. A. *Kiss, Bow, or Shake Hands: How To Do Business in Sixty Countries.* Holbrook, MA: Bob Adams Media Corporation, 1994.

Passport to the World Books is a series of booklets on 22 countries published between 1994–1996. It is available from World Trade Press, 1450 Grant Avenue, Suite 204, Novato, CA 94901, tel: (800) 833–8586 and (415) 898–1124, fax: (415) 898–1080, e-mail: worldpress@ aol.com.

Price Waterhouse Information Guidebooks, a series of business oriented booklets on 119 different countries, are available from PriceWaterhouseCoopers, 1251 Avenue of the Americas, New York, NY

10020–1104, tel: (212) 596–7000, fax: (212) 6620, Web site: http://www.132.174.112/infosrc/pw.

Put Your Best Foot Forward guide books on doing business in Europe, Asia, Mexico, Canada, Russia, and South America are available from Terra Cognita, 300 West 40th Street 314, New York, NY 10019, tel: (888) 262–2099 and (212) 262–4529, fax: 92120 262–5789, e-mail info@terracognita.com.

Worldwide Business Briefings, is a series of briefing booklets on 52 countries (available in print and online), and *International Business Audio Guides*, is a series of audio tapes with booklets on 22 countries. They are available from International Cultural Enterprises, Inc., 1241 Dartmouth Lane, Deerfield, IL 60015, tel: (800) 626–2772 and (708) 945–9516, fax: (708) 945–9614, e-mail: ice@mcs.com.

CD-ROMs

Bridging Cultures is a six-hour interactive CD-ROM–based training program that includes an 80-page workbook. It was developed by Park Li in 1998 and can be obtained from AON Consulting, 400 Renaissance Center, Suite 1500, Detroit, MI 48243–1508, tel: (800) 477–7545 and (313) 259–0116, fax: (313) 567–7292, e-mail: hrcd@aoncons.com.

The Culture Compass, a series of country-specific cross-cultural guides for international business travelers and expatriates, based on Fons Trompenaars' research, is available from United Notions, A. J. Ernstraat 595-d, 1082 LD Amstelveen, Netherlands, tel: 31–20–301-6665/6, fax: 31–20–301–6555, e-mail: info@unotions.nl.

Diversity by Crescendo is a diversity training CD available from ConnectCo, 43 Main Street S. E., Suite 508, Minneapolis, MN 55414, tel: (800) 665–5894 and (612) 617–7703, fax: (612) 617–7706, e-mail: connectco@connecto-products.com.

E.I.U. Country Profiles & Reports, CDs based on the written overviews and reports on 83 countries, are available from the Economist Intelligence Unit, 111 West 57th Street, New York, NY 10019, tel: (800) 938–4685 and (212) 554–0600, fax: (212) 586-1181/2, e-mail: newyork@eiu.com.

The Global Country Series, country-specific cross-cultural CD-based programs for expatriate and international business travelers, are available from Across Frontiers International Inc., 211 East 43rd Street,

Suite 1400, New York, NY 1007, tel: (888) 370–7017 and (212) 370–4915, fax: (212) 370–4918, e-mail: globalsuccess@accrossfrontiers.com.

Herring, S. C. *Computer-Mediated Communication: Linguistic, Social and Cross-Cultural Perspectives.* Amsterdam: John Benjamins Press, 1996.

International Business Negotiations CD, produced in 1997, is available from CD\Works, 365 Washington Street, Boston, MA 02108, tel: (617) 482–2759, fax: (617) 482–0403 and Web site: http://www.negotiations.com.

Terra Cognita CD-ROMs on living and working abroad and business-oriented topics on China, Japan, Mexico, Germany, Morocco, France, and Brazil are available from Terra Cognita, 300 West 40th Street 314, New York, NY 10019, tel: (888) 262–2099 and (212) 262–4529, fax: (212) 262–5789, e-mail: info@terracognita.com.

Training Magazine *Using Technology-Delivered Learning*, Minneapolis, MN: Lakewood Publications, 1996.

Videos and Audiotapes

Intercultural/International

After America . . . After Japan, a two-part videotape oriented toward repatriation issues for Japanese and US expatriates produced by Regge Life is available from Global Film Network, Inc., PO Box 70, East Chatham, NY 12060, tel: (800) 343–5540, fax: (201) 652–1973.

American Communication Patterns: The Business Meeting, an analysis of actual intercultural business meetings produced by Greg Nees in 2000, is available from The German Connection, Inc., PO Box 3332, Boulder, CO 80307, tel: (303) 440–4929, fax: (303) 440-4377 and via e-mail at gregnees@aol.com.

At Ease Asian Etiquette, a series of four videotapes on Japan, Hong Kong, Singapore, and Thailand from At Ease, Inc., 119 East Court Street, Cincinnati, OH 45202, tel: (800) 873–9909, fax: (513) 241–8701, e-mail: atease@eos.com.

At the Heart of Bull is a video on French and American workplace culture, produced by Bull HN Information systems, Inc. *Cold Water* is a 48-minute video about cross-cultural adaptation and culture shock. They are available from Intercultural Press, Inc., PO Box 700,

Yarmouth, ME 04096, tel: (800) 370–2665 and (207) 846–5168, fax: (207) 846–5181, e-mail: interculturalpress@internetmci.com.

Building the Transnational Team is a training videotape available from the American Society for Training and Development, 1640 King Street, Box 1443, Alexandria, VA 223313–2943, tel: (800) 628–2788 and (703) 683–3100, fax: (703) 693–1523, e-mail: csc4@astd.org.

Cross-Cultural Management, a videotape and software program based on Fons Trompenaars intercultural model, is available in four languages from Video Management N.V, Moulstraal 15-B – 1000, Brussels, Belgium.

Doing Business Internationally: The Cross-Cultural Challenges, 43-minute videotape (includes leader's guide, participant workbook, and audio cassette), MultiMedia Inc., 15 North Summit Street, Tenafly, NJ 07670, tel: (800) 682–1992 and Princeton Training Press, 247 Nassau Street, Princeton, NJ 08542, tel: (609) 497–0645, 1994.

The Dynamics of Cross-Cultural Selling: What You Don't Know May Be Costing You Sales is a two-part set of audiotapes focused on Asian and Middle Eastern customers, produced by Deena Levine. It is available from *Cultural Diversity at Work*, The GilDeane Group, 13751 Lake City Way N. E., Suite 106, Seattle, WA 98125–3615, tel: (206) 362–0336, fax: (206) 363–5028, e-mail: editors@diversityhotwire.com.

Going International and *Valuing Differences* is a seven-part video series on a variety of cross-cultural and diversity topics by Griggs Productions, 5616 Geary Boulevard, San Francisco, CA 94121; tel: (800) 210–4200 and (415) 668–4200, fax: (415) 668–6004, e-mail: Griggs @griggs.com.

International Business Audio Guides, a series of audiotapes with booklets on 22 countries is available from International Cultural Enterprises, Inc., 1241 Dartmouth Lane, Deerfield, IL 60015, tel: (800) 626–2772 and (708) 945–9516, fax: (708) 945–9614, e-mail: ice @mcs.com.

International Business Videos, a series of videotapes on 14 countries in Latin America and Asia, is available from Big World Inc., 4204 Tamarack Court, Suite 100, Boulder CO 80304, tel: (800) 682–1261 and (303) 444–6179, fax: (303) 444–6190, e-mail: bigworld@aol.com.

International Straight Talk, a series of videotapes on human resource management issues in 14 different countries, is available from William Drake & Associates, PO Box 2838, Waxahachie, TX 75165, tel/fax: (972) 938–2927, e-mail: bdrake@onramp.net.

New Skills for Global Management, a 39-minute videotape with a booklet, was produced in 1993 by MultiMedia Inc., 15 North Summit Street, Tenafly, NJ 07670, tel: (800) 682–1992.

Peregrine Audio Guides, business-oriented audiotapes on China, Mexico, Japan, and Germany produced in 1992, are available from Peregrine Media Group, PO Box 6721, Yorkville Finance Station, New York, NY 10128.

Summerfield, E. *Crossing Cultures through Film*. Yarmouth, ME: Intercultural Press, 1993.

Terra Cognita videos on living and working abroad and business-oriented audiotapes on China, Japan, Mexico, Germany, Morocco, France, and Brazil are available from Terra Cognita, 300 West 40th Street 314, New York, NY 10019, tel: (888) 262–2099 and (212) 262–4529, fax: (212) 262–5789, e-mail: info@terracognita.com.

West Meets East in Japan is a business-oriented video available from Bryn Mawr, 850 Lancaster Avenue, Bryn Mawr, PA 10910, tel: (800) 622–3610 and (610) 526–9100, fax: (610) 525–2563, and e-mail: training@videolrn.com.

Working with Japan, Managing in China, and *Working with USA for Asians* videos in a series are available from Meridian Resources Associates, Inc., 1741 Buchanan Street, San Francisco, CA 94115, tel: (800) 626–2047 and (415) 749–2920, fax: (415) 749–0124, e-mail: Contact@mera.com.

Workplace Diversity

Age Discrimination: You Be the Judge is a 28-minute video with a leaders' guide and was produced in 1994 by Karen Frankl and Marilyn J. Young. *Sexual Harassment: Prevention, Recognition and Correction*, is a 25-minute video produced in 1993 by Holly Hughes and Rosalie L. Donlon. They are available from the Bureau of Business Practice, 24 Rope Ferry Road, Waterford, CT 06386, tel: (800) 243–0876 ext. 6, e-mail: billt@bbplists.com.

Bridges: Skills for Managing a Diverse Workforce is an 8-video series with trainers' and trainees' manuals. They are available from BNA Communications, Inc., 9439 Key West Avenue, Rockville, MD 20850–3396, tel: (800) 233–6067 and (301) 948–0540, fax: (301) 948–2085, e-mail: cdefilip@bna.com.

California Newsreel offers 11 training videos on cultural diversity and race relations. They are available from California Newsreel at 149

Ninth Street, San Francisco, CA 94103, tel: (415) 621–6196, fax: (415) 621–6522 and via e-mail at contact@newsreel.org.

Competing through Managing Diversity is a 70-minute video produced by R. Roosevelt Thomas, Jr. It is available from American Media Incorporated, 4900 University Avenue, Suite 100, West Des Moines, IA 50266–6769, tel: (800) 262–2557 and (514) 224–0919, fax: (515) 224–0256, e-mail: amil@ammedia.com.

Dynamics of Diversity: Strategic Programs for Your Organization is a training kit including a 26-minute video, leader's guide, and participant booklets. It was produced in 1994 by Odette Pollar, Mary Kay Beeby, and Rafael Gonzalez and is available from Crisp Publications, Inc., 1200 Hamilton Court, Menlo Park, CA 94025, tel: (800) 442–7477 and (650) 323–6100, fax: (650) 323–5800, e-mail: mcrisp@crisplearning.com.

The F.A.I.R. Way To Manage Diversity is a 19-minute video available from Richard Chang Associates, Inc., 15265 Alton Parkway, Suite 300, Irvine CA, 92618, tel: (949) 727–7477, fax: (949) 727- 7007, e-mail: info@rca4results.com.

HR Press Diversity Video Series includes 16 videos on diversity in the workplace. *Workforce Diversity* is a video-based training workshop that includes participant booklets and a leader's guide. They are available from HR Press, PO Box 28, Fredonia, NY 14063, tel: (800) 444–7139 and (716) 672–4254, fax: (716) 697–3177, e-mail: hrpress@netsync.net.

Let's Talk Diversity and *Sexual Harassment-New Roles/New Rules* are training videos available from Edge Training Systems, Inc. 10043 Midlothian Turnpike, Suite C, Richmond, VA 23235, tel: (800) 476–1405 and (804) 272–1711, fax: (804) 272–1683 and e-mail: mail box@edgetraining.com.

The Multicultural Workplace, produced by Jay Anania and Marian Calabro, is a 32-minute video. *Race & Sex Discrimination in the Workplace: What You Need To Know* is a 21-minute video by Perry Schwartz Productions. Both were produced in 1990, and they are available from Coronet/MTI Film & Video, 2349 Chaffee drive, St. Louis, MO 63146, tel: (314) 569–0211, fax: (314) 569–2834, e-mail: phoenixfilms@att.net.

The Winning Balance is a diversity awareness-building video from ConnectCo, 43 Main Street S. E., Suite 508, Minneapolis, MN 55414, tel: (800) 665–5894 and (612) 617–7703, fax: (612) 617–7706, e-mail: connectco@connecto-products.com.

Working Together is a 25-minute diversity training video with a leader's guide and trainee workbooks available from George Simons International, 236 Plateau Avenue, Santa Cruz, CA 95060, tel/fax: (888) 251–3117 and via e-mail at gsimons@diversophy.com.

Assessment/Selection Instruments

Change Agent Profile (CAP) is an assessment tool for developing diversity awareness and skills available from ConnectCo, 43 Main Street S. E., Suite 508, Minneapolis, MN 55414, tel: (800) 665–5894 and (612) 617–7703, fax: (612) 617–7706, e-mail: connectco@connectco-products.com.

Cross-Cultural Adaptability Inventory, developed by Colleen Kelley and Judith Meyers and *GAPtest, Global Awareness Profile,* a self-awareness instrument created by J. Nathan Corbitt, are available from Intercultural Press, Inc., PO Box 700, Yarmouth, ME 04096, tel: (800) 370–2665 and (207) 846–5168, fax: (207) 846–5181, e-mail: interculturalpress@internetmci.com.

The Cross Cultural Assessor, a multimedia-based expatriate assessment focused on attitudes and knowledge developed by Richard D. Lewis, is available from Richard Lewis Communications, 3c New York Inc., 450 West 15th Street, Suite 305, New York, NY 10011, tel: (212) 328–0710, fax: (212) 271–6372, e-mail: ternsing@3cny.com.

Culture in the Workplace Questionnaire is a cultural profile instrument, and *Global Team Process Questionnaire* is a multicultural team training tool. They are available from ITAP International, 268 Wall Street, Princeton, NJ 08540, tel: (800) 659–4827 and (609) 921–1446, fax: (609) 924–7946, e-mail: itap@itapintl.com.

Discovering Diversity Profile, a self-administered instrument, is available with a facilitator's kit from Team Builders Plus, Suite 302, Cherry Hills, NJ 08003, tel: (800) 777–9897 and (609) 596–4196, fax: (609) 489–9228, and via e-mail at info@disctools.com.

Harris, P. R. *Twenty Fully Reproducible Assessment Instruments for the New Work Culture,* Amherst, MA: HRD Press, 1995. See "Intercultural Relations Inventory."

Individual Global Competency Assessment, an intercultural job-related instrument developed by Robert T. Moran and John R. Riesenberger, is available from Robert T. Moran, 5000 N. Wilkinson Road, Scottsdale, AZ 85253, tel: (602) 946–8046, fax: (602) 949–8716, e-mail: bmoran@aztec.asu.edu.

Intercultural Development Inventory, an instrument developed by Mitchell Hammer and Milton Bennett to measure intercultural sensitivity, is available to purchasers who have attended a qualifying seminar. It is offered by the Intercultural Communication Institute, 8835 Southwest Canyon Lane, Suite 238, Portland, OR 97225, tel: (503) 4622, fax: (503) 297–4695, e-mail: ici@intercultural.org.

OAI: Overseas Assignment Inventory is an expatriate selection and counseling instrument developed by Michael Tucker. It is available from Prudential Relocation International, 200 Summit Lake Drive, Valhalla, NY 10595, tel: (800) 356–6834, Web site: http://www. prudential.com/prm. It is also available from Tucker International, 900 28th Street, Suite 200, Boulder, CO 80803, tel: (303) 786–7753, fax: (303) 786–7801, e-mail info@tuckerintl.com and Web site: http:// www.tuckerintl.com/.

PCAT, Peterson Global Awareness Test, developed by Brooks Peterson, is available at Across Culture Inc., 1602 Juno Avenue, Saint Paul, MN 55116, tel: (651) 695–0011, fax: (615) 695–0022, e-mail: info @acrosscultures.net.

Personal Diversity Maturity Index (PDMI), Personal Diversity Maturity Scale (PDMS), and Organizational Diversity Maturity Scale (ODMS) are instruments designed for use in workplace diversity programs. They are available from R. Thomas Consulting & Training, 2872 Woodcock Boulevard, Suite 220, Atlanta, GA 30341–4100, tel: (770) 234–0222, fax: (770) 234–0226, e-mail: info@rthomasconsulting.com.

Perceptual Modality Preference Survey (PMPS) is an instrument for assessing learning styles developed by Clarence E. Cherry and updated in 1997. It is available from the Institute for Learning Styles Research, 103 Ruskin Circle, Maryville, TN 37803, tel: (423) 982–6253, fax: (423) 982–4499, e-mail: llst@prodigy.net.

16PF Profile, an expatriate selection instrument developed by Lou Gilbert and Ron Wonderlin, is available from Ron Wonderlin, 310 Clifton Avenue, Minneapolis, MN 55403, tel: (612) 872–7220, fax: (612) 870–1916 and e-mail ronwunderlin@excite.com.

Questions of Diversity: Assessment Tools of Organizations and Individuals. (6th ed.) Written by George F. Simmons and Bob Abramms in 1994, this title is available from George Simons International, 236 Plateau Avenue, Santa Cruz, CA 95060, tel and fax: (888) 251–3117 and via e-mail at gsimons@diversophy.com.

Supervisor International Evaluation Instrument and *Foreign Assignment Exercise* are expatriate selection tools developed by Barry Kozloff. They are available from Selection Research International, Inc., 8420 Delmar Boulevard, Lobby West, St. Louis, MO, 63124–2181, tel: (314) 567–6900, fax: (314) 567–7782, e-mail: kozloff@sri –2000.com.

Transcultural Communicator/Negotiator is a training instrument with an administrator's guide. It was developed by George F. Simons and is available from ODT, Inc., One East Pleasant Street, Amherst MA 01002, tel: (800) 736–1293, fax: (413) 549–3503, e-mail: 0003475157@mcimail.com.

Games and Simulations

BAFA BAFA is a game that uses two simulated cultures to explore cross-cultural communication and interaction and *Star Power* is a simulation aimed at exploring interpersonal power in culturally diverse contexts. They were developed by R. Garry Shirts and are available from Simulation Training Systems, PO Box 910, Del Mar, CA 92014, tel: (800) 942–2900, fax: (619) 792–9743, e-mail sts@cts.com.

BARNGA: A Simulation Game on Cultural Clashes, developed by Sivasailam Thiagarajan and Barbara Steinwachs, and *An Alien Among Us*, a simulation focused on adaptability fitness for intercultural sojourners created by Richard B. Powers, are cross-cultural training tools. They are available from Intercultural Press, Inc., PO Box 700, Yarmouth, ME 04096, tel: (800) 370–2665 and (207) 846–5168, fax: (207) 846–5181, e-mail: interculturalpress@internetmci.com.

Clues and Challenges: Culture-General Cross-Cultural Orientation, is a simulation focused on cultural awareness and cross-cultural transitions, developed by Sandra Mumford Fowler, Barbara Steinwachs, and Pierre Corbeil. It is available from Youth for Understanding International Exchange, 3501 Newark Street, Washington, DC 20016, tel: (800) 872–0200 and (202) 966–6800, fax: (202) 895–1104, e-mail: info@us.yfu.org.

Cross Culture Tour Game is a board game developed by Richard D. Lewis. It is available from the Institute of Cross Culture Communication, Riversdown House, Warnford, Hampshire, SO32 3LH, UK, tel: 44–1962–771–111, fax: 44–1962–771–105, e-mail: iccc@crossculture.com.

Diversity Bingo, Global Beads, Sh! Sexual Harassment, a simulation game produced by Thiagarajan Sivasailam, and other intercultural and diversity learning games are available from HR Press, PO Box 28, Fredonia, NY 14063, tel: (800) 444–7139 and (716) 672–4254, fax: (716) 697–3177, e-mail: hrpress@epix.net.

DiversiCARD is a series of country-specific playing card decks for learning about doing business with the Canadians, Dutch, Japanese, Mexicans, French, Germans, and US Americans. *Diversophy* is a participative diversity-awareness building game. They are available from George Simons International, 236 Plateau Avenue, Santa Cruz, CA, 95060, tel: (831) 426–9608, fax: (888) 215–3117, e-mail: g.f. simons@gte.net.

ECOTONOS is a simulation that focuses on problem-solving and decision-making in multicultural environments developed by Dianne Hofner-Saphiere. It is available from Nipporica Associates, 10072 Buena Vista Drive, Conifer, CO 80433, tel: (303) 838–1798, fax: (303) 338–1799 and e-mail: nipporica@aol.com.

Grendler, M. *Designing and Evaluating Games and Simulations.* Houston, TX: Gulf Publishing Company, 1994.

Honoring Differences Connection Cards is a diversity awareness-building game from ConnectCo, 43 Main Street S. E., Suite 508, Minneapolis, MN 55414, tel: (800) 665–5894 and (612) 617–7703, fax: (612) 617–7706, e-mail: connectco@connectco-products.com.

Kirby, A. *The Encyclopedia of Games for Trainers.* Amherst, MA: HRD Press, 1992.

Kirby, A. *Great Games for Trainers.* Amherst, MA: HRD Press, 1994.

Markhall is a simulation that explores management styles in different cultures. It was developed by James McCaffery, Daniel Edwards, Judee Blom, and David Bachner. It is available from Youth for Understanding International Exchange, 3501 Newark Street, Washington, DC 20016, tel: (800) 872–0200, e-mail: alamweb@us.yfu. org.

Moran, R. T., and Braaten, D. O. (eds.) *International Directory of Multicultural Resources.* Houston: TX: Gulf Publishing Company, 1996, pp. 55–56. See "Simulations."

Sisk, D. A. "Simulation Games as Training Tools." In S. M. Fowler and M. G. Mumford (eds.), *Intercultural Sourcebook: Cross-Cultural*

Training Methods, Vol. 1, Yarmouth, ME: Intercultural Press, 1995, pp. 81–92.

Thiagarajan, S. *Diversity Simulation Games*. Amherst, MA: HRD Press, 1995.

Wederspahn, G. M. and Kanyane, M. "Board Game Teaches Local Culture." *Cultural Diversity at Work*, Winter 1998, pp. 1 and 12.

8

Intercultural Service Providers

There is no doubt in my mind that . . . the intercultural field has become
the most important calling to which anyone can respond, for it provides
the means of understanding and drawing together the disparate and
often antagonistic peoples of our nation and of the world.

L. Robert Kohls in *Training Know-How
for Cross-Cultural and Diversity Trainers*

Sellers and Buyers

For every buyer, there are several potential sellers of intercultural services. The competition between providers in this "buyers'
market" contributes to the health of the profession by promoting
quality, cost-effectiveness, and customer service. However, this
competition also has caused a proliferation of options to be available. The sophistication and intensity of the marketing and sales
efforts of the vendors have grown as they seek to differentiate
themselves from their competitors. Under these circumstances,
the buyers' power is increased, but so is the difficulty in making
the best choices. Effective teamwork between purchasers and
their suppliers, and high-quality training and development results
depend on selecting the right providers (see Exhibit 8–1).

Finding Suitable Providers

Perhaps the most challenging cross-cultural . . . conflict is between the
intercultural practitioner culture and the business/organizational culture.

                                        Pierre Casse in *Training for the Cross-
                                        Cultural Mind*

Something most practitioners share is a sense of calling that goes beyond just having a job or making a living. This common belief in the
inherent value of their services may make them seem quite similar on
the surface. However, you can differentiate providers by considering
their motivations, backgrounds, organizational capabilities, and professional standings. Distinguishing differences among them in these re-
spects will help you make a good match between your company or
organization and your vendors.

Motivations

What seems to motivate and sustain many providers is the convic-
tion that promoting understanding and harmony among people of diverse cultural backgrounds is a noble and worthwhile endeavor. Most
senior practitioners recall originally being attracted to the intercultural
field for such idealistic reasons, and the many new aspiring interculturalists drawn into the profession each year often express similar motivations.

In addition, many consider it glamorous or exciting to deal with different cultures and countries. Others are stimulated by the intellectual
challenge and learning involved in deciphering subtle cultural factors
and discovering the practical implications of this knowledge. Some
consultants stress the satisfaction they feel in contributing to their
clients' global business competitiveness, productivity, and profitability.
On a personal level, many seek to enhance their professional reputations and advance their careers. Of course, money also can be a strong
motivator.

In reality, each provider has a unique mixture of motivations. Learning why potential vendors are in the intercultural field is a useful first
step in determining which of them are most likely to be in harmony
with your organizations' values and aims. At this level, the key issue of

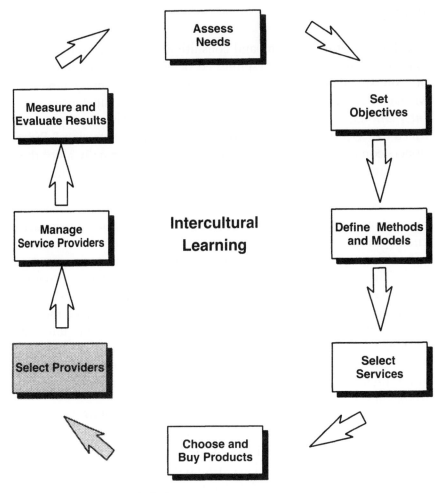

EXHIBIT 8–1. INTERCULTURAL SERVICES CYCLE.

"good chemistry" is often resolved. Having compatible motivations is a necessary, but not sufficient, credential for a particular vendor to be your best choice. Compatibility must be combined with appropriate expertise, skills, and organizational capability in order for a provider to meet your needs.

Backgrounds

The intercultural training and consulting field is relatively new and multidisciplinary. A firmly established or generally recognized course of professional development for interculturalists does not yet exist. As Michael Paige put it in his 1986 article on trainer competencies in the *International Journal of Intercultural Relations*, "There are few established experiential or academic pathways into the profession." Practitioners come from a wide range of backgrounds. Virtually all of them have international or cross-cultural experience. However, the extent and depth of their experience varies greatly.

You are likely to encounter consultants or trainers from the "helping professions" such as former teachers, counselors, pastors, missionaries, and psychologists. Likewise, many people in the field were once members of international development and economic assistance organizations. The various study abroad and international exchange programs also have contributed newcomers to the profession. A number of former corporate expatriate employees and spouses have joined the field. Intercultural consulting and training is a sideline of some university professors, especially sociologists, anthropologists, language teachers, and business/management instructors. Graduates of academic programs on international business and intercultural communications add to the mix.

Talented and competent practitioners come from all of these different backgrounds. Having a particular professional or academic history is neither an asset nor a liability in the intercultural profession. You should consider a provider's background only to the extent that it may give you some indication of the provider's values and viewpoints. Those attributes are important for you to know when you are assessing potential suppliers' compatibility with your company or organizational corporate culture. Also, if they have gone beyond their original backgrounds through education or experience, it demonstrates an ability to change and adapt, which is an essential characteristic of good cross-cultural trainers and consultants.

Integrity

No professional body oversees intercultural service firms and practitioners to guarantee that they comply with an accepted set of ethical standards. Therefore, it is your responsibility as a buyer to be sure that potential suppliers have a high level of integrity. You should satisfy yourself that they are not misrepresenting their experience or qualifications. It also pays to be skeptical of vendors that seem to promise too much. A reputable provider will readily admit to having realistic limitations and constraints. Likewise, be wary of salespeople who focus mostly on their products and services and who show little or no interest in your needs and concerns. In general, you should heed the saying, "Let the buyer beware."

Organizational Capabilities

Providers of intercultural services range from individual freelance practitioners working out of their homes, to small companies servicing a local market, to large firms with many employees and regional, national, and international offices and training facilities. Some are informal networks of associates who work together occasionally. Others are subcontractors or business units of large corporations in related fields, such as accounting and relocation firms, moving companies, and language training suppliers. A few providers specialize by focusing on a specific country or region of the world. Most offer services on any country. Some providers are seasoned veterans with long and successful careers, and others are fledgling newcomers eager to establish themselves in the field. Checking references with clients of prospective suppliers is strongly advisable.

The following questions are helpful when you are considering a provider's organizational capabilities:

❑ Focus: Are intercultural services the vendor's core business? Does the vendor provide its own services directly, or does it use subcontractors? Who is accountable for client satisfaction?
❑ Expertise: Does the provider have the appropriate knowledge base and program design and delivery skills? Is its professional staff well qualified?
❑ Scope: Does the provider's expertise extend to all of the countries and cultures in which your company is interested?
❑ Responsiveness: Are your requests for information, assistance, and services responded to promptly?

❑ Flexibility: Does the provider have a reputation for reacting quickly and positively to client requests for changes in program content, dates, or location?

❑ Accessibility: Are its training facilities and administrative offices conveniently located? Is it able to deliver services in various venues and at international locations?

❑ Versatility: Are the supplier's consultants and trainers capable of handling a variety of assignments?

❑ Organizational depth: Does the vendor have a sufficient number of staff to meet the demand for its services? Are they employees or contractors hired on an ad hoc basis?

❑ Professionalism: Does the organization function in a professional and business-like manner?

❑ Efficiency: Do its clients say that program booking, billing for services, reporting, and business communications are handled efficiently?

Professional Standing

Good standing in the intercultural field is an essential requisite for individual practitioners and providers' core staff. They should be active in their profession and accepted by others as colleagues. They must be knowledgeable regarding the general concepts, information, methods, and techniques used in the field. Suitable providers have a reputation of "knowing what they are doing," and of satisfying their clients.

Applying the following criteria will give you some indication of a practitioner's professional standing:

❑ Involvement: Have they been involved in the intercultural professional society and the international human resource organizations for a significant amount of time (5 years or more)?

❑ Intellectual contributions: Have they contributed to the intercultural field by writing articles or books and making presentations at professional conferences? Have they done research?

❑ Academic credentials: Have they studied intercultural topics in formal academic settings? Do they teach courses? Are academic credentials essential in order to meet your needs?

❑ Continued learning: Have they attended intercultural programs, seminars, and workshops?

❑ Public recognition: Are they mentioned or quoted in human resources and business publications? Have they received awards for their work?

❑ Service record: How long have they been in business? How much experience do they have providing which kinds of services?

❑ Client satisfaction: Do they have a respectable client list? Are their clients willing to give them unequivocally positive references?

❑ Reputation: Are they known in the field? Do they have a reputation for integrity and quality?

Proximity

Other suitability factors being equal, it makes sense to consider the distance of the supplier's training and administrative facilities from locations where the services are needed. Trainees' travel expense often is a significant portion of the overall cost of training. Several providers have established regional client service offices and training centers in order to be more conveniently located for their clients. Others have focused on their local home markets. Virtually all of them are more than willing to deliver programs at their client's locations. But, in these cases, the trainers' travel expenses and the costs of shipping the training materials must be added to the fees charged by the suppliers. You may consult the lists of service providers at the end of this chapter to identify those located in your area. Remember that a national provider may have a regional facility nearby.

Supplier Suitability Considerations

❑ Motivations: Are they compatible with your organization's values and mission?

❑ Backgrounds: Do they have the appropriate expertise and geographical knowledge?

❑ Organizational capabilities: Are they well organized and efficient?

❑ Professional standing: Do they have a good reputation in the intercultural field?

❑ Proximity: Are they conveniently located?
❑ Staff qualifications: Are their consultants and trainers well qualified and experienced?

Supplier Suitability Focus Questions
☑ How would you describe your company or organizational culture? What are its predominant characteristics?
☑ Which of these factors have most influenced its choice of vendors and suppliers? How and why?
☑ Which of your current vendors are most compatible with your organizational culture? What are the attributes that enabled them to achieve this level of compatibility?
☑ What kinds of problems has your company had with its suppliers? Which of these are most important to avoid when selecting intercultural service providers?
☑ Must intercultural service providers have special expertise or capabilities in order to meet your organization's or company's needs? If so, what are these? How would you prioritize them?
☑ Can your intercultural needs be classified into different levels of complexity and importance? If so, does it make sense to use different kinds of providers?
☑ What attributes in an intercultural service provider are most important to you? Why?
☑ How can you best find out about potential providers' reputations and qualifications?
☑ Is the location of training facilities an important consideration?

Intercultural Trainer Qualifications

If you think it is expensive to hire a professional, wait until you hire an amateur!

Red Adair
oil well firefighter

Because most intercultural services involve training programs, the qualifications of provider trainers are important to consider. How well they have mastered their craft and their personal qualities probably have more impact on the outcome of programs than any other factors. They are responsible for making the program designs work and the content stimulating. More importantly, they are teachers, guides, coaches, and models to the trainees. Whether a program is a rewarding and productive learning experience largely depends on them.

The trainers must have a set of specific experiences, knowledge, skills, attributes, and ethics in order to perform their roles effectively. You need to look beyond providers' motivations, backgrounds, and organizational capabilities to assure yourself that their trainers are suitable and well qualified. All the qualifications of the ideal trainer are rarely found in any single individual. Nevertheless, having a clear vision of the best possible trainer gives you a standard for measurement.

International/Intercultural Experience

The amount and type of trainers' international and intercultural experience are critical to their effectiveness. The following questions will help you determine the extent to which backgrounds are suitable:

❑ Depth: Did their assignments abroad require in-depth personal and professional relationships with the local people and involvement in the culture? Did their roles demand that they enter into others' cultural frames of reference?

❑ Duration: Did they stay in the country long enough to undergo the entire expatriate adaptation process and to master cross-cultural skills?

❑ Success: Were their international awareness, assignments successful in terms of cultural adaptation and professional goal accomplishment? Was their success achieved through the application of intercultural awareness, knowledge and skills?

❑ Relevance: Were their experiences in the particular countries and kinds of circumstances in which your organization is interested? A "study abroad" or Peace Corps assignment alone, for example, does not qualify one to offer international business advice.

❑ Breadth: Have the potential providers lived or worked in a variety of cultures in order to be able to distinguish significant differences among them?

❑ Learning: Did they gain useful knowledge and cultural insights from the experiences? Can they articulate what they learned?

Knowledge, Skills, and Attributes

In addition to having the appropriate international and intercultural experience, well-qualified trainers possess a particular set of skills, knowledge, and attributes. The success of training programs and your employees' satisfaction as trainees depend, to a great extent, on these qualities in the people who actually deliver them.

Content and Context Knowledge

The specific areas of knowledge required by intercultural trainers include the following:

❑ The client's international business context or organizational mission
❑ The importance of intercultural competence
❑ Key cross-cultural concepts
❑ Country-specific and regional cultural and business information
❑ The process of cultural adaptation
❑ Trainees' cross-cultural role requirements
❑ Needs assessment and objective setting
❑ Adult learning styles and preferences
❑ Instructional methods, techniques, and aids
❑ The client's outcome expectations
❑ Training program evaluation methods

Trainer Skills

The "toolkit" of essential skills of cross-cultural trainers includes the following:

❑ Individual and organizational needs assessment techniques
❑ Customization of program design and content
❑ Creation of supportive learning environments
❑ Program time management and pacing of activities
❑ Presentation, facilitation, summarization, and feedback skills
❑ Ability to stimulate trainees into participating actively
❑ Accommodation to different learning styles and cultural backgrounds
❑ Competent use of resources: people, training materials, and teaching aids
❑ Effectively use of unanticipated learning opportunities

❏ Ability to provide practical illustrations and examples
❏ Ability to model effective cross-cultural skills
❏ Ability to maintain focus on program objectives

Personal Attributes

Competent intercultural trainers have certain personal qualities that contribute to their credibility and effectiveness. Among these attributes are

❏ Openness to, interest in, and enjoyment of cross-cultural experiences and people
❏ Sensitivity to cultural differences and respecting and valuing them
❏ Cultural self-awareness
❏ Intellectual and behavioral flexibility
❏ Charisma as a trainer and ability to inspire learning
❏ Empathy
❏ Energy and enthusiasm
❏ Interpersonal warmth and approachability
❏ Personal comfort with the client's corporate culture
❏ Commitment to excellence
❏ Sense of accountability for results

Trainer Ethics

By its very nature, intercultural training involves "transformational" learning. It requires trainees to confront their own beliefs and values and to be open-minded about those of people from other cultures. In the process, trainees may change their viewpoints and transform their relationship styles. The potentially strong influence of this type of training on learners imposes a serious responsibility on the trainers. Likewise, trainees could misuse their new intercultural knowledge and skills if they are guided improperly. Therefore, high ethical standards are required of trainers generally the following:

❏ Recognizing and admitting their own limitations as trainers and not extending themselves beyond their current capabilities
❏ Being knowledgeable about cross-cultural ethical issues
❏ Not promoting their own values

❑ Being aware of the potential risks and stresses of intercultural training and avoiding harm to trainees' self-concept and self-confidence
❑ Empowering learners and avoiding the creation of dependency
❑ Cautioning trainees to not extend themselves beyond the limitations of their new learning
❑ Promoting ethical behavior in international relations and business
❑ Preserving the confidentiality of privileged client information
❑ Declining any assignments they consider ethically compromising
❑ Continually learning and upgrading their own knowledge and skills

---

Trainer Qualification Focus Questions

☑ What are the professional and personal qualifications of your company's in-house trainers or those of outside training contractors you have used?

☑ Which of them are most highly rated by your employees? Why?

☑ Which are considered most successful by supervisors? Why?

☑ Are their popularity and success factors relevant to the selection of intercultural trainers? If so, can you articulate and prioritize these factors?

☑ Do your employees have any particular learning style preferences? If so, what are these?

☑ Does information from potential providers include sufficient detail regarding the qualifications of their trainers? If not, what type of information is missing? How can you best obtain it?

☑ Had you established criteria for trainer selection? What are the most important requirements?

☑ To what extent do potential providers' trainers match your profile of the ideal trainer?

☑ Will they let you observe them conducting a training program? Will they do a demonstration?

Assessing Vendors Information

The buyer needs a hundred eyes, the seller but one.

Arab proverb

As a buyer of intercultural services, you undoubtedly will receive marketing brochures and proposals from potential vendors and will be given sales presentations by their representatives. Knowing how to interpret marketing materials and proposals is an important skill for you to develop. It will enable you to filter out the "hype," quickly spot gaps in information, and generate useful follow-up questions. Likewise, possessing criteria with which to evaluate sales presentations and having discriminating questions to ask will help you to distinguish substance from salesmanship. Reputable, high-quality providers are not inhibited by such signs of savvy on the part of potential clients and will welcome the opportunity to discuss substantive issues with you.

Evaluating Marketing Materials

In addition to containing information about providers' services, marketing materials often reveal much about their organizational cultures, standards, and business styles. Such hints may be as important as the descriptions of their services in helping you understand what potential suppliers have to offer and how they work. The following questions will enable you to interpret both the intentional and unintentional messages in promotional materials. These are not provider selection criteria, but they should help narrow your search for the kinds of vendors that best meet your needs and preferences.

❑ Appearance: Are the materials attractive and professional-looking? Making a good first impression reflects a commitment to quality, organizational pride, and business savvy.
❑ Writing quality: Is the text readable, concise, and free from grammatical and spelling errors? Good writing is an indication of clear thinking and attention to detail.
❑ Thoroughness: Do the materials include descriptions of services, organizational structure, capabilities, philosophy, and mission? Do they reveal how long the provider has been in business? Do they contain client lists and profiles of past projects? Major omissions may indicate a lack of thoroughness or might be attempts to mask shortcomings.
❑ Focus: Are the purposes of different kinds of programs well-defined? Are services such as training, consulting, and counseling

clearly distinguished from each other? Ambiguity in this regard may reveal a lack of precision in organizational focus.

❑ Detail: Are the descriptions of services and programs detailed enough to determine, for example, if they are generic or custom-tailored, if family members are included, and where programs can be conducted? This level of detail is needed in order to compare various vendors.

❑ Tone: Is the overall tone business-like, academic, or informal and folksy? Consideration of this factor will help you assess providers' compatibility with your organizational or corporate culture.

❑ Credibility: Are the claims made in the materials believable? Are any testimonials included verifiable? Are any statistics supported by reliable references? Exaggerated claims of being the *foremost, best, leading,* or *most-respected* provider are pompous and self-serving. Furthermore, they are unnecessary if suppliers are fully confident in the quality of their services.

❑ Added value: Are useful items such as article reprints, survey reports, or samples of program materials enclosed? Being willing to share helpful information, without commitment on your part, is a sign that a potential provider is likely to be client-centered.

❑ Rationale: Do the materials provide solid rationale regarding the need for intercultural services? Is it well supported with factual data? Inclusion of this kind of information reflects an understanding of your need to "sell" the services in-house. It also demonstrates an ability to help you meet that challenge.

Dealing with Proposals

Vendors may send you unsolicited proposals. You can assess them using the same criteria applied to marketing materials. Essentially, such proposals are merely a different form of sales literature. However, you should check them for any indications that they were aimed specifically at your company's or organization's needs and cross-border projects. If this were the case, it would be a positive sign that the vendor made an effort to discover what particular topics and country focus might be of interest to you. Such efforts to customize its sales literature may be a clue that it tailors services to clients rather than offering generic "one size fits all" programs and products.

Requests for Proposal

The written request for proposal (RFP) is a procurement tool that traditionally has been used to solicit proposals from potential providers. However, during the past 10 years, its use has declined significantly. Today, it is mostly seen in the public sector and in cases of large training contracts being opened for competitive bidding.

The RFP process normally requires a considerable investment of time and effort on the purchaser's part. It involves gathering input, writing the RFP document, obtaining buy-in from various interested parties, sending the document, answering questions from vendors, receiving the proposals, requesting missing information, organizing review committees, assessing and comparing the proposals received, and advising vendors of your decision. These requirements discourage its use in situations where time and staff resources are significant limitations.

Nevertheless, going through the RFP process has a number of benefits:

❑ It requires purchasers to carefully define their objectives and goals.
❑ It helps build in-house awareness of the need for the services.
❑ It involves various stakeholders in the decision.
❑ It provides a clear basis for evaluation of the services.
❑ It promotes objectivity and fairness in the selection process.

If you decide that it is necessary or desirable to generate an RFP, you may be able to obtain assistance from your in-house procurement or contracting specialists. They are likely to have sample RFPs that could serve as models for you. Also, they can probably give you advice on how to structure your solicitation and review processes. You should make it clear to them that you are purchasing services (rather than materials or products) in order to receive appropriate help. For ideas regarding possible content for RFPs of intercultural services, you may refer to the previous sections on providers' organizational capabilities, motivations, professional standing, and the qualifications of their trainers.

Assessing Proposals

A useful starting point for evaluating proposals is to apply the previously given criteria for assessing marketing materials. However, you should take several additional considerations into account:

1. Was the submission deadline met? Late proposals may indicate deficiencies in a vendor's management capabilities.
2. Is the proposal well-written, error-free, and professional-looking? These factors reflect clear thinking, quality consciousness, and attention to detail.
3. Does it respond to all of your specifications? Incompleteness could show a lack of thoroughness or an unwillingness to follow direction.
4. How well does it respond to your needs? Does it demonstrate expertise in the intercultural field and knowledge of your company?
5. Is it creative? If it merely paraphrases the RFP, the vendor may not be able to help you expand your awareness of needs and possibilities.

A simple and easy way to quickly check whether a proposal is adequate or not is to ask yourself whether it answers the six key questions: Who? What? When? Where? How? Why?

Key Questions About Proposals

☐ *Who* is the proposal from? Is it a quality supplier?
☐ *What* does it include? Is it relevant to your needs?
☐ *When* can the proposed services begin? Do the dates meet your timetable?
☐ *Where* can the services be delivered? Is the location convenient for you?
☐ *How* will the services be delivered? Is the approach compatible with your organization's culture?
☐ *Why* has the vendor proposed these particular services? Does the rationale make sense to you?

Handling Sales Presentations

Most of the qualities of good marketing materials listed also apply to a face-to-face sales presentation. Meeting personally with representatives of service providers gives you an opportunity to assess their companies' capabilities and working styles at much greater depth. The following pointers will help you get the most from their presentations.

❑ Expectations: Be explicit about what you want as outcomes from the presentation and how and when you plan to make your purchasing decision. Having clear expectations on both sides will prevent you from working at cross-purposes and will save time.

❑ Agenda: Arrange, in advance, the topics to be covered. Solicit suggestions and input from the provider. Pose questions raised during your review of the marketing materials. Ask the presenter to come prepared to answer them. Put the primary focus on *your needs* rather than on the providers' services. Make sure that your items of highest priority are first on the agenda.

❑ Meeting atmosphere: The tone of the meeting should be professional and business-like but also cordial. If the presenter and the attendees are at ease, the quality and amount of information shared will be enhanced. Ideally, the presenter should be made to feel like a consultant who is helping you uncover and confront your company's intercultural needs, not merely a salesperson.

❑ Attendees: If possible, include employees or colleagues from different cultural backgrounds. Brief them in advance. Observe how the presenter relates to them. Ask for their feedback on the presentation. Likewise, involve employees who have cross-border responsibilities and experience.

❑ Time management: Ask the provider to send any materials that will be used in the presentation. Reading them in advance will not only save time but may generate additional questions. Recommend that the presenter use visuals and other efficient methods of transmitting information. Post and follow the agenda.

❑ Interaction: Don't accept a generic "canned" presentation. Allow time for questions and answers and discussion. Use this interaction to pursue your interests at greater depth and to determine whether the salesperson is knowledgeable about the core concepts and content of the intercultural field.

❑ Sales resistance: Let the salesperson know that you need to be informed and advised, not persuaded. Ask for verification of claims and sales points. Insist on straight answers to your questions. Don't allow yourself to be rushed, pressured, or intimidated. Resist any attempts by salespeople to manipulate you by making negative comments about their competitors.

❑ Closure: End the meeting by briefly summarizing what was covered, identifying any additional information required from the provider, and listing the next steps, if any. If feasible, set time lines.

❑ Follow-through: Advise providers of your decisions in a timely manner. Request a demonstration or pilot program if your purchase will be substantial. Be sure that providers use the kinds of trainers and resources that would be in the programs you are buying rather than special ones selected merely to impress you.

Vendor Materials and Presentations Focus Questions

☑ Do you have a clear picture of your company's or organization's intercultural needs?

☑ If so, have you defined what to look for in marketing materials and sales presentations?

☑ If not, have you advised potential suppliers that you want help identifying your needs so that they can focus their materials and presentations accordingly?

☑ Do you know what kind of provider is likely to be most suitable and compatible with your organizational culture?

☑ How will you decide from which ones to solicit materials and request presentations? Referrals from colleagues? Recommendations from professional organizations? Use of provider directories? Internet search? Advice from a consultant?

☑ Who in your organization or company should be involved in reviewing marketing materials and attending sales presentations? How can they best be prepared for these tasks?

☑ Have the materials and presentations given you all the information you require? If not, how can you obtain it?

☑ What do they reveal about providers beyond their intended messages? How can these insights help in your decision-making?

☑ Are the materials and presentations well-integrated with your supplier selection process? Are all key decision-makers involved?

☑ Is your sales resistance strong enough to keep you from being manipulated or pressured to make a purchase?

Summary and Suggested Action Steps

This chapter includes an explanation of the qualities and characteristics of different types of providers. It identifies the major attributes and competencies you can use to distinguish among them and to consider when defining your supplier selection criteria. It describes the essential set of knowledge, skills, experiences, and personal traits that typify competent intercultural trainers. It also gives you guidance on how to interpret marketing materials and use sales presentations effectively. Extensive lists of intercultural service providers are included in the resource section at the end of this chapter to help start your search for suitable suppliers.

Here are some ways you can use the content of this chapter:

1. Define your own criteria for supplier compatibility by considering practitioner motivations and backgrounds relative to your company or organizational culture.
2. Use your supplier compatibility factors and this chapter's sections on provider organizational capabilities and trainer competencies to develop selection criteria.
3. Share this chapter with other decision-makers involved in the supplier selection process.
4. If you develop an RFP, discuss relevant sections with the in-house procurement or contracting specialists who can help you.
5. Prepare in-house personnel, who will review marketing materials or proposals and attend sales presentations, by discussing appropriate sections of the chapter with them.
6. Incorporate relevant questions from the sections on organizational capability and professional standing into your list of questions for colleagues from whom you are seeking referrals.
7. Consult the provider list or the directories in the resource section at the end of this chapter to locate the suppliers you want to contact.
8. Create a profile of an ideal intercultural service provider and share it with potential suppliers.
9. For major purchases, consider using a qualified and nonbiased consultant to help you through the purchasing process.

Resources

References on Trainer Qualifications

Bennett, R. "The Effective Trainer Checklist." In J. Prior (ed.), *Gower Handbook of Training and Development.* (2nd ed.) Brookfield, VT: Gower Publishing Company Limited, 1994, pp. 194–202.

"Diversity and Cross-Cultural Trainers: Do They Know What They're Doing? New Survey Results." *Cultural Diversity at Work*, Vol. 5, No. 5, May 1993, pp. 1, 10–14.

Enderle, G. (ed.). *International Business Ethics: Challenges and Approaches*. South Bend, IN: University of Notre Dame Press, 1999.

Kohls, R. L. with Brussow H. L. *Training Know-How for Cross-Cultural and Diversity Trainers*. Duncanville, TX: Adult Learning Systems, Inc., 1995, pp. 66–67.

Kumar, B. N., and Steinmann, H. (eds.) *Ethics in International Management*, Hawthorne, NY: Walter De Gruyter Press, 1998.

Morgan, E. *Navigating Cross-Cultural Ethics: What Global Managers Do Right To Keep from Going Wrong*. Woburn, MA: Butterworth-Heinemann Press, 1998.

Odenwald, S. B. *Global Training: How To Design a Program for the Multinational Corporation*. Homewood, IL: Business One Irwin, 1993. See "Tips for Global Trainers," pp. 143–155.

Paige, M. R., and Martin, J. N. "Ethical Issues and Ethics in Cross-Cultural Training." In D. Landis and R. W. Brislin (eds.), *Handbook of Intercultural Training, Vol. 1*. Elmsford, NY: Pergamon Press, 1983, pp. 36–60.

Paige, M. R., and Martin, J. N. "Ethics in Intercultural Training." In D. Landis and R. S. Bhagat (eds.), *Handbook of Intercultural Training*. (2nd ed.) Thousand Oaks, CA: Sage Publications, Inc., 1996, pp. 35–60.

Paige, M. R. "Intercultural Trainer Competencies." In D. Landis and R. S. Bhagat (eds.), *Handbook of Intercultural Training*. (2nd ed.) Thousand Oaks, CA: Sage Publications, Inc., 1996, pp. 148–164.

Paige, M. R. "Trainer Competencies for International and Intercultural Programs." In M. R. Paige (ed.), *Education for the Intercultural Experience*. Yarmouth, ME: Intercultural Press, 1993.

Paige, M. R. "Trainer Competencies: The Missing Conceptual Link in Orientation." *International Journal of Intercultural Relations*. Vol. 10, 1986, pp. 135–158.

Pedersen, P., R. W. Brislin and T. Yoshida (eds.) "Doing the Right Thing: A Question of Ethics." In *Improving Intercultural Interactions: Modules for Cross-Cultural Training Programs*. Thousand Oaks: CA: Sage Publications, Inc., 1997, pp. 149–164.

Rasmussen, T., and Roe R. L. (eds.). *The ASTD Trainer's Sourcebook: Diversity*. New York: McGraw-Hill, 1995

Training Magazine, *Delivering Training: Mastery in the Classroom.* Minneapolis, MN: Lakewood Publications, 1996.

Wederspahn, G. M., and Daniel, S. T. "Intercultural Business Ethics: A Management Challenge." *Human Resource Professional*, Vol. 11, No. 6, Nov./Dec., 1998, pp. 3–6.

Williams, T., and Green A. *Dealing with Differences: How Trainers Can Take Account of Cultural Diversity.* Hampshire, England: Gower Publishing, 1994, pp. 8–12 and 35–37.

Directories of Providers

The GilDean Group Consultant Listing and Referral Service, 13751 Lake City Way North East, Suite 106, Seattle, WA 98125–8612, tel: (206) 362–0336, fax: (206) 363–5028, e-mail: barbara@diversitycentral.com.

Moran, R. T., and Braaten, D. O. (eds.). *International Directory of Multicultural Resources*, Houston, TX: Gulf Publishing Company, 1996, PO Box 2608, Houston, TX 77252–2608, info@gulfpub.com.

Murray, M., et al. *The 1992 Global Connector: The Complete Resource Directory of International Training and Development.* Sausalito, CA: PASport Publishing International, 1992.

SIETAR International Consultant and Referral Directory, Putney, VT: SIETAR, 1999, PO Box 467, Putney, VT 05346, tel: (802) 387–4785, fax: (802) 387–5783, e-mail: sietar@sover.net.

SIETAR International Membership Directory. Putney, VT: SIETAR, 1998.

Summer Institute for Intercultural Communication: Directory of Selected Resources, 1998. Intercultural Communication Institute, 8835 SW Canyon Lane, Suite 238, Portland OR 97225; tel: (503) 297–4622, fax: (503) 297–4695, e-mail: ici@intercultural.org.

Intercultural Service Providers

Within the scope of this book, it is not feasible to list all intercultural service providers. Those included here are representative of the wide range of practitioners and organizations of different types and sizes that are available. Their inclusion in these resource lists is not an endorsement. The vast variety of types of providers and the equally diverse needs, locations, and budgets of the buyers make the recommendation of a generic set of suppliers impractical. You should apply the criteria and advice in this book and make your selections carefully.

These vendors offer training, assessment, counseling, or consulting directly to their clients. The services are delivered at the suppliers' own facilities or at the purchaser's location. Although the lists in this book are quite comprehensive, you should use them as only a starting point in your search for suppliers. By consulting the directories already given and seeking referrals from the professional organizations listed in Chapter 1, you can find additional potential providers.

Based in the United States

Multiple Location Organizations

The following organizations have their own training facilities and offices in different locations staffed by full-time employees. They offer services at their locations, at rented facilities, and at clients' sites.

Aon Consulting, 400 Renaissance Center, Suite 1500, Detroit, MI 48243–1508, tel: (800) 477–7545 and (313) 259–0116, fax: (313) 567–7292, e-mail: hrcd@aoncons.com.

Berlitz Cross-Cultural, 400 Alexander Park, Princeton, NJ 08540-6306, tel: (800) 528–8908 and (609) 514–3173, fax: (609) 514–3411, e-mail: cross-cultural@berlitz.com.

Cerdant Intercultural, The Bennett Group, One North Franklin, Suite 750, Chicago, IL 60606, tel: (899) 251–9005 and (312) 251–9000, fax: (312) 251–9015, e-mail: consult@bennettassoc.com.

CHP International, 1040 North Boulevard, Suite 220, Oak Park, IL 60301, tel: (708) 848–9650, fax: (708) 848–3191, e-mail: chp@wwa.com.

Clarke Consulting Group, 1840 Gateway Drive, Suite 200, San Mateo, CA 94404, tel: (880) 331–4224 and (650) 591–8100, fax: (650) 591–8269, e-mail: webmasre@clarke.com.

Eaton Consulting Group, Inc., 192 South Street, Suite 300, Boston, MA 02111, tel: (617) 338–8883, fax: (617) 338–8880, e-mail: deaton@eatonconsultinggroup.com.

Inlingua Intercultural Training, 352 South Denver Street, Suite 315, Salt Lake City, UT 84111, tel: (888) 558–3775 and (801) 355–3775, fax: (801) 355–0421, e-mail: inlingua@ix.netcom.org.

International Orientation Resources, 500 Skokie Boulevard, Suite 600, Northbrook, IL 60062, tel: (800) 215–8792 and (847) 205–0066, fax: (847) 205–0085, e-mail: marketing@iorworld.com.

Prudential Relocation International, 200 Summit Lake Drive, Valhalla, NY 10595, tel: (800) 356–6834 and (914) 741–6111, fax: (914) 749–4784, e-mail: relo.webleads@prudential.com.

RHR International Company, 220 Gerry Drive, Wood Dale, IL 60191–1147, tel: (630) 766–7007, fax: (630) 766–9037, e-mail: jdurocher@rhrinternational.com.

Richard Lewis Communications, 3cNew York Inc., 450 West 15th Street, Suite 305, New York, NY 10011, tel: (212) 328–0710, fax: (212) 271–6372, e-mail: ternsing@3city.com.

SoCoCo Intercultural, PO Box 746, Princeton Junction, NJ 08550, tel: (888) 771–0598 and (609) 631–0382, fax: (609) 631–0383, e-mail: culture@sococo.com.

Transnational Management Associates Ltd., 5 Independence Way, Suite 300, Princeton, NJ 08540, tel: (609) 514–5126, fax: (609) 514–5127, e-mail: info@tmaworld.com.

Windham International/ECA, 55 Fifth Avenue, New York, NY 10003, tel: (212) 647–0555, fax (212) 647–0494, e-mail: info@windhamint.com.

Centrally Based Organizations

The following organizations have a central office and training facility. They provide services there, at rented facilities, and at clients' locations.

The Brannen Group, 6200 Antioch Street, Suite 201, Oakland CA 94611, tel: (510) 339–6096, fax: (510) 339–6098, e-mail: brannengrp@aol.com.

Coghill & Beery International, 1490 Devonshire Court, Atlanta, GA 30338, tel: (770) 617–0004, fax: (770) 671–0417, e-mail: beery@coghillbeery.com.

Cornelius Grove & Associates, LLC, 442 47th Street, Brooklyn, NY 11220–1216, tel: (718) 492–1896, fax: (718) 492–4005, e-mail: info@grovewell.com.

Cultural Awareness International, 4560 Belfort Place, Dallas, TX 75205, tel: (214) 559-2742, fax: (214) 559–0904, e-mail: cai@dallas.net.

The GilDean Group, 13751 Lake City Way, N. E., Suite 106, Seattle, WA 98125–8612, tel: (206) 362–0336, fax: (206) 363–5028, e-mail: barbara@diversitycentral.com.

Global Business Access, Ltd., International Square, Suite 400, 1825 I Street N. W., Washington, DC 20006, tel: (202) 429–3702, fax: (202) 466–6249, e-mail: global@globalltd.com.

Global Dynamics, Inc., 19 Wilkinson Road, Randolph, NJ 07869, tel: (873) 927–9135, fax: (873) 927–6936, e-mail: ngoodman @global-dynamics.com.

Global Intercultural Services, 358 5th Avenue, Suite 1101, New York, NY 10001, tel: (212) 695–5493, fax: (212) 695–4615, e-mail: nmithani@globalintercultural.com.

Global Success, 111 West St. John Street, Suite 706, San Jose, CA 95113, tel: (408) 286–8013, fax: (408) 286–4368, e-mail: Farid @ix.netcom.com.

Global Vision Strategies, 88 Honey Ridge Court, St Charles, MO 63304, tel: (636) 928–8880, fax: (636) 922–2012, e-mail: info @globalvisionstrategies.com.

INSERV, 6600 LBJ Freeway, Suite 183, Dallas, TX 75240, tel: (972) 991–2300, fax: (972) 991–6471, e-mail: inserv@inservllc.com.

Intercultural Training Institute, 9201 University City Boulevard, Charlotte, NC 28223–0001, tel: (704) 547–2442, fax: (704) 547–3091, e-mail: gpferrar@unccvm.uncc.edu.

Interlink Consulting Services, Inc., PO Box 211302, West Palm Beach, FL 33421–1302, tel: (561) 792–0453, fax: (561) 792–9375, e-mail: info@interlinkconsulting.com.

International Business Center, Inc., 1400 Computer Drive, Westboro, MA 01581–5043, tel: (800) 783–8569 and (508) 366–1003, fax: (508) 366–0514, e-mail: ibc@ultranet.com.

The International Training and Development Institute, 200 West Mercer Street, Suite 504, Seattle WA 98119, tel: (206) 217–9644, fax: (206) 217–9643, e-mail: ace@cultural.org.

ITAP International, 268 Wall Street, Princeton, NJ 08540, tel: (800) 659–4827 and (609) 921–1446, fax: (609) 924–7946, e-mail: itap@ itapintl.com.

Komei, Inc., 101 West Ohio Street, 20th floor, Indianapolis, IN 46204–4204, tel: (317) 684–6715, fax: (317) 684–6810, e-mail: solutions@komei.com.

Meridian Resources Associates, Inc., 1741 Buchanan Street, San Francisco, CA 94115, tel: (800) 626–2047 and (415) 749–2920, fax: (415) 749–0124, e-mail: tdale@meridianglobal.com.

PRISM International, Inc., 321 West First Street, Suite 310, Sanford, FL 32771–1205, tel: (888) 997–7476 and (407) 325–5290, fax: (407) 324–0148, e-mail: linda@prism-international.com.

NiS International Services, 1321 Murfreesboro Road, Suite 610, Nashville, TN 37217, tel: (800) 366–0945 and (615) 367–5000, fax: (615) 361–6448, e-mail: r.terhune@nisintl.com.

Savoir Faire, Inc., 5 Raymond Street, Suite 202, Lexington, MA 02173, tel: (617) 863–1445, fax: (617) 863–5011, e-mail: savfaire@aol.com.

SRI, Selection Research International, Inc., 8420 Delmar Boulevard, Lobby West, St. Louis, MO 63124–2181, tel: (314) 567–6900, fax: (314) 567–7782, e-mail: kozloff@sri – 2000.com.

W. Shabaz Associates, Inc., 5415 North Lakeshore Drive, Holland MI 49424, tel: (616) 786–4500, fax: (616) 786–0417, e-mail: wayne @shabaz.com.

Thunderbird American Graduate School of International Management, 15249 North 59th Avenue, Glendale, AZ 85306–6000, tel: (602) 978–7100, fax: (602) 439–5432, e-mail: admissions@t-bird.edu.

Training Management Corporation, 600 Alexander Road, Princeton, NJ 08540, tel: (609) 951–0525, fax: (609) 951–0395, e-mail: info@tmcorp.com.

Training Resources Group, Inc., 909 North Washington Street, Suite 305, Alexandria, VA 22314, tel: (703) 548–3535, fax: (703) 836–2415, e-mail: info@trg-inc.com.

Tucker International, 900 28th Street, Suite 200, Boulder, CO 80303, tel: (303) 786–7753, fax: (303) 786–7801, e-mail: mtucker@tuckerintl.com.

Window on the World, Inc., 100 North 6th Street, Suite 300A, Minneapolis, MN 55403, tel: (612) 338–3690, fax: (612) 338–3037, e-mail: kcermak@windoontheworldinc.com.

Wordsmart, Inc., 595 Blossom Road, Suite 110, Rochester, NY 14610, tel: (800) 836–9948 and (716) 654–7420, fax: (716) 654–6916, e-mail: ctan@acspr1.acs.brockport.edu.

World Learning, Kipling Road, PO Box 676, Brattleboro, VT 05302–0676, tel: (802) 257–7751, fax: (802) 258–3248, e-mail: info@worldlearning.org.

WorldWise, Inc., 4725 Quail Creek Lane, Boulder, CO 80301, tel: (800) 571–8831 and (303) 530–0680, fax: (303) 530–0305, e-mail: everhart@worldwise-inc.com.

Individual and Associate Group Practices

The following practitioners work independently or with associates and provide services at clients' locations or rented facilities.

Across Cultures, Inc., Brooks Peterson, 1602 Juno Avenue, St. Paul, MN 55116, tel: (651) 695–0011, fax: (651) 695–0022, e-mail: info @acrosscultures.net.

Advance International, Ltd., Kate Evert, PO Box 641801, Chicago, IL 60613, tel: (312) 447–1590, fax: (312) 477–1588.

At Ease, Inc., Ann Marie Sabath, 119 East Court Street, Cincinnati, OH 45202, tel: (800) 873–9909, fax: (513) 241–8701, e-mail: atease@eos.com.

Janet and Milton Bennet, Intercultural Communication Institute, 8835, SW Canyon Lane, Suite 238, Portland OR 97225–3304, tel: (503) 297–4622, fax: (503) 297–4695, e-mail: ici@intercultural.org.

J. Stewart Black, University of Michigan Business School, 701 Tappan Street, Ann Arbor, MI 48109–1234, tel: (888) 446–4685, fax: (877) 846–4685, e-mail: sblackgli@aol.com.

Buma Associates, Inc., Kyoji Buma, 43 Arnold Avenue, Closter, NJ 07642, tel/fax: (201) 768–5830.

Cambio International, Cynthia H. Livingston, 5 Putman Street, Boston, MA 02129, tel: (617) 242–3694, (617) 242–2048.

Charis Intercultural Training, Marian Stetson-Rodriguez, 5674 Stonedale Drive, Suite 112, Pleasanton, CA 94588, tel: (925) 469–6000, fax: (925) 469–6001, e-mail: M.S.Rodiguez@chariscorp.com.

Jorge Cherbosque, 11911 San Vicente Boulevard # 240, Los Angeles, CA 90049, tel: (310) 207–5100, fax: (310) 981–2991.

John Condon, University of New Mexico, 1801 Roma NE, Albuquerque, NM 87131, tel: (505) 277–5811, fax: (505) 829–9134, e-mail jcondon@jemez.com.

Cross-Culture Communications, Edward Retta, PO Box 141263, Dallas, TX 75214–1263, tel: (214) 827–8632, fax: (214) 824–9861, e-mail: edwret@aol.com.

Cross Cultural Resources, Marilyn Richey, 448 Parker Drive, Pittsburgh, PA 15216, tel: (412) 344–1558, fax: (412) 344–8444, e-mail: crosscultr@aol.com.

Cross-Cultural Services, Sally Normand McReynolds, 1992 Hayes Street, San Francisco, CA 94117, tel/fax: (415) 387–2710, e-mail: ccssnm@earthlink.net.

Cultural Exchange Service, Carlos Nagel, 240 East Limberlost, Tucson, AZ 85705, tel: (520) 887–1188, fax: (520) 887–1575.

Cultural Diversity Group, Syed and Joyce, Zafar, 4031 Levonshire Drive, Houston, TX 77025, tel: (713) 587–6935, fax: (713) 667–2686, e-mail: szafar@compassnet.com.

The Culture Exchange, Nancy Babcock, 2870 Peachtree Road, Suite 209, Atlanta, GA 30305, tel: (404) 842–3835, fax: (404) 816–1371, e-mail: nbabcock@ibm.net.

Culture Interaction, Erika L. Seid, 88 Chenery Street, Number 1, San Francisco, CA 94131, tel/fax: (415) 642–6542, e-mail: info@cultureinteraction.com.

Cultural Link, Inc., Amy E. Kahn, 2929 North Central Avenue, Phoenix, AZ 85012, tel: (800) 883–4367 and (602) 266–8676, fax: (602) 788–4365, e-mail: culturelnk@aol.com.

Culture to Culture, Susan F. Keith, 5708 Tinnin Road North West, Albuquerque, NM 87017, tel: (505) 237–2070, fax: (505) 345–8807.

D.C.W. Research Associates International, David C. Wigglesworth, PO Box 5469, Kingwood, TX 77325–5469, tel: (281) 359–4236, fax (281) 359–4238, e-mail: dcwigg@aol.com.

William Drake & Associates, PO Box 2838, Waxahachie, TX 75165, tel/fax: (972) 938–2927, e-mail: bdrake@onramp.net.

East-West Business Strategies, Steven D. Jones, 41 Octavia Street, Suite 8, San Francisco, CA 94102, tel: (415) 241–9506, fax: (415) 487–0466, e-mail: info@ewbs.com.

The East West Group, Dean W. Engel, 1204 Lattie Lane, Mill Valley, CA 94941, tel: (415) 383–0285.

Expat Forum, Inc., Jeff Freeburg, 40 King's Way, Suite 405B, Waltham, MA 02451, tel: (781) 672–2587, fax: (781) 830–9577, e-mail: hrint@expatforum.com.

Sandra Mumford Fowler, 4020 Linnean Avenue, N. W., Washington, DC 20008–3805, tel: (202) 244–8337, fax: (202) 686–5466, e-mail: sfowler@apa.org.

The Geneva Global Group, Ltd., Maryalice Mazzara, The Hudson Cliff Building, 825 West 187th Street, Suite 6-K, New York, NY 10033, tel: (212) 928–7586, fax: (212) 678–4048, e-mail: genevaltd@aol.com.

GeoAgenda, Larry Caldwell, 1909 Spruce Street, Boulder, CO 80302, tel: (303) 440–5343, e-mail: caldwell@geoagenda.com.

The German Connection, Greg Nees, PO Box 3332, Boulder, CO 80307, tel: (303) 440–4929, fax: (303) 440–4377, e-mail: gregnees@ aol.com.

Global Bonding, Marianne Brandt, 19584 Crystal Lake Drive, Northville, MI 48167–2524, tel: (313) 845–8616, fax: (313) 390–2314, e-mail: mbrandt1@ford.com.

Global Business Access, Ltd. Charles A. Schmidz, 1825 I Street North West, Suite 400, Washington, DC 20006, tel: (202) 429–2702, fax: (202) 466–6249.

The Global Group, Jillian Austin and Priscilla Nelson, PO Box 23830, Knoxville, TN 37933–1830, tel: (423) 893–0242, e-mail: jillian@globals.com.

Global Human Resource Service, Ltd., Catherine Tiemann, PO Box 353, Great Falls, VA 22066, tel: (703) 759–7070, e-mail: 7544.1416@compuserve.com.

Global Interact, Stephan M. Branch, 2911 Turtle Creek, Suite 300, Dallas, TX 75219, tel: (214) 520–0911, fax: (214) 528–7778.

Global Management, LLC, Richard R. Gesteland, 2564 Branch Street, B2, Middleton, WI 53562, tel: (608) 836–0088, fax: (608) 0087, e-mail: rrgestel@aol.com.

Global Workplace Dynamics, Patricia Zakian Tith, 2400 Virginia Avenue NW, Suite C312, Washington, DC 20037–2612, tel: (202) 293–7748, tax: (202) 466–3376, e-mail: pattith@globalworkplace.com.

Hal B. Gregersen, Brigham Young University, Provo, UT 84604, tel: (801) 378–2902, fax: (801) 478–8098, e-mail: hal_gregersen@byu.edu.

Hale & Associates, LLC, 395 Sierra Vista Lane, Valley Cottage, New York, NY 10989, tel: (914) 358–3575, fax: (914) 358–3844, e-mail: info@hale.com.

Mitchell R. Hammer, Conflict Mediation Across Cultures, PMB #705, North Potomac, MD 20878, fax: (301) 926–7450, e-mail: docmitch@email.msn.com.

Harris International, Ltd., Philip R. Harris, 2702 Costebelle Drive, La Jolla, CA 92037, tel: (858) 453–2271, fax: (858) 453–0788, e-mail: philharris@aol.com.

Integrated Resources Group, Robert Scott, Bank One Building, Suite 505, 3444 North First Street, Abilene, TX 79603, tel: (915) 676–2290, fax: (915) 676–1383, e-mail: irg@expat-repat.com.

Intercultural Business Solutions, Gary M. Wederspahn, 4838 West Moorhead Circle, Boulder, CO 80303, tel: (303) 494–5403, e-mail: gwederspahn@mailcity.com.

Intercultural Development, Selma Myers, 755 San Mario Drive, Solana Beach, CA 92075, tel: (858) 755–3160, fax: (858) 755–8637, e-mail: gwederspahn@mailcity.com.

Intercultural Management Training & Consulting, Marvina Shilling, 2520 North Buchanan Street, Arlington, VA 22207, tel/fax (703) 527–0909, e-mail: marvishill@aol.com.

Intercultural Training Associates, Inc., Sandra Hagman, 836 South Williams Lake Road, White Lake, MI 48386–3529, tel: (248) 363–9441, fax: (248) 363–8306, e-mail: 102120.3120@compuserve.com.

Inter-Face International, Suzanne Salimbene, 3821 East Street, Suite 197, Rockford, IL 61108, tel: (815) 965–7535, fax: (815) 965–4960, e-mail: IFI4you@aol.com.

Interglobe Cross-Cultural Business Services, Rita Wuebbler, 743 Virginia Avenue North East, Suite 201, Atlanta, GA 30306, tel: (404) 733–5688, fax: (404) 888–9416, e-mail: rwuebbler@aol.com.

International Adaptations, Nancy Mueller, 1612 North West 67th Street, Seattle, WA 98117, tel: (206) 784–8277, fax: (206) 783–2547, e-mail: dorkis1@ccnmail.com.

International Business Protocol, Dorothy Manning, PO Box 990074, Boston, MA 02199, tel: (617) 267–6268, e-mail: msi@ultranet.com.

International Counseling Institute, Dvora Lazarov, 211 West 56th Street, New York, NY 10019, tel: (212) 265–8480, fax: (212) 489–8011.

International Institute of Language and Culture, Steven L. West, 1506 North 15th Street, Boise, ID 83702, tel: (208) 331–8382, fax: (208) 331–0818 e-mail: iilcwest@micron.net.

Japan Business Consultants, Ltd., Glenn Howard Mazur, 1140 Morehead Court, Ann Arbor, MI 48103–6181, tel: (313) 995–0847, fax: (313) 995–3810, e-mail: gmazur@engin.umich.edu.

Karani Lam & Associates, Managing Across Cultures, Zareen Karini Lam de Arooz, 12, Chesterford Road, Winchester, MA 01890, tel: (718) 721–7546, fax: (718) 721–7543, e-mail: zkaraoz@channel1.com.

L. Robert Kohls, 1362 Vallejo Street, #B, San Francisco, CA 94109–0701, tel: (415) 474–0552, fax: (415) 561–0468, e-mail: robkohls @ix.netcom.com.

The Lett Group, Cynthia Lett, 13116 Hutchinson Way, Silver Springs, MD 20906–5947, tel: (301) 946–8208, fax: (603) 462–5779, e-mail: clett@lettgroup.com.

Lhamby & Associates, Lynda Hamby, 1012 Asbury Avenue, Evanston, IL 60202–1165, tel: (847) 864–8092, fax: (847) 864–8093, e-mail: ichamby@earthlink.net.

Moran Associates, Robert T. Moran, 5000 North Wilkinson Road, Paradise Valley, AZ 85253, tel: (480) 946–8046, fax: (480) 949–8716, e-mail: moranr@t-bird.edu.

Multinational Related Services, Inc., Dennis Canavaugh, 26555 Evergreen, Suite 1061, South Field MI 48076, tel: (810) 354–4080, fax: (810) 354–5279.

Neil W. Currie & Company, 1385 Washington Valley Road, Bridgewater, NJ 08807, tel: (908) 725–2297, fax: (908) 725–0477.

Nipporica Associates, Dianne M. Saphiere, PO Box 1343, Conifer, CO 80433–1343, tel: (303) 838–1798, fax: (303) 838–1799, e-mail: dianne@nipporica.com.

The Odenwald Connection, Inc., Bill Matheny, 5918 Long Cove, Garland, TX 75044, tel: (972) 867–9390, fax: (972) 496–3905, e-mail: odenwald@odenwaldconnection.com.

Overseas Training and Orientation Program, JoAnn Craig, 10 Tapia Way, San Francisco, CA 94132, tel: (415) 377–8393.

Alexander Patico, 5448 Hound Hill Court, Columbia, MD 20145, tel: (301) 596–6375.

The Palladian Group, Elayne L. Gallagher, 114 West Del Norte Street, Colorado Springs, CO 80907, tel: (719) 633–5970, fax: (719) 578–8099, e-mail: elgallaghe@aol.com.

Pelikan Associates, Helen Pelikan, 6501 Bannockburn Drive, Bethesda, MD 20817–5431, tel: (301) 229–8550, fax: (301) 229–6609.

Pirie Associates, Barbara Pirie, 1414 Heulu Street, Honolulu, HI 96822, tel: (808) 943–9120, fax: (808) 941–4035, e-mail: bjpirie @alaho.net.

The Protocol School of Washington, Dorothea Johnson, 1401 Chain Bridge Road, Suite 202, McLean, VA 22101, tel: (703) 821–5613 and (877) 766–3751, fax: (703) 821–5615, e-mail: protocol@erols.com.

Renwick & Associates, George Renwick, Trade Center, Suite A – 105, Box 5007, Carefree, AZ 85377–5007, tel: (480) 488–9566, fax: (480) 488–9388, telex: 7101115411.

Lawrence Reynolds Associates, 3105 Pioneer Circle, Waco TX, tel/fax: (817) 848–4545.

Rhinesmith and Associates, Inc., Stephen H. Rhinesmith, One Devonshire Place, Suite 3513, Boston, MA 02109, tel: (617) 720–1884, fax: (781) 272–0463, e-mail: SHRglobal@aol.com.

Rowland & Associates, Inc., Diana Rowland, 14084 Mango Drive, San Diego, CA 14082, tel: (858) 794–9637, fax: (858) 794–9638, e-mail: Diana@InternationalExcellenc.com.

Sherisen International, Inc., Sondra Sen, 29 Arden Road, Mountain Lakes, NJ 07046, tel: (973) 625–5916, fax: (973) 625–1035, e-mail: ssitsi@att.net.

Fanchon Silberstein, 6621 32nd Street, NW, Washington, DC 20015–2309, tel: (202) 363–3823, fax: (202) 363–7664, e-mail: fsilber@aol.com.

George Simons International, George F. Simons, 236 Plateau Avenue, Santa Cruz, CA 95060 and Residence L'Argentiere, Batiment A, Boulevard de las Tavermiere, 06210, Mandelieu La Napoule, France, tel: (831) 426–9608, fax: (888) 215–3117, e-mail: gsimmons@ diversophy.com.

Snowdon International Protocol, Inc., Sondra Snowdon, 235 East 57th Street, Suite 7E, New York, NY 10022, tel: (212) 247–4152, fax: (211) 750–0390.

Jeremy Solomons, 303 East Gurley Street, Suite 221, Prescott, AZ 86301, tel/fax: (520) 636–5106, e-mail: jersols@aol.com.

The Starkey Group, Inc., Judith A. Starkey, 333 West Wacker Drive, Suite 700, Chicago, IL 60606–1225, tel: (312) 444–2025, fax: (312) 614–3096, e-mail: azdbc@aol.com.

Strange Lands International Assignment Specialists, Gary Fontaine, 47–403B Ahuimanu Road, Kaneohe, HI 96744, e-mail: gmfontaine @cs.com.

Craig Storti and Associates, 436 Bankard Road, Westminster, MD 21158, tel: (410) 346–7336, fax: (410) 346–7846, e-mail: cstorti @compuserve.com.

Success Across Borders, Heather A. Robinson, 23723 51st Avenue South, Kent, WA 98032–3301, tel: (253) 852–0903, fax: (253) 854–5401, e-mail: har5055@aol.com.

Sondra B. Thiederman, 4585 48th Street, San Diego, CA 92115–3236, tel: (800) 858–4478 and (619) 583- 4478, fax: (619) 583–0304, e-mail: stphd@thiederman.com.

Transcultural Services, Nessa P. Loewenthal, 712 NW Westover Terrace, Portland, OR 97210, tel: (503) 497–1066, fax: (503) 497–1080, e-mail nessa@transport.com.

Transnational Business Development Corporation, Henry Ferguson, 5 Chestnut Hill North, Albany, NY 12211–1606, tel: (518) 436–1651, fax: (518) 436–7654, e-mail: speakerHF@cs.com.

The Uni-Pro Group, Abby Molano, 111 North Market Street, Suite 1000, San Jose, CA 95113, tel: (408) 866–6770, fax: (408) 866–6776, e-mail: amolano@uniprogroup.com.

The Web of Culture, Eileen F. Sheridan, 236 Plateau Avenue, Santa Cruz, CA 95060, tel/fax: (813) 273–6074, e-mail: webmaven@ webofculture.com.

Al Wight, PO Box 890, Basin, WY 82410, tel: (307) 568–2621, e-mail: arwight@netscape.net.

Jackson Wolfe, 2455 Franklin Avenue, Louisville, CO 80027, tel: (303) 664–9022, e-mail: jacksonwolfe69@cs.com.

World Wide Synergy, Camilla Bleau McGill, 4803 Meadowglen Drive, Pearland, TX 77584–8621, tel: (281) 997–7882, fax: (281) 997–7633, e-mail: wwsyn@neosoft.com.

Celia Young & Associates, PMB 134, 24040 Camino del Avion #A, Monarch Beach, CA 92629, tel; (949) 388–7882, e-mail: celiayong@ home.com.

Based Outside of the USA

International Networking Contacts

SEITAR Brazil, Lucy Piaxio Linhares, International Cultural Assistance, Av. Graça Aranha, Number 81, Sala 613, Cebtro, Rio de Janeiro, 20030–002, RJ Brasil, tel/fax: 55–21–5330388, e-mail: sie tarbrasil@infolink.com.br.

SIETAR Canada, Laura Sarino van der Smissen, York University, 201 York Lanes, 4700 Keele Street, North York, Ontario, M3J 1P3, Canada, tel: (416) 736–5177, fax: (416) 736–5176.

SIETAR Deutschland, Bernd Muller-Jacquier, Technical University Chemnitz-Zwickau, Interkultturelle Kommunikation, Postfach 964, D – 09107 Chemnitz, Germany, tel: 49–371–531–3966, fax: 49–921– 511–020, e-mail: mue-jac@phi.tu-chemnitz.de.

SIETAR Europa, Marie-Therese Claes, Shyla de Clippele, c/o ICHEC, 2 Boulevard Brand Whitlock B, 1150 Brussels, Belgium, tel/fax: 33–1–45–28–58–27, e-mail: sietareu.ichec@euronet.br.

SIETAR France, Andre Cresson, 5 rue Adele, 93250 Villemomble, France, tel/fax: 33–1–45–28–58–27, e-mail: sietar.france@wanadoo.fr.

SIETAR Indonesia, Irid Rachman Agoes, Jalan Tebet Barat X/18, Selatan, Jakarta, 12810, Indonesia, tel: 6221–829–5385, fax: 6221–830–6955.

SIETAR Israel, Varda, Perl, Z Heshvan 23, Ramat Hasharon, 47220, Israel, tel: 972–3–547–2118, fax: 972–3–547–0225, e-mail: ishahar@netmedia.co.il.

SIETAR Japan, Shoko Araki, Obirin University, 3758 Tokiwa-cho, Machida-shi 0427–97–2661, tel: 044–989–0069, fax: 044–989–1474, e-mail: shokoark@obrin.ac.jp.

SIETAR Korea, Yunhee Choe, Department of Journalism and Mass Communication, University of Suwon, Suwon PO Box 77, Kyonggido, Republic of Korea, tel: 0331–220–2265, fax: 02–425–0249, e-mail: ychoe@mail.suwon.ac.kr.

SIETAR Nederlande, Simone Dermijn, Vordensbinnenweg 8, 7231 BC Warnsveld, The Netherlands, tel: 31–575–52–48–23, e-mail: dermijn@worldonline.nl.

SIETAR Taiwan, Kaoru Y. Oba, # 4 Lane 254, Shan Chaio Road, Ta Hwa Village, Niao Song Kaohsiung Hsien, Taiwan, tel 888–7–370–7716, fax: 888–886–379–0576, e-mail: oba2u@mx27.hinet.net.

SIETAR United Kingdom, Terry Mughan, Anglia Polytechnic University, School of Languages and Social Sciences, East Road Cambridge, CB1 1PT, United Kingdom, tel: 44–1223–36271, fax 44–1223–352973, e-mail: t.mughyan@anglia.ac.uk.

Organizations and Practitioners

Asia Pacific

AmAsia, Inc., Lions Building, Suite 601, 1–3–1 Marunouchi, Naka-Ku, Nagoya 460–0002, Japan, tel: 81–52–212–1003, fax: 81–52–212–1007, e-mail: inquiry@amasia.co.jp.

AMM-Expat, Judith R. Phillips, 12–01 Silverton Condos, 88 Persiaran Gurney, 10250 Penang, Malaysia, tel/fax: 60–4–229–9451, e-mail: jphils@pc.jaring.my.

Celine J. Castillo-Macy, 435 Duke Street, Greenhills East 1502, Metro-Manila, Philippines, tel: 632–637–4427, fax: 632–635–2864, e-mail: aiti@iconn.com.ph.

Insoo Cho, #308–204 Mokdong Apartment, Yang-Ku, Seoul, Korea, tel: 82–2–654–4589, fax: 82–2–393–7272, e-mail: ysgsis@bubble.yonsei.ac.kr.

Cross-Cultural Management Co., LTD., Harry Holmes, First floor, Rimco House, 139 Ekamai, Sukhumvit Road, Klongton-nua, Wattana Bangkok 10110, Thailand, tel: 662–391–8586–7, fax: 662–391–8589, e-mail: e-mail: crosscul@loxinfo.co.th.

CSC Management Consulting, Maura, GPO 712, Hong Kong, Hong Kong, tel: 852–2522–6071, fax: 852–2522–8967, e-mail: mfallon @hk.super.net.

Cultural Dynamics, Shirley Harper, PO Box 343, Drummoyne, Sydney, NSW 2047, Australia, tel: 612–9904–4435, fax: 612–9904–4436, e-mail: sharpe@s055.aone.net.au.

Executive Orientation Services, Wisma Bank Dharmala, Lt. 12, Jl. Jend., Sudirman Kav. 28, Jakarta, Indonesia, tel: 62–21–523–9179, fax: 62–21–523–9191, e-mail: eostek@server.indo.net.id.

Global Interface Ltd., Karen Huchendorf, PO Box 432, Milsons Point, NSW 2061, Australia, tel: 61–2–9953–9450, fax: 61–2–9953–4190.

Globalinx Corporation, Sato Estate Number 3 47, 2–5, Sarugaku-Cho, Shibuya-Ku, Tokyo 150–0033 Japan, tel: 81–3–5456–0191, fax: 81–3–5456–8977, e-mail: gixdeane@gol.com.

Indonesian Foundation for Intercultural Learning, Jasmin Jasin, Jl. Cibulan Number 11, Kebayoran Baru, Jakarta, 12170 Indonesia, tel: 62–21–720–3617, fax: 62–21–720–2320, e-mail: Jazz@cbn.net.id.

The Institute for International Business Communication, Sanno Grand Building 9th Floor, 2–14–2, Nagata-Cho, Chiyoda-Ku, Tokyo 100, Japan, tel: 81–33–580–0286, fax: 81–33–581–5608, e-mail: kyasiro@reitaku.u.ac.jp.

Intec Japan, Karukozaka-tanaka Building, 2–16 Kagurazaka, Shinjuku-Ku, Tokyo 162, Japan, tel: 81–03–3267–5988, fax: 81–03–3335–2550, e-mail vreyens@gol.com.

Kyungae Jin, LG Academy, 165 Haeweol-Ri, Majang-Myun, Inchun-City, Kyunggi-Province, 467–810 Korea, tel: 82–336–30–6720, fax: 82–336–30–6767, e-mail: kajin@iga.lg.co.kr.

Oba Y. Kaoru, Number 4 Lane, 254, Shan Chiao Road, Ta Hwa Village, Niao Song, Kaohsiung, Taiwan, tel/fax: 886–7–385–7716, e-mail: kaoruo@mail.nsysu.edu.tw.

K/H Business Communications and Consulting Co. Ltd., Joel Hastings, 12th Floor, Korea Herald Building, 1–12 Hoehyon-Dong Chung-Gu, Seoul, 100–771, Korea, tel: 82-2-773-1631, fax: 82-2-773-1633.

Steven J. Kulich, SISU Foreign Experts, Building 306, Guang Ling Yi-Lu 121, Shanghai, 20083 China, tel: 86–21–654–23070 ext. 306, fax: 86-21-654-4-8852, e-mail: kulis@chinaonline.com.cn.net.uninet.com.cn.

Kiyoharu Nakajima, 60 Nakano-Cho, Sakae-Ku, Yokohama 247, Japan, tel: 81–45–894–2961, fax: 81–45–894–3313, e-mail: kiyonak@wa2.so-net.ne.jp.

Nandani Lynton, Guang Ming Apartments 3/16, Liangmaqiao Road, Chaoyang District, Beijing, 100016 China, tel: 86–19–65919008, fax: 86–10 64677655, e-mail: lyncc@chinaonline.com.cn.net.

Sing Chee Ling, 15 East Shelford Road, Singapore, 1128 Singapore, tel: 772–3722, fax: 775–5571, e-mail: fbolsc@leonis.nus.sg.

Rebecca Long, PO Box 747, Hsinch, Taiwan, tel: 35·772121x58100, e-mail: rlong@cc.nctu.edu.tw.

Oak Associates, Aoki Building 3F, 4–1–10 Toramon, Minato-Ku, Tokyo 105, Japan, tel: 81–3–5472–7077, fax: 81–3–5472–7076, e-mail: oakkk@gol.com.

Organisational Consultants, Ltd., Lichia Yiu, Prince's Building, 8th Floor, Central Hong Kong, Hong Kong, tel: 852–2521–4288, fax: 852–2845–9175, e-mail: saneryiu@csi.com.

David J. Pauleen, Wellington Polechchnic, Private Bag 756, Wellington, New Zealand, tel: 64–4–801–2794 ext 8432, fax: 64–4–801–2693, e-mail: davidp@directorate.wnp.ac.nz.

Philip Merry Consulting Group Pte. Ltd., Level 36-Hong Leong Building, Raffles Quay, Singapore, 04581, Singapore, tel: 607–221–0727, fax: 607–221–0728, e-mail: pmerry@pacific.net.sg.

Monica Rabe, Villa 69731 An Dien, An Phu Duc District, Ho Chi Minh City, Vietnam.

Tokyo Centre for Language & Culture, Sanshin Building 1–20–1 Shibuya, Shibuya-Ku, Tokyo 150, Japan, tel/fax: 81–3–3486–9627, e-mail: terryhakes@aol.com.

P. T. Visi Konsultama, Irid Agoes, Jl. Tebet Barat X/18, Selatan, Jakarta, Indonesia, tel: 62–21–829–5385, fax: 62–21–830–6955, e-mail: 671–708@mci.mail.

Europe

Pierre Casse, 15 Rte Suisse, 1296 Coppet, Switzerland, tel: 41–22–776–9450, fax: 41–22 776–9446, e-mail: 100652.2656@compu serve.com.

Castle Consultants International, Walt Hopkins, 9 Drummond Park, Crook of Devon, Kinross KY13 0UX, Scotland, United Kingdom, tel: 44–1577–840–122, fax: 44–171–681–1445, e-mail: walt@hopkins. net.

Centre for Inter-Cultural Development, John 27 Langland Gardens, London, NW3 6QE, United Kingdom, tel: 44 (0) 171–431–1712, fax: 44 (0) 171 431–6060.

Centre for International Briefing, Farnham Castle, Farnham, Surrey GU9 0AG, United Kingdom, tel: 44 (0) 1252–7204, fax: 44 (0) 1252–719277, e-mail: marketing@cibfarnham.com.

Cornelius Görres Communications, Weissenburger Platz Number 8, 81667 Munich, Germany, tel: 49–89–48–999–838, fax: 49–89–999–839, e-mail: 100754.662@compuserve.com.

Consultants Interculturele Communicatie, Marnixstraatr 154-I, 1016 TE Amsterdam, The Netherlands, tel: 31(0) 20–624–2212, fax: 31 (0) 20–624–1513, e-mail: bvhouten@euronet.nl.

Cross-Cultural Consulting, Gay Tischbirek, 52 rue du Docteur Blanche, F – 75016 Paris, France, tel/fax: 33–1–4524–3361.

Cross Cultural Relations Centre, Jean Phillips-Martinsson, Far-things, 44 Warwick Park, Tunbridge Wells, Kent, TN2 5EF, United Kingdom, tel/fax: 44–1892–549492, e-mail: jeanpws@compuserve. com.

Culture Crossings Ltd., Polly Platt, 51 rue de Bellechasse, 75007 Paris, France, tel: 33–1 4556–0462, fax: 33–1–4555–8186, e-mail: polly@pollyplatt.com.

Oyvind Dahl, Gamleveien 45, N – 4030 Hinna, Norway, tel: 47–515–6273, fax: 47–515–6272, e-mail: od@misjonshs.no.

Danida's Kursuscenter, Skovvej 7, DK – 3100 Hornbaek, Denmark, tel: 45–70–1000, fax: 45–70–1073, e-mail: danida-hbh@danida-hbh.dk.

Europublic SA/NV, Richard Hill and Karin Minke, Avenue Winston Churchill 11, Box 21, B – 1180, Brussels, Belgium, tel: 32–2–343–7726, fax: 32–2–343–9330, e-mail: info@europublic.com.

Face to Face Training, Sandra Roding, Frodvagen 6, S – 85741 Sundsvall, Sweden, tel/fax: 46–60–155933.

William Fasse, OULU Ploytech, Henttulantie 21, FIN – 91500 Muhos, Finland, tel: 08–5331–427, e-mail: william.fasse@hermes.okol.oamk.fi.

Helmut Fennes, Interkulturelles Zentrum, Kettenbruckenpasse 23, A – 1050 Wien, Austria, tel: 43–1–586–7544–0, fax: 43–1–586–7544–0, e-mail: helmut.fennes@blackbox.at.

Joao Viegas Fernandes, Urbanizacao De S Luis, Lote D – 7th, 8000 Faro, Portugal, tel: 351–089–813168, fax: 351–089–864675.

Focus Consultants International, Ruth Ann Lake, Via Primo Maggio 8/7, 20078 San Colombano al Lambro, Milano, Italy, tel/fax: 39–371–200027, e-mail: lakejabb@pmp.it.

Global Integration, Kevan Hall, PO Box 7086, Hook, RG41 0YG, United Kingdom, tel: 44 (0) 118–973–6282, fax: 44 (0) 118–973–6283, e-mail: global_integration@compuserve.com.

Greater Europe Mission, Dianne Collard, Muvelodes ut 21–27, H – 1223 Budapest, Hungary, tel/fax: 36–1–277–2735, e-mail: 100324.2556@compuserve.com.

GroupeMeyer Cross-Cultural Consulting, 29 rue du Loing, 77690 Montigny sur Loing, France, tel: 33 (0) 1–6478–3650, e-mail Julie_meyer@yahoo.com.

Gert Hofstede, Den Brul 15, 6881 AN Velp, The Netherlands, tel: 31–26–364–2648, fax: 31–23 661–1021, e-mail: secretariat@iric.unimaas.nl.

IMD-International Institute for Management Development, Chemin de Bellerive 23, PO Box 915, CH – 1001, Lausanne-Ouchy, Switzerland, tel: 41–21–618–0111, fax: 41–21–618–0707, e-mail: info@imd.ch.

IOR UK Limited, Three Whitehall Court, Suite 55, London, SW1A 2EL, United Kingdom, tel: 020–7930–7090, fax: 020–7930–7088, e-mail: msims@iorukltd.com.

Intercultura-Italy, Roberto Ruffino, Via Gracco Del Secco 100, Colle Val D'Elsa, Sienna, 1–53034, Italy, tel: 39–577–921427, fax: 39–577–920948, e-mail: ruffino@intercultura.it.

Intercultural Solutions Group, Uhlandstrasse 16, D – 91074 Herzo-genaurach, Germany, tel: 49–9132–40466, fax: 49–9132–40478, e-mail: training@isg_international.com.

Interkulturel Utbildning, Anne-Charlotte Sukhia, Kalovagen 17, S – 13234 Saltsjo-Boo, Sweden, tel: 46–8715–8703, fax: 46–8715–3969, e-mail: anna.sukhia@interkulturellutbuildning.se.

Interkulturelles Zentrum, Helmut Fennes, Kettenbruckenpasse 23, A – 1050 Wien, Austria, tel: 43–1–586–7544–0, fax: 43–1–586–7544–9, e-mail: helmut.fennes@blackbox.at.

Interlink, Susan Vonsild, Hasselvej 15, DK – 9530, Stovring, Den-mark, tel: 45–98–37–4433, fax: 45–89–37–1864.

International Focus, Margaret E. Mander, Number 28 NaVypichu, Prague, 6–16200, Czech Republic, e-mail: focus@cream/cybertia.cz.

International Institute-Professional Development, Anna Varga, 11–17 Leninsky Street, Moscow, 117049, Russia, tel: 7–095–237–3829, fax: 7–095–332–6377.

Institute of Cross Culture Communication, Riversdown House, Warnford, Hampshire, SO32 3LH, United Kingdom, tel: 44–1962–771–111, fax: 44–1962–771–105, e-mail: iccc@crossculture.com.

Instituut voor Inter-Etnisch Management, Toernooiveld 100, PO Box 31367, 6503 CJ Niijmenegen, The Netherlands, tel: 31–24–360–6760, fax: 31–24–360–5602.

Insead-Institute Europeen d'Administration des Affaires, Boulevard de Constance, F – 77305 Fontainebleau, Cedex, France, tel: 33–(0)–1–607–2400, fax: 33–(0)–1–60–7455–00, e-mail: webmaster@insead.fr.

LCT Consultants, Eric Lynn, Adam-Kraft-Strasse 45, D – 90419 Nuremberg, Germany, tel: 49 (0) 911–39–7702, fax: 49(0) 911–33–1477, e-mail: ericlynnlct@compuserve.com.

LTS Training and Consulting, Phillip E. O'Conner, 5 Belvedere, Lans-down Road, Bath, BA1 5ED, United Kingdom, tel: 44–1–22–544–8148, fax: 44–1–22–544–8149, e-mail: 100074.15@compuserve.com.

Roberta Maierhofer, Instituti Fur Amerikanistik, Karl-Franzens Uni-versitat Graz, A – 8010 Graz, Austria, tel: 43–316–380–2469, fax: 43–316–3848–98, e-mail: maierhr@email.kfunigraz.ac.at.

Plamen Makareiv, Sophia University, 14 Tsar Osvoboditel Boule-vard, 1504 Sofia, Bulgaria, tel: 359–2–986–5579, fax: 359–2–973–3338, e-mail: makariev@phls.uni-sofia.bg.

Nomadic Life Management Consultants, Fredrik Fogelberg, Rou-bosiaan 30B, 2252 KR Voorschoten, The Netherlands, tel: 31–71–561–8936, fax: 31–71–562–1470, e-mail: fredrikfogelberg@nomadic.

nl. Organisational Consultants, Ltd., Raymond Saner, 4 Place Des Alpes, 1201 Geneva, Switzerland, tel: 41–22–906–1160, fax: 41–22–906–1169, e-mail: saneryiu@csi.com.

Pharos Corporation, Banu Golesorkhi, and Robert Brown, IFL Centre, 31 Place de Brouckere, B – 1000 Brussels, Belgium, tel: 32–2 227–1390, fax: 32–2–227–1392, e-mail: robert.brown@infoboard.be.

George Simons, Residence L'Argentiere-Batiment A, 637 Boulevard de la Taverniere, 06210 Mandelieu-La Napoule, France, tel: 33–4–92–97–5735, fax: 33–1–53–01–3504, e-mail: gsimons@diversophy.com.

Carina Skareby, c/o Isaksson, 231 rue de Kirchberg, L – 1858 GD de Luxembourg, Luxembourg, tel: 352–4300–2780, fax: 352–42–1378, e-mail: cskareby@interway.lu.

TMA Europe, 211 Picadilly, London W1V 9LD, United Kingdom, tel: 44–171–917–2784, fax: 44–171–2785, e-mail: info@2tmaworld.com.

Johnny Tobiassen, Kyrkjelemyra 3, N – 5300 Kleppesto, Norway, tel: 55–31–0550, e-mail: johnny.tobiassen@paych.uib.no.

Transcultural International, Monica Armour, Reguliersgracht 104A, 1017 LW Amsterdam, The Netherlands, tel: 31–20–623–0445, fax: 31–20–620–5770, e-mail: mramour@wxs.nl.

Trans-Cultural Relations, Enid Kopper, Klusstrasse 42, CH – 8032 Zurich, Switzerland, tel/fax: 41–1–383–1925, e-mail: kopper. kiechl@bluewin.ch.

Transnational Management Associates, 211 Piccadilly, London, United Kingdom, W1V 9LD, tel: 0171–917–2784, fax: 0171–917–2785, e-mail: pbanks@netcomuk.co.uk.

United Notions BV, Fons Trompenaars, A.J. Ernstraat 595-d, 1082 LD Amstelveen, The Netherlands, tel: 31–20–301–6666, fax: 31–20–301–6555, e-mail: info@unotions.nl.

Jeremy Williams, Handshaikh Ltd., PO Box 123, Alresford, Hampshire, SO24 0ZF, United Kingdom, tel: 44–0–1962–771699, fax: 44–0–1962–771814, e-mail: info@handshaikh.com.

Canada

Nancy J. Adler, Faculty of Management, McGill University, 1001 rue Sherbrooke Ouest, Montreal, Quebec, H3A 1G5, Canada, tel: (514) 398–4031, fax: (514) 398–3876, e-mail: info@jaims.org.

Cross-Cultural Communication Centre, Louis Chrysostom, 2909 Dundas Street West, Toronto, Ontario, M6P 1Z1, Canada, tel: (416) 760–7855, fax: (416) 760–7911.

The Cross Cultural Group, Suite 200, 275 Portage Avenue, Winnipeg, Manitoba, R3B 2B3, Canada, tel: (204) 949–1144, fax: (204) 949–1372, e-mail: hass@ccci.ca.

The Expatriate Group, Inc., Tom Boleantu, Suite 280, 926 5th Avenue SW, Calgary, Alberta, T2P 0N7, Canada, tel: (403) 232–8561, fax: (403) 294–1222, e-mail: expatriate@expat.ca.

FGI, 10 Commerce Valley Drive East, Suite 200, Thornhill, Ontario, L3T 7N7, Canada, tel: (905) 886–2157, fax: (905) 886–4337, e-mail: csimmons@fgiworld.com.

Global Transitions, Jill Koch, 702 Rideau Road SW, Calgary, Alberta, T2S 0R6, Canada, tel: (403) 287–9669, fax: (403) 287–1925.

Golden Bridges & Associates, Daneal Charney, 46 Alexis Road, Thornhill, ON, L3T 6Z9, Canada, tel: (905) 886–5605, fax: (905) 886–6503, e-mail: charney@idirect.com.

Intercultural Management Development, Inc., Werner R. Draegestein, 716–3000 Yonge Street, Toronto, ON M4N 2K5, Canada, tel: (416) 440–1332, e-mail: draegestein@sympatico.ca.

International Briefing Associates, Michael Miner, 116 Promenade Du Portage, Hull, Quebec, J8X 2K1, Canada, tel: (819) 776–9985, fax: (819) 776–9776.

Pasargadae International Expatriate Management, Roxanna Husain, 115 Mayfair Cresent, Regina, Sakatchewan, S4S 5T9, Canada, tel: (306) 584–9847, fax: (306) 352–7351, e-mail: pasargadae @sk.sympatico.ca.

Square One Management Ltd., Ruben Nelson, PO Box 2699, Canmore, Alberta, Canada, tel: (403) 673–3537, fax: (403) 673–2114.

Transcultural International, Monica Armour, 175 Cumberland Street, Suite 2009, Toronto, Ontario, M5R 3M9, Canada, tel: (416) 929–0270, fax: (416) 962–9271, e-mail: monicati@interlog.com.

Latin America/Caribbean
Building Blocks Training and Consulting, Edisonia Kook, Kaya HRD, Youngbloed 25, Curaçao, Nederland Antilles, Curaçao, tel: 59–9–937–1205, fax: 59–9–996–4930.

Center for Research and Continuing Education, Yves J. Joseph, PO Box 13373 Delmas, Port-au-Prince, Haiti, tel: 509–22–5500, fax: 509–23–9603.

Laura Graziela Gomes, Rua Pereira Nunes, 68/1002 Inga, Niteroi, RJ24.21u – 430, Brazil, tel/fax: 021–620–6746, e-mail: grazeila @web4u.com.br.

Maria Elena Hoffmann, PO Box 51291, Caracas, 1050-A, Venezuela, tel: 58–2–743025.

International Cultural Assistance, Lucy Paixao Linhares, Av. Graça Aranha, Number 81, Sala 613, Centro Rio de Janeiro, 20030–002, RJ Brasil, tel/fax: 55–21–5330388, e-mail: ica@infolink.com.br.

International, Ltd., Richard J. Good, Calle 9 Number 3–11, Bogotá, Colombia, tel: 57–1–283–2913, fax: 57–1–282–3420.

MundialMente, Adriana Arzac, Bosque del Comendedor 2, Bosques de la Herradura, CP 52570, Huixilucan Edo de Mexico, Mexico, tel: 52–5–294–7079, fax: 52–5–294–7076, e-mail: arzac@servidor.unam. mx.

Bertha C. Murrieta, Escuela par Estdiantes Extranjeros, Universidad Veracruzana, PO Box 440, Zamora 25 Xalapa, Veracruz, 91000, Mexico, tel: 52–28–178687, fax: 52–28–186413.

PG Consultants, Patricia Ghany, 2 Hobson Street, San Fernando Trinidad, West Indies, tel: 80–9–652–4351, fax: 80–9–653–9650, e-mail: esau@trinidad.net.

Maria Martin Thacker, PO Box FL 239, Smith's Parish, FL BX Bermuda, tel: 441–232–0803, fax: 441–236–7148, e-mail: jthacker @ibl.bm.

Jorge Torres, CETALIC, Ando Postal 1–201 CP, 62001 Cuernavaca, Morelos, Mexico, tel: 52–73–170850, fax: 52–73–132637, e-mail: cetlalic@mail.giga.com.

Barbara Vilar, PO Box 10027, Carolina, Puerto Rico, 00988, tel: (787) 760–8127, fax: (787) 761–6069, e-mail: brvilar@aol.com.

Interculturalists at Other Locations

The following members of the intercultural profession may be able to provide services directly or give referrals to others at their locations.

Nancy Frampton, 1081 Corniche El Nil, Garden City, Cairo, Egypt, tel: 20-2-517-3721, fax: 20-2-517-0740, e-mail: bfcielp1@frcu,eun.eg.

Peter T. Govert, CHP International, PO Box 754, Naivasha, Kenya, tel: 254-3-112-1108, fax: 254-3-112-1109.

Handshaikh Ltd., PO Box 7979, Dubai, United Arab Emirates, tel: 971-4-3517624, fax: 971-4-3521033, e-mail: info@handshaikh.com.

Jennifer Hanson, Robert College, PKI Arnavutkoy, 80820, Turkey, tel/fax: 90–212–229–3006, e-mail: jhanson@ku.edu.tr.

Bethany Barron Naizian, PO Box 155, 31001, Haifa, Israel, tel: 972-4-835-8358, fax: 972-4-835-8591, e-mail: bethany@bmc.org.

Ralph P. Metzger, Box 17541, Gulshan-E-Iqbal, Karachi, 75300, Pakistan, tel: 922-1-454-6453, fax: 922-1-773-8659, e-mail: rpmetz @ibm.net.

Eunice Olurante Okelana, PO Box 1411, Ikej, Lagos, Nigeria, tel: 234-1-763-1860.

Vivek Paranjpe, Diversity Education, HP India, Paharpur Business Centre, 21, Nehru Place, New Delhi, 110019, India, tel: (415) 857-2402, fax: (415) – 857-8115.

Mark William Simpson, Box 10617, Dhahran, 31311, Saudi Arabia, tel: 966-3-877-2734, fax: 966-3-872-0113.

Melissa Steyn, University of Cape Town, Rodenbosch, 7701, Cape Town, Republic of South Africa, tel: 272-165-03409, fax: 274-165-03408, e-mail: mes@education.uct.ac.za.

Diversity Service Providers

The primary focus of this book is on international intercultural services. However, in some cases, domestic diversity issues may be mixed with the cross-border challenges that face transnational companies and organizations. In these instances, it is helpful to involve diversity service providers. The following list of providers is not intended to be exhaustive, nor does it imply any endorsements. Rather, it is merely meant to give you a useful starting point for locating practitioners and suppliers.

Advanced Research Management Consultants, 1014 South Second Street, 2nd Floor, Philadelphia, PA 19147, tel: (800) 237-9856 and (215) 551-5340 fax: (215) 551-3710, e-mail: armc-hr@aerols.com.

Battaglia, Ltd., 2237 North Westwood Avenue, Santa Ana, CA 92706, tel: (714) 542-2233, fax: (714) 543-7375, e-mail: beverly @leveragingdiversity.com.

Bridges in Organizations, Inc., 4811 St. Elmo Avenue, Bethesda, MD 20814, tel: (301) 718-9040, e-mail: info@bridges-in-orgs.com.

Camelot, 1150 Silverado Street, Suite 115, La Jolla, CA 92037, tel: (619) 283-8269, fax: (619) 288-7279, e-mail: psj@tns.net.

Cor Communications, LLC, 19197 Twin Oaks Lane, Sonoma, CA 95476, tel: (800) 397-6256 and (707) 935-8576, fax: (707) 935-8605, e-mail: mheim@corcommunications.com.

Diversitas New York, Inc., 353 7th Avenue, New York, NY 10001, tel: (212) 643-9745, fax: (212) 643-1621.

The Diversity Group, Inc., 714 North Scott Street, Wheaton, IL 60187, tel/fax: (630) 784–0647, e-mail: thediversitygroup@hotmail. com.

The Diversity Training Group, 11654 Plaza America Drive, Suite 747, Reston, VA 20190, tel: (703) 728–9191, fax: (703) 709–0591, e-mail: maurciov@diversitydtg.com.

Diversity Training University International LLC, PO Box 720207, San Diego, CA 92172–0207, tel: (619) 888–1778, fax: (619) 615–2055, e-mail: billy@diversityuintl.com.

Diversity Training-Workplace Solutions, Inc., 17 Beresford Court, Williamsville, NY 14221, tel: (716) 656–2000, fax: (716) 565–2002, e-mail: lkorn@diversitytraining.com.

DTG, Inc., PO Box 2412, Pearland, TX 77588–2412, tel: (888) 788–1027, fax: (713) 436–0731, e-mail: consult2@consult-dtc.com.

Edge Training systems, Inc., 10043 Midlothian Turnpike, Suite C, Richmond, VA 23235, tel: (800) 576–1045 and (804) 272–1711, fax: (804) 272–1683, e-mail: mailbox@edgetraining.com.

Empowerment Workshops, Inc., 251 Newbury Street, Boston, MA 02116, tel: (617) 266–9100, fax: (617) 266–7270, e-mail: info@ empowermentworks.com.

Executive Diversity Services, Inc., 1139 34th Avenue, Unit B, Seattle, WA 98122, tel: (206) 224–9293, fax: (206) 328–3050, e-mail: exec div@ricochet.net.

Gardenswartz & Rowe, 12658 West Washington Boulevard, Suite 105, Los Angeles, CA 90066, tel: (310) 823–2466, fax: (310) 823–3923, e-mail: mail@gardenswartzrowe.com.

The GilDean Group, 13751 Lake City Way North East, Suite 106, Seattle, WA 98125–8612, tel: (206) 362–0336, fax: (206) 363–5028, e-mail: gildeane@diversitycentral.com.

Griggs Productions, 5616 Geary Boulevard, San Francisco, CA 94121, tel: (800) 210–4200 and (415) 668–4200, fax: (415) 668–6004, e-mail: griggs@griggs.com.

Harbeck Company, Inc., 5600 W. Lovers Lane, Suite 116–398, Dallas, TX 75209, tel: (214) 520–2921, fax: (214) 520–1230, e-mail: info@harbeck.com.

Hubbard & Hubbard, Inc., 1302 Holm Road, Petaluma, CA 94954–1164, tel: (707) 763–8380, fax: (707) 763–3640, e-mail: hubahuba99@aol.com.

Inter-Change Consultants, 255 West 108th Street, New York, NY 10025, Suite 6CI, tel: (212) 316–2604, e-mail: interchnge@aol.com.

International Training and Development Services, Leslie, Aguilar, PO Box 592562, Orlando, FL, 32859, tel: (407) 859–1191, fax: (407) 859–7217, e-mail: info@inclusiveservice.com.

The Kaleel Jamison Consulting Group, Inc., 279 River Street, Suite 40, Troy, MI 12180, tel: (888) 552–4662 and (518) 271–7000, fax: (518) 271–4400, e-mail: bbrave@kjcg.com.

Kochman Communications Consultants, Ltd., 120 North Oak Park Avenue, Oak Park, IL 60301, tel: (708) 383–9235, fax: (708) 383–9084, e-mail: tkkdd@aol.com.

Meridian Associates, 3320 East Second Avenue, Denver, CO 80206, tel: (800) 238–6747 and (303) 399–5006, fax: (303) 399–4600, e-mail: aipsaro@meridassoc.com.

Moorhead Kennedy Associates, 45 John Street, New York, NY 10038, tel: (212) 964–0649, fax: (212) 964–1364.

National Association of Gender Diversity Training, 4621 East Abraham Lane, Phoenix, AZ 85050, tel: (480) 473 0426, fax: (480) 473–0427, e-mail: info@gendertraining.com.

National Multicultural Institute, 3000 Connecticut Avenue North West, Suite 438, Washington, DC 20008–2556, tel: (202) 483–0700, fax: (202) 483–5233, e-mail: mmci@mmci.org.

D. B. Pargman Diversity Training, 624 Third Avenue, Decatur, GA 30030, tel: (404) 377–2189, fax: (404) 373–9539, e-mail: contact @dbpargman.com.

ProGroup, Riverplace, One Main Street South East, Suite 200, Minneapolis, MN 55414, tel: (800) 652–4093 and (612) 379–7223, fax: (612) 379–7048, e-mail: psvennson@progroupinc.com.

Pope and Associates, Inc., 1313 East Kemper Road # 350, Cincinnati, OH 45246, tel: (513) 671–1277, fax: (513) 671–1815, e-mail: pbenson@pope-diversity.com.

R3, Laura Ricci, PO Box 26249, Austin, TX 78755, tel: (512) 347–9666, e-mail: lricci@R3.com.

Loden Associates, Inc., 70 Gilmartin Drive, Tiburon, Ca 94920, tel: (415) 435–8507, e-mail: mail@loden.com.

Sybil Evans Associates, 244 Madison Avenue, New York, NY 10016, tel: (212) 697–0974, fax: (212) 797–9104, e-mail: sybil@ sybilevans.com.

Simmons Associates, Inc., 31 North Sugan Road, PO Box 712, New Hope, PA 18938, tel: (800) 520–0072 and (215) 862–3020, fax: (215) 862–3077, e-mail: info@simassoc.com.

SMBC Incorporated, 1769 Aberdeen Circle, Crofton, MD 21114, tel: (410) 721–1512, fax: (410) 721–5247, e-mail: lou@smbcinc.com.

R. Thomas Consulting & Training, 2872 Woodcock Boulevard, Suite 220, Atlanta, GA 30341–4100, tel: (770) 234–0222, fax: (770) 234–0226, e-mail: info@rthomasconsulting.com.

Tulin DiversiTeam Associates, 5 Curtis Park Drive, Wyncote, PA 19095, tel: (215) 884–7325, fax: (215) 886–5515, e-mail: info@ diversiteam.com.

9

Working with Suppliers

The important thing to recognize is that it takes a team, and the team ought to get credit for the wins and losses. Successes have many fathers; failures have none.

Philip Caldwell
former chairman and CEO of Ford Motor
Company

Client-Supplier Teamwork
Successful management of intercultural service suppliers is based on establishing mutually beneficial relationships with them, setting clear standards for their performance, and working closely together as a team (see Exhibit 9–1). The client and the suppliers must openly confront and discuss the problems and issues that affect their shared endeavors. They should seek to continually improve the services and use cooperation, evaluation, and feedback to achieve that end. Increasing the intercultural effectiveness of the client's expatriates, host-country counterparts, international business travelers, and other cross-border employees is the purpose of client-supplier teamwork and the ultimate measure of its success.

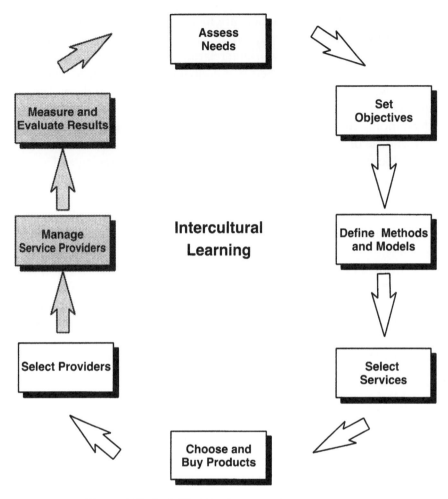

EXHIBIT 9–1. INTERCULTURAL SERVICES CYCLE.

Managing the Relationship

> When crew and captain understand each other to the core, it takes a
> gale and more . . . to put their ship ashore.
>
> **Rudyard Kipling** in *Together*

Selecting and hiring suppliers are merely the first steps in providing intercultural services to your organization or company. Establishing and maintaining effective working relationships with them ensures that they will be able to make their best contributions. Therefore, you need to be aware of the issues that typically cause friction, and you should give careful attention to how the relationships are structured. By understanding the different options for client-supplier arrangements, you can choose or design one that best meets your needs and one that lays a solid foundation for on-going collaboration. By foreseeing and avoiding the problems that typically hinder client-supplier relations, you will have a significant head start.

Types of Supplier Relationships

Providers of intercultural services and their clients have developed a variety of ways to work together. The different options are neither rigidly defined nor static. They are structured according to the clients' preferences and requirements, and they are modified frequently in response to changing client needs and circumstances. Several basic types of contractual arrangements and service delivery methods can be identified.

Simple Fee-for-Service
This is the simplest business arrangement. It merely requires payment for a product or service upon delivery, and it implies no commitment by either the buyer or seller beyond the current transaction. The services are performed on an ad hoc basis. This approach is commonly used in cases in which the client's need is low volume or sporadic and difficult to forecast. Also, purchasers often prefer a fee-for-service relationship while they are comparing various vendors. Although this arrangement is referred to as "fee-for-service," of course suppliers also are paid fees in other types of transactions.

Preferred Provider
In this scenario, the supplier and the client make a verbal or written agreement that the provider is the client's first choice. No guarantee of business is given to the supplier. The purchaser agrees to first offer any intercultural work to the vendor but remains free to use other suppliers if prices or other terms of service cannot be agreed upon. In exchange, the provider typically invests time in becoming well-acquainted

with the client's business and international projects and often designates a specific client representative to handle its requests. In addition, the client may be given priority when conflicts arise in scheduling programs or assigning preferred trainers or consultants. Large companies, with numerous business units, may have several preferred providers.

Sole Supplier

An exclusive relationship may be entered into when a supplier has delivered consistently outstanding services over time or if it possesses a particular expertise that the purchaser values highly. Under this arrangement, the vendor may offer price concessions, develop company-specific training materials, ensure the availability of preferred staff, or create a service team specifically dedicated to the client. In return, the client may commit to giving the provider a minimum volume of business during the period of the agreement or may contract for a specific dollar amount of work.

Outsourcing

In this approach, the buyer contractually delegates to the supplier the responsibility for administering the services in addition to delivering them. The provider deals directly with the client's employees and may help implement policies, organize and schedule services, keep records, and produce reports. This method was developed to increase the capabilities of understaffed international human resources departments, to add expertise missing in the purchaser's organization, and to gain more thoroughness and consistency in the application of international assignment policies. In some cases, it is used to achieve economies of scale by integrating the management of various international assignment functions, such as relocation, visa facilitation, counseling, and expatriate children's educational services.

Consulting Agreements

Intercultural consultants work under all the different arrangements familiar in the consulting profession. These include hourly, daily, weekly, monthly, or project-based fees and indefinite service contracts. Retainers may also be used to ensure the availability of consultants who are in high demand. Some consultants sell blocks of time in advance to be used, as needed, during the period of their contracts.

Delivery Options

Aside from the various arrangements for structuring client-supplier relationships, different modes of service delivery exist. Where the services occur and how they are managed help define the various options. They each have their own advantages and drawbacks. You need to become familiar with them and consider which ones best meet your organization's or company's needs.

Provider's Location

The larger intercultural service suppliers have their own facilities for training programs and counseling sessions. Usually their training rooms are well suited and properly equipped for their purposes. The availability of the provider's administrative staff to readily solve any logistical problems that may occur is an advantage. In addition, having your employees attend programs at the provider's facilities removes them from their routine work environment and helps them focus on the learning task of the moment. On the other hand, the requirement that program attendees travel to the vendor's location adds to the overall expense and may cause inconveniences.

External Facilities

Suppliers often rent training rooms at hotels or conference centers for group programs. The cost of the facilities and amenities may be included in the project fee or billed separately. Your company or organization might directly rent these facilities if there are cost savings in doing so. The logistics involved in ensuring that audiovisual equipment, flip charts, and other instructional aids are available and in good working order can be time-consuming. Likewise, arranging for suitable meals and refreshments is an additional administrative task. Nevertheless, the prospect of participating in a learning activity in a pleasant off-site setting may be attractive to your employees and help increase program attendance.

Client Site

It is common for providers to deliver their services in training or conference rooms at the client's location. This alternative saves employee travel time, is usually less expensive, and avoids the logistical challenges already mentioned. Also, the program's visibility helps build organizational awareness of the intercultural activities. Another advantage of client site programs is that you can easily arrange for key in-house sponsors to observe portions of them. However, the participants are prone to being interrupted by phone calls and colleagues calling them out of the sessions. Your administrative staff may find it burdensome to support the programs on an ongoing basis.

In-House Service Centers

Vendors may be contracted to staff in-house service centers so they can manage training or counseling facilities on their client's premises. In this case, the trainers, counselors, and administrators remain employees of the supplier. This arrangement may or may not be part of an outsourcing contract. With a competent contractor, an in-house service center offers you a relatively trouble-free way to deliver intercultural training and counseling, especially when a large number of employees are involved. At the same time, such an arrangement enables you to maintain adequate direction and supervision. This mode of delivery is frequently combined with the provision of other international relocation services. You might consider it as a means to deal with head count limitations or to reduce your staff overhead.

On-Site Service Representatives

A supplier may assign an employee to work full-time at the client's location. This representative may be a qualified interculturalist who directly provides consulting, training, or counseling to employees as needed. Alternatively, this person could be a coordinator or administrator who merely arranges for the services. Having an on-site supplier representative offers several benefits—your employees have immediate access to the services; the representative gains insight into your company's business operations and organizational culture, which helps improve the relevance of the supplier's training program designs. However, office space and facilities must be provided, and the liability issues of having a non-employee working on your premises have to be addressed and resolved.

Relationship Issues

Despite the good will of both suppliers and clients, many issues may cause friction and even failures in their relationships. By being aware of the most common pitfalls and taking steps to prevent them, you can maximize the effectiveness of the services your company purchases and make working with your providers more enjoyable. Some of the more common problems are due to lack of clarity or the absence of explicit agreements in the following areas.

Scope of Work

A supplier and client may have different understandings regarding the service to be provided. For example, a company may hire a consultant to deliver a workshop on managing cultural differences thinking the program will address its concern about the resistance of some of its employees to promoting female subordinates. However, the consultant could easily miss this nuance and focus on cultural diversity in the workplace, dealing with gender issues only in passing. This type of misunderstanding is often due to the provider not delving deeply enough into the client's needs and concerns and to the client being too subtle or indirect when describing sensitive problems. Bringing your suppliers fully into your confidence, communicating with them clearly and unambiguously, and being sure that they truly understand your organization's needs will help prevent such misunderstandings.

Lead Time

In order to deliver a high-quality training or orientation program, providers need adequate preparation time. This requirement is especially important for custom-tailored programs. It takes time to gather information on participants' needs, interests, and backgrounds, to assemble an appropriate multicultural training team, and to create or modify program designs and materials. Unfortunately, in response to the rapid pace and unpredictability of international business, clients often request programs on very short notice. Giving your suppliers as much advance notice as possible is very important to the success and quality of the programs and reduces stress in the relationship.

Professional Confidentiality

Reports on suitability assessments and counseling sessions of potential expatriates frequently contain personal and sensitive information. For these services to be effective, the people using them must feel that their privacy will be protected. Therefore, the provider, client, and the potential expatriate employees (and their spouses, if involved) must thoroughly understand and agree exactly who will have access to the information and how it will be used. Likewise, participants in cross-cultural training programs should know whether their trainers are expected to assess and report on the trainees' suitability for an international assignment based on their performance during the programs. Establishing explicit and transparent guidelines regarding the confidentiality of services is key to preserving their integrity and credibility in the eyes of your employees.

Fee Negotiations

Reaching agreement regarding the fees for services can be stressful to both the buyer and the vendor. Prices vary greatly among different providers according to factors such as their size, experience, and reputation. Comparison-shopping is difficult because products and programs that may appear identical in written descriptions often are quite different under the surface. For example, a one-day training program or workshop may be much more in-depth and intensive than a one-day briefing or orientation and, therefore, may justify a higher price. In negotiating fees for intercultural services, you are best advised to focus on value and quality before cost. Also, you should know what your colleagues in other companies are paying for comparable services, and you should understand the pricing structure variables described here.

Pricing Structures

The prices of intercultural programs may be based on a set program fee or on the number of attendees. They also typically vary according to the length, location, and type of program. Custom-tailored programs cost more than generic ones. In some cases, special features or extra resources may influence prices. Sliding scales or group discounts may be offered. Other costs, such as preprogram trainee needs assessment, trainer travel expenses, and post-program evaluations and reports, may be included in the program fee or billed separately. Some providers allow client observers to attend programs free of charge, but others do not. Be sure that you thoroughly understand the pricing structure. Doing so will help prevent tension during price negotiations and avoid billing disputes later.

Billing

Suppliers' billing policies may require extra charges for canceling or rescheduling programs and for late payment of invoices. Some providers charge a premium for rush assignments. It is important for you to discuss and, if necessary, negotiate the conditions under which these charges would be made. Failure to do so often leads to unnecessary friction and frustration. In some cases, delayed invoices from suppliers cause accounting problems for purchasers. Therefore, both parties should clearly communicate their billing and payment turnaround time expectations.

Staffing

Some providers use the same set of trainers to staff most, or all, of their programs. Others temporarily hire different trainers when they are available and if they are appropriate for the type of program being conducted. Suppliers may share information on the qualifications and backgrounds of the trainers with their clients prior to the programs, or they may expect clients to trust their staffing decisions without reviewing trainer biographies. Therefore, if you strongly prefer particular trainers or if you are concerned about trainers' qualifications, it is important for you to discuss providers' staffing policies with them. Most suppliers have a cadre of qualified trainers available. It is generally a good policy to allow flexibility in trainer selection as long as program results consistently meet or exceed your expectations.

Use of Subcontractors

In some cases, your suppliers may want to use subcontractors to deliver some of the services you have purchased. This practice is common among third-party providers who "bundle" different kinds of services for sale as a package. Another situation in which subcontracting may be used is when a supplier is overextended and has made more commitments to its clients than it can fulfill with its own staff. Likewise, unanticipated program scheduling conflicts or unusual requirements may cause providers to turn to outside practitioners or firms to perform part of their work. Suppliers' use of subcontractors is not necessarily a cause for concern. However, you should know in advance and agree with their decision to do so. Also, it is wise to make explicit your expectation that the prime contractor will be accountable for the quality of the services.

Ownership of Materials

Misunderstanding and disagreement regarding the ownership of materials developed for custom-tailored programs can be another source of friction. Copyright issues need to be resolved before any developmental work is commissioned. Depending on the agreement reached, materials may belong to either party or be shared by them. You should obtain permission from your suppliers if you want to copy or distribute their instructional materials or share them with employees who did not attend the programs in which they were used. Likewise, authorization must be obtained from the vendor before videotaping any portion of a program.

Sensitive Client Information

You should require trainers or authorized representatives of the providers' organization to sign nondisclosure agreements if sensitive company information is likely to be discussed during the programs. Likewise, vendors should obtain permission before using your company name or logo in their marketing materials. The same rule should apply to quoting trainees' comments from background questionnaires and program evaluations or using employee testimonials for commercial purposes. In practice, satisfied clients do endorse their suppliers. But it should be done with your full knowledge and consent in order to avoid discord later.

Business Interface

To ensure accountability and consistency in the handling of your requests for services, ask vendors to designate a single point of contact for your company's account. Dealing with several administrators increases the risk of having program confirmations delayed, billing mistakes being made, and other communication problems occurring. In contrast, a manager specifically dedicated to your account will soon become familiar with your organization or company's procedures, policies, and requirements and will develop a sense of obligation to you. Having one contact person is especially important when using larger intercultural service providers that have multiple offices and training sites.

Multiple Providers

It is common for larger purchasers of intercultural services to use more than one vendor. This practice enables clients to tap a broad base of talent and expertise in order to meet their diverse needs. It also gives them more options for scheduling programs and selecting training sites. In addition, competition between the suppliers helps moderate price increases and promotes customer service values. However, providers may be concerned that their proprietary materials, proposals, prices, and training program designs could be seen by their competitors. And, they naturally dislike feeling that they might be pitted against each other. Their uneasiness can be a source of irritation in your client-supplier relationships with them. It may also undermine the spirit of teamwork that will help you obtain the best service from your providers. Demonstrating a high level of professionalism, fairness, and trustworthiness in your dealings with them is essential to preventing these problems.

Hiring Providers' Personnel

Difficulties often arise when clients hire their providers' trainers, consultants, or counselors to perform similar functions directly in-house. The ethical issues involved are ambiguous because these practitioners may not be full- or even part-time employees of the supplier. To reduce the risk of damaging the client-supplier relationship, engage all interested parties in an open discussion of your company's intentions before offering employment to anyone you met through a service provider.

Supplier Relationship Focus Questions

☑ How does your organization or company deal with its vendors and suppliers?

☑ What are the issues and problems that typically affect those relationships? How can they be prevented or avoided in your relationships with intercultural service providers?

☑ What type of relationship do you really want?

☑ Are you convinced of the value of teamwork with your suppliers?

☑ What type of contractual or functional arrangement with them makes the most sense for your organization or company?

☑ Are outsourcing, on-site provider service coordinators, or in-house service centers options worth considering?

☑ Have you consulted with colleagues in other companies about the provider relationship issues they face and how they deal with them?

☑ Have you discussed issues such as lead-time requirements, pricing structure, and staffing policies with your providers?

☑ Have you made your requirements and expectations clear? Do your suppliers understand and accept them?

Improving Supplier Performance

We're supposed to be perfect our first day on the job and then show constant improvement.

Ed Vargo
major league baseball umpire

Although surveys suggest clients generally are satisfied with the intercultural services they receive, reputable, high-quality providers are committed to constantly improving what they offer. In fact, a key hallmark of good relationships between clients and suppliers is that they work together to continually upgrade the products, programs, and processes. Openness to feedback, willingness to change, and a spirit of mutual helpfulness characterize their cooperation.

Helping improve your suppliers' performance is a means to an end: achieving optimal results from the services your organization or company purchases. Probably the most important tools used for this purpose are evaluation, feedback, application of findings, and assistance with follow-through. Therefore, understanding the basics in each of these areas is extremely useful to you as a purchaser and user of intercultural services.

Evaluating Intercultural Learning Activities

Effectively evaluating the learning activities conducted by your intercultural service providers requires that you understand the basic principles of evaluation and that you examine the entire process of planning and implementing the activities.

Basic Evaluation Principles

The aim of evaluation is to improve outcomes. It requires comparing the results with the objectives originally set, determining the extent to which the objectives were achieved, and assessing the resources and processes used. Evaluation findings may be used to measure benefits obtained, to enhance processes, or to refocus objectives. They help managers decide whether they are doing the right things and whether they are doing things right.

Effective evaluation depends on a set of conditions. First, thorough needs assessment must be done in order to select appropriate objectives. Second, the objectives should be defined in terms that are measurable or observable. Third, the results have to be measured by methods and standards that are consistent with the objectives. Finally, the findings of the evaluation should be put to good use. Therefore, evaluation is an integral part of a system, not merely an isolated event or activity.

The principles of sound evaluation certainly apply to the learning activities that are the basis of most intercultural services. However, the evaluator faces some special challenges. Culture, the object of study, is complex and hidden from direct observation. The concepts and knowledge usually are quite novel to the learners. Many of the changes sought in the learners tend to be subjective, subtle, and difficult to measure. Nevertheless, as a purchaser, you need to be sure that the expatriate training and cultural awareness programs, international business seminars, and cross-cultural counseling and coaching services you buy are properly evaluated.

Who Evaluates?

Both purchasers and vendors have important reasons for conducting evaluations. Buyers need evaluation data in order to determine the benefits and the cost-effectiveness of the learning activities from their perspectives as clients. They also use the information to help justify their expenditures and to build in-house support for future purchases. Sellers use evaluation findings to improve services to all of their customers. Ideally, because they have a common interest, providers and purchasers can share the responsibility of ensuring that programs are evaluated consistently and effectively. In practice, the clients generally approve the content and methods used, and the suppliers conduct the evaluations and report the findings. However, this joint effort requires that they agree on what to measure and how to do it.

Evaluating the Learning Achieved

It is essential that evaluators determine to what extent the participants have actually accomplished their learning objectives. Usually the trainer, observers from the client organization, and the trainees' job supervisors share this responsibility. The major categories for measurement are the following:

1. Trainees awareness of the nature and power of culture, consciousness of their own cultural self-identity, the impact of cultural differences, and the challenge of cross-cultural adaptation
2. Knowledge of factual information about the physical environment, history, current events, business conditions, and culture (beliefs, values and customs) of the host country or countries being studied
3. Skills in cross-cultural communications, cultural stress management, cross-border business relations, plus information-gathering and problem-solving in a different cultural environment
4. Attitudes such as empathy, positive acceptance of cultural and ethnic differences, avoidance of stereotyping, interest in learning about other cultures, and willingness to adapt
5. Results achieved by applying intercultural learning on the job (better expatriate/repatriate retention rates, increased cross-border customer satisfaction, and fewer international joint venture disputes, for example)

Common Evaluation Methods

Evaluators have a choice of many different methods to use when measuring the amount of learning achieved. The most common of these are
- Observing the learners' behaviors during the program or event
- Testing their knowledge and skills before and after the program
- Surveying the participants' reactions and feelings by means of interviews, questionnaires, or group debriefings

❑ Rating their subsequent performance and practical application of the things they have learned

Evaluating Intercultural Learning

Most formal intercultural learning occurs within the context of workshops, seminars, and training programs. The key elements and components of these activities should be evaluated to measure their contributions to the learning process. Typically, the trainees and observers from the client's organization assess the following:

❑ Goals and objectives: Were they clear, relevant, and achievable?
❑ Training staff: Were the trainers and cultural resource people qualified, competent, and effective?
❑ Materials: Were they appropriate, well-designed, and useful?
❑ Teaching aids: Was the presentation enhanced by the effective use of graphics and audiovisual presentations?
❑ Instructional methods: Were they engaging and suitable for the trainees? How well did they support the program objectives?
❑ Environment: Was the setting comfortable and conducive to learning?
❑ Pace: Was the time managed well?
❑ Trainee satisfaction: Were the trainees satisfied with the amount learned and the training experience?

In most cases, written questionnaires are used to evaluate intercultural training and orientation programs. These are usually two to four pages in length and focus on the items already listed. They may use many different techniques including rating scales, open-ended questions, checklists, sentence completion, ranked ordering, multiple choice, and comparisons of most-effective versus least-effective activities. Exhibit 9–2 is a sample of a simple post-program evaluation questionnaire.

1. Overall, to what extent are you satisfied with the training program you just completed?
   Not at all satisfied   1   2   3   4   5   Very satisfied
2. The program addressed my intercultural needs and concerns.
   Not at all satisfied   1   2   3   4   5   Very satisfied

Name _____

Company _____

Program Title _____

Program Dates _____

Program Location _____

Trainer _____

EXHIBIT 9–2. INTERCULTURAL TRAINING PROGRAM EVALUATION.

3. The program materials (handouts, visuals, and so on) contributed to my learning.
   Not at all satisfied   1   2   3   4   5   Very satisfied
4. The site, amenities, and support were adequate.
   Not at all satisfied   1   2   3   4   5   Very satisfied
5. How strongly would you recommend this program to others?
   Not at all satisfied   1   2   3   4   5   Very satisfied
6. Which part of the training was most helpful and why?

   _____

   _____

7. How could the training be improved?

   _____

   _____

Please rate the trainer:

	Not at all				Completely
8. Knew the content; was well-prepared	1	2	3	4	5
9. Maintained a good pace	1	2	3	4	5
10. Created a productive learning environment	1	2	3	4	5
11. Was responsive to my concerns	1	2	3	4	5
12. Facilitated discussion effectively	1	2	3	4	5

Any other comments on the program?

   _____

   _____

Thank you!

Timing of Evaluations

Most designers of training evaluations focus on four key measurement points in the learning process. Which or how many of these are used for a particular program depends on the aims of the evaluators and the degree of thoroughness required. Evaluations often are done at the following points:

1. Pre-training: This type of evaluation is often conducted to establish a baseline measurement of the trainees' knowledge and skills. It may also be used to confirm the appropriateness of the planned/ projected program content and objectives.
2. During training: Periodic spot checks may be done, formally or informally, while the training program is in progress. These enable the trainer to make corrections in the direction, approach, or pace of the course. This is especially useful in multi-day programs.
3. Post-training: Most frequently, training is evaluated immediately following the program. This timing helps capture trainee opinions, reactions, and feelings while they are fresh.
4. Follow-up: The evaluation process may include an assessment of the long-term impact of the training program by having trainees complete a survey six months to a year following their program. Typically, it measures subsequent changes in the performance of the learners based on feedback from their supervisors or from the content of self-reports.

Some Cautions

Your evaluation efforts are much more likely to be effective if you avoid some common mistakes made by purchasers of intercultural services. The first pitfall is to accept a provider's evaluation process and instruments without question or discussion. Actively involving yourself in the selection and design of evaluation methods and tools is essential to ensure that your company's requirements are met and that its resources have been spent wisely. Most suppliers would be pleased to have your involvement in this area.

Another error is to rely too heavily on trainee reactions to judge the success of programs. Glowing evaluation questionnaires, sometimes called "happy sheets," do not necessarily correlate with objective measurements of learning. This does not mean that bored or alienated trainees learn well. Positive feelings about a program seem to be a necessary, but not sufficient, condition for its success. Nevertheless, placing too much emphasis on these feelings may encourage trainers to stress entertainment over learning.

A third pitfall is that purchasers sometimes become so focused on the training objectives proposed by the vendors that they fail to refer back to the output of their own needs assessments. The success of the program can be determined only if its objectives are tightly linked to your needs. For example, the original need may have been for your international business travelers to negotiate more effectively with Brazilian business counterparts. If the supplier's training objective focused on "learning to do business in Brazil," your need may or may not have been met. Obviously, if an adequate needs assessment was not conducted, no meaningful evaluation can be done.

Support for evaluation of training programs often is undermined because the questionnaires are long and complicated, or they are administered too frequently. In these cases, trainees tend to respond to them superficially and perfunctorily, if at all. The amount and quality of information obtained are generally increased when you strictly limit the questions to high-priority topics. Exercising restraint by eliminating extra "nice to know" items will enhance the evaluation process. Likewise, you should avoid surveying the same people more than is absolutely necessary.

Another way support is lost is when the evaluation findings apparently are not applied to solving the company's intercultural problems. Trainees need to know that their input and recommendations have been considered and that some of them actually have been used to make improvements. Reporting to employees how their feedback has made a difference is an easy and effective way to increase the level of their cooperation. Future program attendees also will be more responsive if they believe that evaluation is a meaningful exercise.

Applying Findings

Different stakeholders can use the findings produced by evaluations in a variety ways. Ask yourself who needs the information and how they can best apply it to improve the overall learning process. Summary evaluation reports should be given to key in-house sponsors of the intercultural services to help strengthen their support. Your training managers and administrators are likely to be interested in the outcomes of the programs. Likewise, the supervisors of the "graduates" should be advised what their subordinates learned by attending the courses. This will encourage them to reinforce and reward the attendees' new intercultural knowledge, skills, and attitudes on the job and use these assets for the benefit of your organization or company.

The findings also should be shared with the program participants to demonstrate to them that their input is being used. However, probably the most important application is giving feedback to your providers' trainers, program designers, curriculum developers, administrators, and managers for fine-tuning future programs. The final step is to revisit your original objectives and reassess your needs in light of what you have learned from the evaluation process.

Giving Feedback to Suppliers

Webster's New World College Dictionary defines feedback as "a process in which the factors that produce a result are themselves modified, corrected, or strengthened by that result." Giving feedback to your providers is essential for helping them improve their performance and for maintaining a robust, healthy relationship with them. One of the main reasons for gathering evaluation data is to share it with suppliers and to discuss how improvements may be made. Virtually all vendors of intercultural services are eager to please their clients. They will want to know how they can support you better. Therefore, your feedback will be welcomed in most cases. If you should encounter resistance, you might remind them of the Rotary International motto: "He profits most who serves best."

Rules for Feedback

Ineffective attempts to give feedback can easily cause defensiveness and resistance to change on the part of the recipient. These reactions are the opposite of what the giver intends and desires. You can increase the likelihood that your feedback will be well received and that it will have a positive impact if you know the qualities of effective feedback and apply the basic rules that follow.

Expected

Ideally, both parties should perceive feedback as a normal and fundamental aspect of their relationship. This expectation needs to be fostered from the very beginning and reinforced as the relationship develops. By becoming a regular, even routine, way in which you and your supplier communicate with each other, feedback sheds the negative connotation it sometimes has. The goal is that it becomes "no big deal" in both of your minds.

Two-Directional

Even though, as customer, you obviously have the most power in the relationship, feedback needs to flow in both directions in order to be effective. In many cases, the success of intercultural services depends on quick responses by both the client and supplier to solve problems. Therefore, receiving feedback from providers, as well as giving it, is in your own interest. Also, demonstrating that you welcome feedback is a very effective way to encourage the same attitude on their part.

Balanced

Too often feedback is seen as criticism in a negative sense and is mentioned only when there is a deficiency of some kind to be corrected. In a healthy relationship feedback also conveys positive messages, not only negative ones. You should use it to motivate and reward your providers in addition to helping them to identify and solve problems. This balanced approach will be an incentive for them to accept feedback.

Helpful Intent

Whether feedback is positive or negative, its purpose is to be helpful and nonthreatening to the party receiving it. Therefore, feedback is not meant to be a means for the giver to vent feelings or relieve stress. Expressing or displaying frustration, displeasure, and disapproval is not feedback. Likewise, to be constructive, feedback should focus on something (a behavior, practice, procedure, or policy) that your vendor is able to change.

Objective

Feedback should be based on data, facts, and objective information upon which you and your vendor agree. Both quantitative and qualitative data are appropriate, but personal impressions and subjective opinions are not useful. For these reasons, clear, specific, and explicit objectives and measurement indicators are required. If these conditions are met, little opportunity exists for disputing the accuracy of the feedback.

Goal-Referenced

The content of feedback should be tied to the goals and objectives that were originally established and agreed upon. It generally focuses on the extent to which the goals were achieved and on the efficiency and effectiveness of the means used to accomplish them. Extraneous topics and issues should be avoided because they detract from this central focus.

Nonjudgmental

Although feedback is related to the evaluation process, it does not include making or expressing value judgments about "good and bad" or "right and wrong." Feedback describes behavior and performance but does not attribute moral qualities or motives to people. Keeping your feedback value-free in this sense helps avoid triggering defensiveness and denial on the part of your suppliers. However, this does not mean that you downplay the consequences of a supplier's failure to use the feedback to correct problems identified.

Timely

Periodic feedback sessions between you and your provider should be a regular part of the relationship. Depending on the volume of services, these could be done on a monthly or quarterly basis. The key is to set aside and commit to a designated time. In cases where feedback is required due to an unforeseen event, it should be given as soon as possible so the facts and circumstances are fresh.

Assisting Suppliers

Helping your suppliers do their best for your company or organization is the rationale for giving them assistance. Working with them to prevent or solve problems is a logical extension of evaluation and feedback. It also strengthens often your relationship and sense of teamwork. The amount and nature of the help you provide obviously will depend on the type of problems discovered and the time and resources you have available. The following are a few of the ways in which clients have found it worthwhile to invest in supporting their providers.

Giving Company Orientations

Taking the initiative to ensure that your suppliers understand as much as possible about your company or organization's products, services, operations, and management culture makes a great deal of sense. The credibility of their trainers, consultants, and counselors and the relevance of what they contribute will be significantly enhanced if they have this knowledge. You should send your providers documents such as annual reports, marketing brochures, and product descriptions. Likewise, you could share with them videotapes used to orient your new employees. You might invite them to attend portions of in-house meetings or conferences that would help them understand your international vision and goals. A visit to a production facility might also be instructive. And, you should insist that their key staff review your Web site, if one exists. Learning about clients is their responsibility, but any assistance you can give them usually has excellent payoffs.

Providing Program Design Support

While programs are in the early stage of development, you should help your providers set the learning objectives and select the training activities. Spending the time required to help them define and fine-tune program designs is a good investment because it results in the learning activities being tailored to meet the intercultural needs you have identified. Any real examples or short case studies of intercultural problems faced by your employees that you can provide will make the training more relevant. Your assistance is most essential in the areas of program objectives and content, but your guidance regarding which methods and techniques are most appropriate for your employees is also important.

The key in providing program design support is to be actively engaged in the process rather than merely being a passive "consumer" of programs.

Facilitating Information Exchange
Intercultural service providers and practitioners vary greatly in their levels of sophistication and capacity in the management and sharing of business information. In many cases, they have come from nonbusiness backgrounds: Their strengths often lie in teaching and training, not management. Nevertheless, they may be very talented and effective interculturalists. Therefore, it might be worthwhile for you to suggest ways to upgrade their program booking and billing systems and procedures. Deficiencies in these areas are likely to have a direct negative impact on your business communications and undermine your relationship.

These problems might be avoided or lessened if you are able to furnish some timely technical assistance. In particular, advice and consultation in management information system design and training department administration could be very beneficial. Establishing electronic links for the requisitioning, booking, scheduling, and billing of services, recommending the required hardware and software, and providing training are ways to greatly facilitate the information exchange.

Problem-Solving
Problems are inevitable given the complexity of intercultural services and the pressured environment in which they frequently are delivered. The client's response when problems occur reflects the quality of the teamwork it has built with its providers. A senior international human resources executive of a major entertainment corporation advises, "Don't fire them for failing to live up to unspoken expectations and unspecified needs; fire them if they fail to live up to clearly delineated and communicated expectations and needs." If it becomes necessary to terminate a service contract, your decision and the reasons for it should not come as a surprise to the supplier. Giving them clear feedback on a regular basis as recommended will avoid such an unpleasant end to your relationship with them.

Generally, it is not wise (or fair) to drop suppliers the first time they fail. To do so wastes the time and energy you have invested in them. It may inhibit their successors' creativity and willingness to accept challenging assignments. In the long term, that may be more damaging than a single incident of failure. Most vendors will give you greater loyalty and dedication if, instead of seeking to establish blame or threatening punishment, you take initiative to determine the cause of problems and to work together to solve them.

Provider Partnership

The degree of closeness and collaboration between clients and suppliers varies greatly. At one end of the spectrum, services and products are considered commodities to be bought on a completely impersonal basis. At the other end, relationships with vendors are viewed as business alliances, and providers are treated as "partners." During the 1990s, most articles on supplier management recommended partnering as the preferred option. The typical rationale is that value-added results such as increased vendor loyalty and responsiveness, better service, synergy, and long-term benefits can be obtained.

Many executives responsible for purchasing goods, products, and services for their corporations seem to agree. For example, Raymond Greer, Senior Vice President and General Manager of Global Operations of Ryder Integrated Logistics, was quoted in CIO magazine recently. He advised, "The word *vendor* implies a transaction. I've never referred to my technical partners as vendors. That would suggest the mind-set that this relationship is just a transaction, and that's not how I want them approaching the job." Likewise, Jeff Winston, Vice President of IS Technology and Operations of Allergen, Inc. said, "We try to treat vendors as if they were an extension of Allergen's staff. If you treat vendors like a third party, then they will behave like a third party."

In deciding which model of vendor relationship makes sense for your company or organization, you should consider at what point on the spectrum a win-win scenario is most likely. If you opt for "partnership," that concept must be more than a catchword that masks a traditional buyer-seller relationship. It requires balancing the needs and interests of both parties and implies the idea of shared risks, rewards, and mutual strategies. Although establishing provider partnerships is not easy, the payoffs make it worthwhile for you to try.

Improving Provider Performance Focus Questions
☑ Have you defined standards of provider performance? If so, how do you measure them?

(continued on page 294)

☑ Have you communicated them to your suppliers? Do they accept the standards?

☑ Does your evaluation process link program outcomes to the learning objectives? Are the objectives linked to the needs identified by your needs assessment process?

☑ Do you intend to play an active role in the evaluation process? If not, why not?

☑ Have you created a favorable environment for giving and receiving feedback?

☑ Who should receive evaluation reports? How will your organization use the evaluation findings?

☑ Do you see the value of assisting your providers? Is there in-house support for doing so?

☑ Do your providers understand your company or organization well enough to provide high-quality service?

☑ How efficient is your exchange of business information?

☑ Do your suppliers welcome your help? If not, why not?

☑ Does your company or organization treat its suppliers as "partners?" If not, why not?

☑ How can you best create win-win scenarios with them?

Summary and Suggested Action Steps

This chapter contains guidance on how to establish and manage effective relationships with your service providers. The focus is on teamwork, synergy, and win-win scenarios. Tips are offered for preventing and resolving common problems in client-vendor relations, and criteria are given for evaluating and improving provider performance. Overall, the aim of the chapter is to promote a standard of high-quality, cost-effective service and productive, harmonious collaboration.

Here are some ways you can use the content of this chapter:

1. Define your ideal provider(s), taking into account the needs, circumstances, and culture of your organization or company.
2. Check with your colleagues and build an in-house consensus regarding the type of provider that would be most appropriate.
3. Consult with your counterparts in other organizations about the nature of their relations with vendors of intercultural services.

4. Use the models for client-supplier teamwork to structure and manage relations with your providers.
5. Review the common pitfalls and problems in client-supplier relations in order to avoid these difficulties.
6. Apply the advice on evaluation and feedback to ensure a consistently high level of provider performance.
7. Consider using a qualified third-party evaluator.
8. Use evaluation summaries and comments from program participants to promote interest in intercultural training. You may post this type of information on your intranet or publish it in your in-house newsletters.

Resources

Client-Supplier Relations

Baldwin, H. "Vendor Relations Overview: Is There a Happily Ever After?" *CIO*, Aug. 1, 1998, pp. 30–33.

Ellram, L. M. "A Managerial Guideline for the Development and Implementation of Purchasing Partnerships." *The Journal of Supply Chain Management*, Vol. 3, No. 2, Spring 1995, pp. 9–16.

Field, T. "Vendor Relations: Breaking Up Is Hard To Do." *CIO*, Aug. 1, 1998, pp. 52–54.

Field, T. "Vendor Relations: Tying the Knot for Better or Worse." *CIO*, Aug. 1, 1998, pp. 44–51.

Foster, R. D. "Strategic Expatriate Management through Outsourcing." *Mobility*, Mar. 1997, pp. 39–40.

Gruner, S. "The Smart Vendor Audit Checklist." *Inc.*, Apr. 1995, p. 93.

Landeros, R., and Plank, R. E. "Maintaining Buyer-Supplier Partnerships." *The Journal of Supply Chain Management*, Vol. 3, No. 3, Summer 1995, pp. 2–10.

Lewis, J. D. *The Connected Corporation: How Leading Companies Win through Customer-Supplier Alliances.* New York: Simon & Schuster Free Press, 1995.

Maurer, R. "Outsourcing—Today It Has a Whole New Meaning." *Human Resource Professional*, Vol. 11, No. 6, Nov./Dec. 1998, pp. 17–20.

Outsourcing Institute. "Creating New Business Synergies through Outsourcing." *Business Week*, Nov. 23, 1998, special section.

Schell, M. S., and Stern, E. M. "Outsourcing Your International Relocation Program: What To Consider." *International HR Journal*, Vol. 5, No. 2, Summer 1996, pp. 53–57.

Stuart, F. I. "Supplier Partnerships: Influencing Factors and Strategic Benefits." *The Journal of Supply Chain Management*, Vol. 29, No. 4, Fall 1993, pp.21–28.

Van Mieghem, T. *Implementing Supplier Partnerships: How To Lower Cost and Improve Service.* Englewood Cliffs, NJ: Prentice-Hall, Inc., 1995.

Evaluating Supplier Performance

Blake, B. F., Brislin, R., and Curtis, S. C. "Measuring Impacts of Cross-Cultural Training." In D. Landis and R. S. Bhagat (eds.), *Handbook of Intercultural Training.* (2nd ed.) Thousand Oaks, CA: Sage Publications, Inc., 1996, pp. 441–464.

Bragg, D. D. "Working Together To Evaluate Training." In J. H. Woods and J. W. Cortada (eds.), *1997 ASTD Training and Performance Yearbook.* New York: McGraw-Hill, 1997, pp. 345–353.

Brethower, D. "Level IV Evaluation: Why, What, & How." In J. H. Woods and J. W. Cortada (eds.), *1997 ASTD Training and Performance Yearbook.* New York: McGraw-Hill, 1997, pp. 322–331.

Brewster, C., and Pickard, J. "Evaluating Expatriate Training." *International Studies of Management & Organization.*, Vol. 24, No. 3, Fall 1994, pp. 69–79.

Dixon, N. M. "New Routes to Evaluation." In J. H. Woods and J. W. Cortada (eds.), *1997 ASTD Training and Performance Yearbook.* New York: McGraw-Hill, 1997, pp. 354–359.

Keller, J. M., and Young, A. *Evaluating Diversity Training.* San Francisco, CA: Jossey-Bass Inc., 1995.

Kirkpatrick, D. L. "Evaluation." In R. L. Craig (ed.), *ASTD Training and Development Handbook.* (4th ed.) New York: McGraw-Hill, 1996, pp. 294–312.

Kohls, R. L., with Brussow H. L. *Training Know-How for Cross-Cultural and Diversity Trainers.* Duncanville, TX: Adult Learning Systems, Inc., 1995, pp. 179–190.

Kohls, R. L., and Knight J. M. *Developing Intercultural Awareness: A Cross-Cultural Training Handbook*. (2nd ed.) Yarmouth, MA: Intercultural Press, Inc., 1994, pp. 123–126.

Mager, R. F. *Measuring Instructional Results: How To Find Out If Your Instructional Objectives Have Been Achieved*. (3rd ed.) Atlanta, GA: Center for Effective Performance Press, 1997.

Phillips, J. J. *The Handbook of Training Evaluation and Measurement Methods*. (3rd ed.) Houston, TX: Gulf Publishing Company, 1997.

Phillips, J. J. "Measuring the Results of Training." In R. L. Craig (ed.), *ASTD Training and Development Handbook*. (4th ed.) New York: McGraw-Hill, 1996, pp. 313–341.

Pruegger, V. J., and Rogers, T. B. "Cross-Cultural Sensitivity Training: Methods and Assessment." *International Journal of Intercultural Relations*. Vol. 18, 1994, pp. 369–387.

Rae, L. *Evaluation Approaches for Training and Development: A Complete Resource Kit*. London: Kogan Page Press, 1997.

Sims, R. R. *Reinventing Training and Development*. Westport, CT: Quorum Books, 1998. See "Training Evaluation," pp. 113–156.

Training Magazine. *Evaluating Training's Impact*. Minneapolis, MN: Lakewood Publications, 1996.

Wynne, B., and Clutterbuck, D. "Using Evaluation Techniques." In J. Prior (ed.), *Gower Handbook of Training and Development*. (2nd ed.) Brookfield, VT: Gower Publishing Company Limited, 1994, pp. 230–242.

10

The Case for Intercultural Services

What ever is worth doing at all is worth doing well.

Earl of Chesterfield

Promoting Services In-House

Frequently, the managers responsible for the productivity and morale of cross-border employees are convinced that their companies and organizations require intercultural services. However, they may face skepticism and resistance on the part of key decision-makers who must approve the purchase of services. Advocates need compelling rationale and evidence that purchasing intercultural programs and products is a worthwhile investment of resources in order to "sell" them in-house. They must be prepared to answer questions such as "Why are intercultural services necessary?" "What do we gain by using them or lose by not doing so?" "Do they really work?" "Are they cost-effective?"

The fundamental rationale for using intercultural services is that they are required in order to conduct cross-border business effectively. This rationale is based on doing the *right* thing for your people from a humanistic perspective and doing the *smart* thing for your company or organization from a cost-benefit perspective. These two factors have powerful impacts on international success or failure. And, in many ways, they are tightly interwoven. Giving high-priority attention to both of them is a hallmark of a globally competitive organization. However, knowing what are the *right* things and the *smart* things to do depends on your understanding of the cross-cultural demands on your people and organization.

The global arena is qualitatively and substantially different than your employees' domestic environment. New knowledge, skills, and attitudes are required on the part of those who hope to survive and thrive globally. Basic common sense and concern for your employees dictate giving them the tools they must have in order to succeed. To present a persuasive case for buying intercultural services, you should arm yourself with evidence that the human and financial costs of failing to do so are prohibitive. In addition, you must convince decision-makers that significant potential gains and competitive advantages are possible for those companies and organizations that do use these services (see Exhibit 10–1). The following downside and upside considerations can provide you with "ammunition" for developing your rationale.

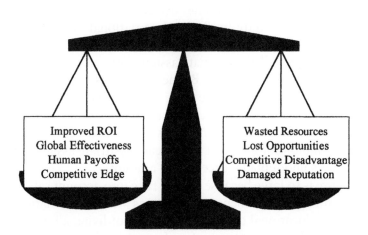

Improved ROI	Wasted Resources
Global Effectiveness	Lost Opportunities
Human Payoffs	Competitive Disadvantage
Competitive Edge	Damaged Reputation

Utilizing the Services   **Neglecting the Services**

EXHIBIT 10–1. THE CASE FOR INTERCULTURAL SERVICES.

The Downside Considerations

Risk comes from not knowing what you're doing.

Warren Buffett
prominent investor and chairman of
Berkshire Hathaway

The first set of arguments in favor of using intercultural services hinges on considering what is likely to be lost or wasted by not doing so. The potential for damage may be less important, in the long run, than the possibility of benefits to be gained, but identified risks usually command the attention of key decision-makers. Examining the amount of investment your organization or company has made in its international ventures and assessing the likelihood and costs (financial and human) of failure are good starting points for developing a compelling rationale.

Protecting Investments at Risk

Many needs for intercultural services are generated by the international relocation of employees and their families. How well they are selected, trained, supported, and guided has a great impact on both the people deployed and the business outcomes sought. The cost of relocating employees and their families overseas represents a very large investment at risk. A study by Berlitz International and HFS Mobility Services, the "1996–97 International Assignee Research Project," reports that a single failed expatriate assignment can cost a corporation well over $1,000,000. Richard Bahner, who was Global Human Resources Director at AT&T at the time, mentioned this figure as early as 1994. A senior expatriate services manager at ALCOA was quoted in the January 1995 issue of *HR News* as saying that her company budgeted $1.3 million for a typical three-year expatriate assignment. Current expenses undoubtedly exceed that amount.

The figure is so large because it must take into account salaries, benefits, and foreign assignment premiums, as well as international relocation fees, educational costs, housing, cost of living allowances, and foreign taxes. For example, the fees for a school year in the international high school in Geneva, Switzerland, range from $18,000–

$20,000 per student. In some cases, expatriates also receive completion incentive payments and hardship or danger bonuses. In addition, certain high-price locations such as Tokyo, Brussels, Mexico City, and Hong Kong drive up the average cost of expatriate assignments. In 1996, according to Lynn Holms of Prudential Relocation Global Services, a typical US manager's total annual compensation in Hong Kong easily could reach $600,000. When a company has numerous international assignments, these expenses quickly become a very significant cost of doing business.

The Financial Costs of Failure

If a family fails to adjust to their host country and must be brought home prematurely, all that has been invested in them is lost. Furthermore, new expenses are required to prepare and send their replacements. Therefore, keeping your expatriate attrition as low as possible is an important business priority. The actual worldwide average failure rate of US international assignees is difficult to determine. Various surveys during the 1990s have reported widely differing results. The lowest figure for failed assignments was reported by *Personnel Journal* in 1993 at around 5%. The February, 1995, issue of *International Business* noted that as many as 40% of US managers did not complete their assignments. Other surveys have indicated attrition rates in the 20–30% range. What is clear is that even a single failed overseas assignment is exceedingly expensive and well worth preventing by proper selection, training, and support.

A real, but hidden, cost to international companies is the "brown out" effect. Many expatriate employees perform at suboptimal levels. Handicapped by the lack of the intercultural knowledge and skills they need and not possessing the appropriate attitudes to gain the cooperation and support of their host-country counterparts, they accomplish much less than they should. Also, concerns about the adjustment difficulties of their spouses and family members may distract them from their focus on work.

No rigorous studies have been made, but researchers Allan Bird and Edward Dunbar have estimated that 30–50% of expatriates function at a minimal level of effectiveness. Considering the high cost of sending these people abroad and maintaining them there, their low level of productivity is especially regrettable. It does not make good business sense to go to the expense of sending your employees to other countries without giving them the tools and support they need to perform well there.

Aborted and ineffective overseas assignments add to the overall cost of international business in other ways. The unfortunate circumstances of an employee's early return may make a very negative impression on potential expatriates. They frequently conclude that international assignments are difficult, risky, and likely to be damaging to their careers. This makes them consider overseas postings undesirable. Unfortunately, that assumption tends to increase their demands for salary and benefits to compensate for the perceived risk, which raises the cost to the company of future assignments. In addition, this assumption causes the most talented employees to avoid being sent abroad—a serious handicap for a company or organization trying to "go global."

Understanding the reasons for expatriate failure is essential to finding the means to reduce it. With regard to the causes of early returns, the surveys vary somewhat. Many of them, such as a 1998 study by Atlas Van Lines, have pointed to lifestyle adjustment difficulties of the employee's spouse or partner as the number one reason. A survey by Living Abroad Publishing, Inc., reported that the top three causes were that the assignee was unable to adjust to the culture, that the family was unable to adjust to life abroad, and that the employee faced cross-cultural difficulties on the job.

Most studies have agreed that the cultural adaptation challenge outweighed other factors such as compensation, working and living conditions, location, or length of assignment. For example, a 1995 survey by Prudential Relocation Intercultural Services found that 35% of respondents listed cross-cultural adaptability and flexibility as key success factors compared to 22% who cited job, technical, and management skills.

Looking at expatriate selection practices as a factor in failed international assignments, a survey by the NFTC and Selection Resources International stressed the impact of faulty staffing decisions. Too often candidates were selected because of their availability rather than their suitability. In addition, they found that having long tenure and being well-known within the company often was more important than having a record of high performance. In some cases, line managers overruled the cautions and concerns expressed about candidates by the in-house human resource professionals.

In general, too little attention has been given to the psychological suitability of candidates for overseas assignments. According to the *1997 Survey of Human Resource Trends* report by Aon Consulting, only 11% of the 1,700 US international organizations surveyed used a psychological profile in their expatriate selection process. Because the technology for rigorous assessment is available, this low level of use by multinational companies is a mistake and an overlooked opportunity to protect their investments in overseas assignments.

Another point at which the international assignment can fail is upon return. Even successful expatriates may leave their companies if their repatriation is not handled well. The loss of status and benefits compared to what they enjoyed overseas and the unexpected stress of having to readjust to life and work at home cause many to them to experience "reentry shock." In some cases this problem is made worse because they feel that their international knowledge is not recognized, used, or valued. As a result of these factors, organizations and companies lose employees who have gained precious (and costly) global savvy.

RHR International, a human resources consulting firm, cited a survey by the Institute of International Human Resources indicating that only 15% of expatriates felt their reentry had been handled well by their employers. In 1998, *CFO* magazine reported the staggering statistic that roughly 40% of repatriated employees switch employers within two years of returning to the US. This large drain of internationally experienced managers reflects a serious failure of transnational organizations and companies to plan and manage their expatriates' career paths effectively. It is also a waste of their investments in the overseas assignments. Despite the magnitude of the problem, only 38% of companies surveyed in a 1997 study by Arthur Andersen and Bennett Associates provided formal repatriation programs.

The Human Impact of Failure

Aside from the financial losses caused by the failure of international corporations and organizations to equip their expatriates with the intercultural tools they need, there is a heavy human cost. Employees' marriages are put under stress, their careers are damaged, and their self-concepts are harmed. Settler International, a worldwide relocation assistance company, reports that the divorce rate among expatriate couples is 40% higher than their domestic counterparts and that the school dropout rate of their children is 50% higher than in their home countries. The tragedy is that most of these unhappy outcomes could have been prevented with proper assessment, selection, counseling, training, and overseas support. Your employees' goodwill and trust are very valuable assets. Too often, the mishandling of international assignments squanders them.

Cross-Border Business Pitfalls

Another set of rationale relates to the cross-cultural pitfalls facing your employees who do business in other countries without living abroad. They not only have to function competently as business people within unfamiliar cultural environments, but they must also act as informal ambassadors. How well they play these two roles often determines the reputation and financial success of your company and organization overseas. If they fail, your company or organization has wasted the cost of their trips, but the major loss is the lack of fulfillment of international business potential—the opportunities lost as a result of the traveler's lack of intercultural skills.

Lost Opportunities

The cost of international business opportunities lost due to cross-cultural incompetence is huge but incalculable. This kind of loss is extremely difficult to document, much less to measure. Inept international business people generally are unaware of, or minimize, the cultural causes of their failures. Frequently, they attribute their problems to the attitudes of their foreign counterparts or the "unusual" circumstances surrounding their dealings with them. And, in any case, lack of success is seldom advertised. Therefore, the size and impact of the lost opportunities have to be estimated indirectly and on a case-by-case basis.

For example, two US aerospace companies were competing for a major contract with the Canadian Air Force in the late 1980s. The technical performance of the fighter aircraft from both of the manufacturers met the requirements of the customer, and their prices were very similar. However, one vendor used a fairly aggressive "hard sell" approach, and the other invested in relationship-building and used a consultative sales approach. Other considerations being more or less equal, the Canadians selected the company whose marketing and negotiating styles were most compatible with their own cultural values.

The result was a multimillion dollar deal lost by one company and gained by another largely on the basis of intercultural competence. If this can happen in dealings between US and Canadian counterparts, it is undoubtedly a much greater risk in situations where the cultural differences are greater. After experiencing this setback, the company that lost the sale started using intercultural training on a regular basis as a way to increase its international competitiveness.

In another case, a major fast food chain missed an opportunity to significantly expand its business in Mexico. The newly appointed vice president, who had a reputation for hard-driving efficiency in the US domestic market, was assigned Mexico as part of his territory. During his first visit to Mexico City to meet current and potential franchisees, he kept them waiting for a half hour while he went to his hotel room to check and respond to his e-mail. His rationale was that Mexicans have a reputation for being late to meetings so he had no need to be on time. Unfortunately, the potential franchisees (serious business people of high social standing) were greatly offended by his behavior. Expecting him to be punctual, they felt that he was acting arrogantly, and few of them chose to do business with him. Subsequently, his company sent him for individualized, "remedial" cross-cultural business training.

You are likely to find some cultural causes of lost international sales or unsuccessfully negotiated cross-border contracts in your own company or organization if you carefully debrief the business travelers involved and analyze the processes and outcomes from an intercultural perspective. Identifying real examples of wasted opportunities and sharing them with your colleagues is an excellent way to highlight the importance of cross-cultural issues. Using other cases in your industry or area of specialization also is a credible way to create awareness.

False Starts

Even if international sales are made and agreements are successfully concluded, cross-border commercial deals may become undone in their initial stages due to the cross-cultural deficiencies of those who must seek repeat sales, implement the contracts, and build positive relationships with the overseas customers or partners. Anthropologist Michael Agar was called in as a consultant to a newly formed alliance of Mexican and US partners who had established a business to distribute rebuilt diesel engine parts in Mexico. He reported in an article in the *International Journal of Intercultural Relations* that the project

" . . . had ground to a halt." Only after he had established a friendship with one of the Mexican partners did he discover that the crisis was due to a lack of trust on the part of the Mexicans. From their point of view, the US business travelers were too blunt, excessively task-oriented, and impersonal. It required some intense intercultural communications facilitating to get the venture back on track.

The dramatic failure of Unidata, the European company formed to challenge IBM's domination of the global computer market, was a false start on a much larger scale. It was a high-profile alliance of Dutch, German, and French computer producers. Many multicultural business and technical teams were formed. After several years of acrimonious in-fighting, the entire venture was dissolved without launching a single product. Another memorable failure was the aborted joint venture of Siemens and Westinghouse. They planned to team up to sell a wide range of industrial automation and control systems worldwide. The project never survived the protracted negotiations. The announced cause, "lack of common ground between the partners," has long been a code expression for cross-cultural misunderstanding and friction. A spectacular case in the automobile industry was the collapse of the proposed merger of Renault and Volvo companies. According to the January 1994 issue of *Ward's Automotive International*, the deal failed due to "overwhelming cultural differences."

Failures in Follow-Through

Most international business efforts must be sustained over the long term for their full payoffs to be realized. This implies that effective on-going maintenance of cross-cultural relationships is required. The high failure rate of cross-border joint ventures described in Chapter 4 is strong evidence that more emphasis needs to be placed on the knowledge, attitudes, and skills that international employees need to avoid failures in follow-through.

According to a 1995 Columbia University study, 57% of cross-cultural joint ventures end in failure. Their average life span was only three and a half years. A survey of 200 companies in 60 industries conducted by Larraine Segil, reported in the November 1998 issue of *Global Workforce* magazine, stressed that cross-border alliances are much more challenging than domestic ones. She found that they take two to three times longer to create and at least half of them fail. Seventy-five percent of the companies surveyed believed the failures were caused by incompatibility of national or corporate cultures.

Many such disasters occur because the due diligence is focused on legal and financial considerations as opposed to cultural ones, according to Jacalyn Sherriton, president of Corporate Management Developers, Inc., a post-merger consulting firm. A Coopers and Lybrand/Yankelovich survey in the mid–1990s reported that as many as 5,000 hours are typically required to create an international joint venture and that only about 4% of that time is focused on human resource issues including training. The negligible emphasis placed on the cultural interaction needs of the people engaged in these ventures seems a very unwise decision considering the risks and challenges they face. Many, perhaps most, of the failures might have been prevented if the investment made in creating these ventures had been protected by providing effective intercultural training, coaching, and support.

Damaged International Images

The public image and reputation of your company or organization is an important asset abroad. The impressions your international business travelers make on host-country counterparts, customers, associates, and partners determine, to a very large extent, the success or failure of your ventures in their countries. For example, if your representatives are perceived as being sophisticated, well-informed, and cross-culturally competent, attracting and retaining talented local employees will be easier. In the increasingly tight labor market for internationally experienced managers in Asia and Latin America, this is an important advantage. With a good local image, your company or organization is unlikely to be seen as an easy target to be manipulated or exploited and might be considered a good candidate for a joint venture partnership. If, however, your people (expatriates and business visitors) are viewed as being arrogant, naive, and culturally ill prepared, the opposite is true.

Unfortunately, the image of the "ugly American" is still far too prevalent overseas. Reactions from local people in many places around the world strongly indicate that more intercultural training of US international personnel is required. For example, a local Czech business person is quoted in a February 26, 1997, article in *USA Today* as saying that he has seen coworkers driven to tears by the rugged management style of some US companies. In the same article, Patricia Digh, editor of two global human resource newsletters, asserted that, "Too many US managers believe US culture can be exported as the world's culture."

In her book *Management in Two Cultures*, Eva Kras quotes a local CFO of a US company's operation in Mexico. He said, "I have great admiration for the technical knowledge and administrative skills of the North Americans. However, when they attempt to impose their methods on us, incredible problems arise and we all feel frustrated and resentful but don't know what to do about it. In my experience, the US executive seems to be a cold, impersonal, discourteous, and critical individual. His main objective seems to be to dehumanize business as much as possible, and to convert people into robots."

An article in the March 10, 1997, issue of *Forbes*, entitled "Damn Yankees," reveals the negative images US international business people have with local executives in 11 countries. A Colombian executive said, "What drives me crazy is the American need for information—right now! Americans are too straightforward, too direct." The senior vice president of a Japanese company adds, "We would do more business with Americans if there were more consistency, more trust." A Swiss CEO felt that American executives tend to oversell themselves and that they are sometimes too quick to make decisions.

Larry Caldwell, an intercultural business trainer, reports that some of his German clients complain that US business people fail to respect the "wall" separating their work time and their personal time by calling them after working hours or on the weekends at home. He adds that many Europeans feel that US Americans are far too informal and use first names too quickly. According to consultant Greg Nees, German business people often think US counterparts are making false promises when they are merely talking about possibilities with a confident "can do" attitude.

Farid Elashmawi, an Egyptian interculturalist, quotes some of his Asian colleagues as saying about Americans "When they need you, they are your buddy. When they do not need you, you are nobody." Swiss management consultant Raymond Saner comments that during international negotiation sessions he observed "The American's need to be in control often exceeds the non-American's tolerance for subservience." Noel Miner, intercultural specialist on China, quotes a Chinese business executive saying, "Many business people from the United States seem to be in such a rush. They may only spend two to three days in my country. Often I have to spend several days meeting with my staff after one of these visits to determine how we will respond to the 'suggestions' made by the Americans."

Ed Ockerby of the Research Institute Group, a human resources information company, admits that he was " ... embarrassed by seeing many of my fellow Americans throwing their weight around during my 13 years abroad as a expatriate." It is important to keep in mind that most of these negative impressions are caused by conflicting cultural values and expectations combined with insufficient international savvy on the part of many Americans. Likewise, it is not accurate or fair to exaggerate the negative image of US business people abroad. Many of their traits such as optimism, industriousness, inventiveness, decisiveness, enthusiasm, and friendliness are mentioned in positive ways. Nevertheless, it is worthwhile to be aware of the negative perceptions of foreign counterparts and to make sure that your cross-border employees, expatriates, and international travelers are not adding to them.

Underestimated Obstacles
Surveys of the obstacles facing US business people abroad present a similar picture. An Ernst & Young survey reported in the September 25, 1994, *Houston Chronicle* confirmed that the biggest barrier to expansion of the respondents' business overseas is the "lack of understanding of foreign customers and markets." A poll of 100 firms by Kroll Associates was described in the July/August 1997 issue of *International Business*. Two-thirds of the companies had entered new international markets during the past year, and two-thirds of these were experiencing difficulties operating overseas. "Not knowing enough about local business partners" was an issue for 52% of them and "not knowing the unwritten rules in foreign countries" was an issue for 49%.

The Institute of International Education surveyed 217 international firms and banks in the late 1980s. Researcher Stephen Korbrin noted in the report that international managers believed the most important factor contributing to effective management overseas is having cross-cultural people skills. That ability ranked above functional and technical skills, knowledge of the company, and industry. It was considered even more important than having factual information about the host country.

A study of 12 leading multinationals by the International Consortium for Executive Development, in which 1,500 international directors and managers were interviewed in Asia, Europe, and North America, was reported in the May 1995 issue of *International Business*. One of its "surprising" conclusions was that most companies put little emphasis on such issues as managing culturally different workforces, cross-border alliances, transnational teams, and international assignments. Apparently, many corporations are not yet heeding the warnings that cross-cultural incompetence is a serious handicap when doing business globally.

The Upside Considerations

> Opportunities multiply as they are seized.
>
> **Sun Tzu** in *The Art of War*

It is essential to go beyond the damage control mentality when trying to promote the use of intercultural services and products in-house. The benefits and advantages to be obtained probably outweigh the losses and risks of failure. By highlighting the positive rewards and payoffs of intercultural competence, your rationale will appeal to the forward-thinking decision-makers in your organization or company. You can borrow ideas and examples from the best practices of successful global corporations and present the evidence for a positive return on investments made in intercultural services. Likewise, you can report the results of studies that indicate that intercultural training is effective and that employees who have participated in such programs perceive them to be highly valuable. Perhaps, the most potent upside argument is that effective use of intercultural services is a way to gain a competitive edge in the global business arena.

Best Practices

A useful means of promoting intercultural services in-house is to point out what major multinational companies consider the best practices for managing cultural issues in their global operations. Regarding the need to "internationalize" managers' thinking and skills, researchers Brooklyn Derr and Gary Oddou conducted a survey of 105 large European multinational companies. They found that the three most widely used practices were sending home-country employees on developmental expatriate assignments, providing international business seminars, and sending executives on extended cross-border trips for learning purposes.

According to a study of the changing global human resource function by the Conference Board in 1994, "A best-practice recommendation is to provide survival-level instruction prior to departure, with more cultural training once the expatriate is in the country." It advises that " . . . cross-cultural training programs improve expatriates' job performance, adjustment to the new culture, and development of cross-cultural skills." The Conference Board also recommends that companies institute a systematic expatriate selection process and that they actively manage the readjustment of repatriating employees and their families.

The 1996 Conference Board report on managing expatriates' return listed expatriate career-path planning, managing returning expatriates' expectations, and facilitating spouse and family repatriation as best practices. It noted that 76% of the 152 companies participating in the survey provided predeparture briefings that focused on the impact of the international assignment on the spouse and children. However, only 25% had formal repatriation programs.

Many studies and surveys during the 1980s and 1990s stressed the importance of selecting expatriates based on their suitability for international assignments and their cross-cultural adaptability. As a recommended best practice, using a formal selection procedure has steadily grown as the cost of failed overseas assignments has increased. A 1994 benchmark study by the Human Resource Management Association of Chicago found that "only 20% of those responding believe they have selection criteria that are good predictors of success on an overseas assignment." The 1998 Prudential Relocation survey reported that 43% of the responding companies used a "specific selection process for international assignments." Clearly, there is still a gap between the recommendation and application of systematic expatriate selection as a best practice. You can help close that gap by proposing that your company or organization use the best available technology when choosing its international assignees.

The *Global Relocation Trends 1998 Survey Report* of the Windham International and the NFTC found that 70% of the 177 companies responding provided some form of cross-cultural training and that 55% address career planning issues with expatriates. According to survey data, the employment of intercultural training and orientation by international companies has risen to its current level from about 30% during the early 1980s. It now seems generally accepted as a standard component of preparation for expatriate assignments.

Another practice that is growing is the use of external intercultural service providers. The 1999 Windham/NFTC report noted that the percentages for consultant-delivered services were higher in every category compared to the previous year. For example, suppliers conducted 62% of the cross-cultural preparation, whereas only 12% was done in-house. (No preparation was provided in 26% of the cases.) The 1998 ORC *North American Survey of International Assignment Policies and Practices* reported that use of outside consultants more than doubled between 1993 and 1998.

Return on Investment

One way to estimate how well companies are managing their international human capital is to measure their perceived return on investment (ROI) for expatriate assignments. In the 1998 Windham/NFTC survey, executives were asked to judge the success of expatriate assignments in their companies in terms of ROI. Fifty-three percent of the 117 respondents rated it average, 35% rated it good or excellent, and 12% rated it fair or poor.

These moderately positive results reflect the kinds of companies and organizations surveyed and their relatively high level of use of intercultural services. They were mostly experienced internationally and had a collective expatriate population of more than 51,000 employees. According to the 1996 Conference Board report on managing expatriates' return, companies with 55–100 expatriates exhibit lower levels of best practices than do those with fewer than 55 or more than 100 expatriates. Apparently, mid-sized corporations do not prepare their expatriates as well as they could.

Posing questions about ROI is a good way to focus the attention of senior management on the preparation and use of expatriates. In order to do this, however, you will need to gather fairly accurate financial data on your international business profits and losses and on your expatriate compensation and benefits, plus their relocation expenses.

Effectiveness of Training

A key question many potential buyers of intercultural training have is, "Does it really work?" This is not an easy question to answer definitively. To scientifically prove that training makes a positive difference in expatriate or international business traveler performance and productivity, it would be necessary to have experimental and control groups matched in aptitude and background and placed in identical circumstances overseas. All variables, except for training, would have to be the same. Such a rigorous study would be extremely difficult and costly to conduct. Consequently, indisputable "hard" data is not available. Daniel Kealey and David Protheroe reported their assessment of research on this topic in a 1996 article in the *International Journal of Intercultural Relations* (IJIR). They "think it probable that the literature's consensus is objectively correct, (but) it remains a concern that the empirical investigation of the effectiveness issue appears inadequate." Nevertheless, a number of studies strongly suggest that cross-cultural training is effective.

Rabi S. Bhagat and Kristin O. Prien summarized 16 cross-cultural training research studies from 1990 to 1993 in their article, "Cross-Cultural Training in Organizational Contexts," in D. Landis and R. S. Bhagat (eds.), *Handbook of Intercultural Training*, 2nd ed., Thousand Oaks, CA: Sage Publications, Inc., 1996, pp. 216–230. They described results such as "Employee perceptions of overseas assignments more positive and lower costs to organizations if training is provided," "High levels of trainee retention," "Predeparture training has a significant, positive impact on organizational commitment," and "Individuals reporting more adequate training also report higher levels of job satisfaction." Their conclusion was that "Some evidence suggests that training for expatriates will have beneficial consequences for the organization, the individual, and the members of the host country who will come into contact with the expatriate and his or her family."

In a 1991 IJIR article, J. Stewart Black and Mark Mendenhall, two well-known interculturalists, reviewed the research and reported that nine studies showed a positive relation between cross-cultural training and adjustment and that 11 of 15 studies found a significant positive impact on expatriate performance. Previous studies by Earley (1987), Worchel and Mitchell (1972), Lefley (1986), and O'Brien (1970) all used independent measures of performance and found a positive connection between training and performance.

In 1992, researchers Satish Deshpande and Chockalingam Visweswaran conducted a "meta analysis" designed to reduce possible margins of error and to control for differences in sampling procedures.

They concluded in their IJIR article that "Cross-cultural training has a strong and positive impact on cross-cultural skills development, cross-cultural adjustability, and job performance in individuals." They add, "Cross-cultural training in general is effective, and this study should remove any doubts that corporate leaders have about the effects of cross-cultural training."

Although the studies mentioned here may not meet a skeptical manager's desire for "proof," they do offer evidence that a reasonable and open-minded executive would find persuasive. If you combine this kind of information with the other types of rationale in this chapter, you can make a strong case for the effectiveness of intercultural training.

Perceived Value of Intercultural Services

Intercultural services are perceived as useful and helpful both by the people for whom they are purchased and the international human resources managers who buy them. According to the 1998 Windham/ NFTC survey, 85% of the respondents viewed their cross-cultural training programs as positive. From the mid 1980s to the mid 1990s, a major intercultural service provider sent 12-month, follow-up evaluation questionnaires to expatriates who had attended predeparture training programs. After living and working abroad for a full year, 94% indicated they would recommend cross-cultural training to others.

A high level of trainee ratings of intercultural programs was reported by Shirley Fishman, assistant vice president for Executive and International Compensation at Northern Telcom. In the April 1, 1996, issue of *Canadian Business Review*, she described a custom-tailored predeparture program she observed for expatriates bound for China. She noted that the overall satisfaction score from evaluations was 93% and that the participants felt the training built their confidence and improved their preparedness.

Richard Jackson, vice president of personnel for Reynolds International, was so pleased with the results of the cross-cultural services received by his company that he agreed to give a "testimonial" on his provider's marketing videotape. Describing a project in Venezuela involving large numbers of expatriates, he said "We were having a rapid return rate to the United States. Once we got into the program, our return rate dropped to zero and our people made an easier adjustment to living and working in Venezuela." On the same videotape, Jim Fisher, expatriate program coordinator for General Motors, said that his company's expatriates always gave positive feedback following the programs.

The vice president for organization and management development for a major multinational soft drink manufacturer started monitoring expatriate attrition rates in 1992 when his company began using a combination of structured selection procedures and predeparture cross-cultural training. By mid–1995, he had reported no early returns due to cultural adjustment problems in 223 international assignments. Certainly, the benefits of intercultural services were obvious to him. Using testimonials and success stories like those mentioned, especially if they are from companies or organizations similar to yours, is a excellent way to convince reluctant or skeptical decision-makers of the value of the services.

Given the general perception among users that intercultural training is of high value and considering the positive feedback from people who have attended programs, there is little risk that introducing such services will draw criticism. On the contrary, the participants in the programs and their supervisors are very likely to become vocal supporters of the training.

Affordability

Considering that a typical expatriate assignment costs more than a million dollars and that failures of international business ventures are vastly more expensive, the use of intercultural services makes good economic sense. They add very little to the overall expense of an international assignment, and they are likely to make the difference between success and failure in some instances. Given the magnitude of the investments at risk, just one or two assignments or projects saved will make the services highly cost-effective.

According to the 1999 Windham/NFTC survey, the average cost of cross-cultural preparation programs was $3,380 per expatriate. The figure for repatriation counseling was $2,567. An informal sampling of US vendors' prices also in 1999 revealed that a two-day program for both types of training ranged from about $5,000 to $7,000 per person. The per person tuition for programs of similar length in the United

Kingdom was quoted at £675 by one provider. In general, however, the prices in Europe for consulting and training seem to be somewhat higher than in the United States.

International assignee selection services vary from around $5 for a simple self-scored questionnaire to approximately $300 for a professionally scored one including a report. Selection interviews cost from $2,000–3,000 per couple, plus travel expenses for the assessor. This cost is a very small factor in the expense of an overseas assignment.

Companies that regret their heavy costs of expatriate failure and loss generally conclude that investing in intercultural services makes excellent business sense. The key question is, "Can your organization or firm afford *not* to invest in them?"

Competitive Advantage

Another argument for using these services is that quite a few companies are overlooking this powerful business tool. Their failure to profit from using these resources gives your company an opportunity to gain a significant competitive edge by employing intercultural services. This advantage will be increasingly important in the global business environment of the new century. You will have brought a major benefit to your company or organization if you can convince your fellow managers of this fact.

Despite the research and business reasoning supporting the use of intercultural services, absolutely indisputable proof of their effectiveness remains elusive. Therefore, internationally minded managers still must exercise judgment when deciding which services are appropriate and justifiable, just as they have always done. However, with the evidence and rationale you have available in this chapter, you can help them make much better-informed and sound decisions than they could have in the past.

Convincing Others

In essence, leadership appears to be the art of getting others to want to do something you are convinced should be done.

Vance Packer in *The Pyramid Climbers*

You will be showing leadership and be making a valuable contribution if you can convince those with the power to buy intercultural services to do so. Your role is not to be a salesperson advocating the use of a particular service, product, or vendor. Instead, you are acting as an in-house consultant concerned about the success of your company or organization and the morale and effectiveness of your employees. Focusing attention on solutions is merely the logical conclusion of the process of identifying needs and problems.

Be Convinced Yourself

If you are doubtful of the rationale for using intercultural services, you are not prepared to convince others with the assurance and integrity required. Therefore, your first task is to be sure that you are thoroughly persuaded that the justifications are sound and credible. In this process, it is helpful to visualize yourself in the roles of expatriates, international business travelers, host-country counterparts, and other employees with cross-border responsibilities. Likewise, you should consider the issue of intercultural competence from the viewpoint of those who have to manage budgets and control costs.

Do Your Homework

A review of the challenges posed by cultural differences and the cross-cultural adjustment process described in Chapter 2 and the demands of new cross-border roles covered in Chapter 4 will give you a good grasp of your employees' needs for intercultural services on an individual basis. The impact of cultural issues on cross-border organizational relationships is dealt with in Chapter 3. Those chapters, with their references and resources, give you abundant information on the "what," "how," and "why" of the reasons for using the services.

You also must be prepared to address the question, "So what?" Gleaning concrete examples and hard data from this chapter and from the resources listed will give you the kind of information demanded by skeptical results-oriented colleagues. They invariably require quantifiable figures or, at least, very plausible evidence of the implications of using or not using intercultural services. Remember that associates in other companies and organizations and service providers often are good sources of this type of information.

Have a Strategy

If you feel that it is worthwhile to try to convince others of the value of intercultural services, it is important to have a strategy for doing so. Without a well-planned approach and specific goals, you will run the risk of wasting your time and failing to enlist the support of the key people who must be convinced. To be effective, your particular goals and strategy must conform to the unique mission, values, and circumstances of your company or organization. Therefore, no generic prescriptions can be given to guide you in your effort. Nevertheless, a few pointers may be helpful:

❑ Define goals that are recognizable when they are achieved.
❑ Set goals that are feasible given the limitations of your time and resources.
❑ Incorporate the input of as many stakeholders as possible.
❑ Know whom you must convince and what rationale they will find persuasive.
❑ Identify and enlist the support of "opinion leaders" who have influence on others.
❑ Develop practical en route objectives and steps toward their achievement.
❑ Have a timeframe for accomplishing your goals and stick to it.
❑ Recruit allies at all levels of your organization or company.
❑ Share successes widely with others.

Be Confident

As you seek to present the rationale for intercultural services, you can be optimistic and confident. The inexorable process of globalization will make the need for these services ever more obvious to international managers. The evidence in favor of using them will be increasingly persuasive as more rigorous research results become available. The growing diversity of the workforce will provide you with supporters who understand and appreciate the value of what you are trying to accomplish. Time is on your side.

Rationale Focus Questions

☑ What type of rationale will be most compelling in your corporate or organizational culture? Human considerations or financial ones? Or both?

☑ Who must be persuaded to approve the purchase of intercultural services? What kind of information would capture the attention of these decision-makers?

☑ Do you have reasonably accurate data on the costs of your expatriate relocations and the profit/loss of your international business? If not, how can you best gather them?

☑ What are your expatriate failure and returnee attrition rates? What are the causes?

☑ Are your international business travelers effectively protecting and enhancing the image of your company or organization?

☑ How does your performance in these areas compare to others in your industry or field of specialization?

☑ What are their "best practices" in intercultural management? To what extent are you using these practices?

☑ Are you aware of any dramatic examples of failed international assignments or projects in your company that illustrate the waste of human or financial resources? Can you use these cases to support your rationale?

☑ Do you need help promoting intercultural services? Do you have allies or supporters in-house? How can you enlist their support?

☑ Do you have a well-planned promotional strategy?

☑ Could a consultant be useful for helping you to plan and implement your strategy?

Summary and Suggested Action Steps

This chapter explains the most compelling rationale for using intercultural services. It supplies evidence and information to support the rationale. The needs for these services are summarized from both a business-oriented and humanistic perspective. Concrete examples, research findings, and "best practices" in the area of intercultural management provide tools for in-house promotional efforts. The references at the end of the chapter include many additional resources to help strengthen the case for using intercultural training, selection, and consulting.

Here are some ways you can use the content of this chapter:

1. Thoroughly review the rationale and evidence to be sure that they are credible and convincing to you. If necessary, consult the appropriate references and Chapters 2–6 to satisfy yourself that the case for using intercultural services is clear and compelling.
2. Identify who in your organization must be persuaded to approve the purchase of these services and determine which aspects of the rationale will most influence them.
3. Plan a strategy for promoting the services. Seek the advice and assistance of colleagues, consultants, and providers.
4. Gather examples of the need for cross-cultural services from your own organization and from others in your industry or field. Use them to buttress the points made in this chapter.
5. Collect evidence of savings made and benefits gained through the use of intercultural services by your organization or company and by others. Publicize these successes.
6. Consult counterparts in leading international companies to ascertain what are their best practices. Share this information with skeptical colleagues.
7. Use portions of this chapter, recommended resources, and the examples you have gathered as content for discussion papers and readings for groups of employees who have international responsibilities.
8. Recruit a senior-level mentor or champion to guide and advise you in your promotional initiatives.
9. Use the online resources listed in this book to keep abreast of new information from surveys, research studies, and reporting in the international business press that can support your rationale.

Resources

The Need for Services

Agar, M. "The Intercultural Frame." *International Journal of Intercultural Relations*, Vol. 18, No. 2, 1994, pp. 221–237.

Axtell, R. A. *Do's and Taboos Around the World.* New York: John Wiley & Sons, Inc., 1993.

Caudron, S. "Surviving Cross-Cultural Shock." *Industry Week,* July 6, 1992, pp. 35–38.

Earley, P. C., and Erez, M. *The Transplanted Executive: Why You Need To Understand How Workers in Other Countries See the World Differently.* Oxford, UK: Oxford University Press, 1997.

"Expat Neglect Strafes Bottom Line: Lack of Training is a Major Factor." *Corporate University Review*, Vol. 6, No. 2, Mar./Apr. 1998, pp. 40–41.

Feldman, D. C., and Thompson, H. B. "Expatriation, Repatriation, and Domestic Geographical Relocation: An Empirical Investigation of Adjustment to New Job Assignments." *Journal of International Business Studies*, Third Quarter 1993, pp. 507–529.

Hannon, K. "The Fast Track Now Leads Overseas." *U.S. News & World Report*, Oct. 31, 1994, pp. 94–98.

Haslbeger, A., and Stroh, L. K. "Premature Return of Expatriates: Reasons and Remedies." *Mobility*, Oct. 1993, pp. 59–68.

Herrera, S. "Damn Yankees." *Forbes*, Mar. 10, 1997, pp. 22–23.

Hodge, S. "Culture Shock Bewilders Business Travelers." *Mobility*, Dec. 1997, pp. 24–27.

Ioannou, L. "It's a Small World After All." *International Business*, Feb. 1994, pp. 82–88.

Kanter, R. M. *World Class: Traveling Locally in the Global Economy.* New York: Simon & Schuster, 1995.

Kurtis, C. "World Full of Trouble." *International Business*, Vol. 10, No. 5, July/Aug. 1997, pp. 12–18.

Laurent, A. "The Cross-Cultural Puzzle of Global Human Resource Management." In V. Pucik, N. M. Tichy, and C. K. Barnett, (eds.), *Globalizing Management: Creating and Leading the Competitive Organization.* New York: John Wiley & Sons, Inc., 1993, pp. 174–186.

Lewis, R. D. *When Cultures Collide: Managing Successfully across Cultures.* Sonoma, CA: Nicholas Brealey Publishing, 1996.

Marx, E. *Breaking through Culture Shock: What You Need To Succeed in International Business.* Sonoma, CA: Nicholas Brealey Publishing, 1999.

Mcnerney, D. J. "Global Staffing: Some Common Problems and Solutions." *HR Focus,* June 1996, pp. 1–6.

Moran, R. T., and Riesenberger, J. R. *The Global Challenge: Building the New Worldwide Enterprise.* London: McGraw-Hill, 1994.

"Recognizing and Heeding Cultural Differences Can Be Key to International Business Success." *Business America,* Oct. 1994, pp. 8–11.

Ricks, D. A. *Big Blunders in International Business.* Cambridge, MA: Blackwell, 1993.

Schell, M. S., and Stoltz-Loike, M. "Importance of Cultural Preparation to International Business Success." *Journal of International Compensation & Benefits,* Jan./Feb., 1994, pp. 47–52.

Schneider, S. C., and Barsoux, J. L. *Managing across Cultures.* London: Prentice Hall Europe, 1997.

Solomon, C. M. "Success Abroad Depends on More Than Job Skills." *Personnel Journal,* Apr. 1994, pp. 51–60.

Swaak, R. A. "Expatriate Failures: Too Many, Too Much Cost, Too Little Planning." *Compensations & Benefits Review,* Nov./Dec., 1995, pp. 47–55.

Trompenaars, F. *Riding the Waves of Culture,* Burr Ridge, IL: Irwin Professional Publishing, 1994.

Tung, R. L., "Expatriate Assignments: Enhancing Success and Minimizing Failure." In M. Mendenhall and G. Oddou (eds.), *Readings and Cases in International Human Resource Management.* Boston: PWS-Kent Publishing Company, 1991, pp. 205–220.

Wederspahn, G. M. "International Relocation: An Emotional Roller Coaster Ride." *Relocation/Realty Update,* Vol. 8, No. 1, Jan. 1992, pp. 5–7.

The Effectiveness of Services

Bird A., Heinbuch, S., and Dunbar, R. "A Conceptual Model of the Effects of Area Studies Training Programs and a Preliminary Investigation of the Model's Hypothesized Relationships." *International Journal of Intercultural Relations,* Vol. 17, 1993, pp. 415–535.

Black, J. S., and Mendenhall, M. "Cross-Cultural Training Effectiveness: Review and a Theoretical Framework for Future Research."

Academy of Management Review, Vol. 15, No.1, Jan. 1990, pp. 113–136.

Conway, B. *Expatriate Effectiveness: A Study of European Expatriates in South-East Asia.* New York: John Wiley & Sons, 1998.

Cushner, K. "Assessing the Impact of a Culture-General Assimilator." *International Journal of Intercultural Relations*, Vol. 13, No. 2, 1989, pp. 125–146.

Deshpande, S. P., and Viswesvaran, C. "Is Cross-Cultural Training of Expatriate Managers Effective? A Meta Analysis." *International Journal of Intercultural Relations*, Vol. 16, 1992, pp. 295–310.

Dinges, N. G., and Baldwin K. D. "Intercultural Competence: A Research Perspective." In D. Landis and R. S. Bhagat (eds.), *Handbook of Intercultural Training*. (2nd ed.) Thousand Oaks, CA: Sage Publications, Inc., 1996, pp. 106–123.

Gregersen, H. B., Black S. J., and Hite, J. M. "Expatriate Performance Appraisal: Principles, Practices, and Challenges." In J. Selmer (ed.), *Expatriate Management: New Ideas for International Business.* Westport, CT: Quorum Books, 1995, pp. 173–196.

Hammer, M. R., and Martin, J. N. "The Effects of Cross-Cultural Training on American Management in a Japanese Joint Venture." *Journal of Applied Communication Research*, Vol. 20, 1992, pp. 161–182.

Hayles, R. "Intercultural Training: The Effectiveness Connection." In S. M. Fowler and M. G. Mumford (eds.), *Intercultural Sourcebook: Cross-Cultural Training Methods, Vol. 1.* Yarmouth, MA: Intercultural Press, Inc., 1995, pp. 215–223.

Hocking, J. B. "Developing an Assignment Success Scoreboard." *International HR Journal*, Vol. 7, No. 4, Winter 1999, pp. 5–10.

Kealey, D. J. "A Study of Cross-Cultural Effectiveness: Theoretical Issues, Practical Applications: An Assessment of the Literature on the Issue." *International Journal of Intercultural Relations*, Vol. 13, 1989, pp. 387–428.

Kealey, D. J., and Protheroe, D. R. "The Effectiveness of Cross-Cultural Training for Expatriates: An Assessment of the Literature on the Issue." *International Journal of Intercultural Relations*, Vol. 20, 1996, pp. 141–165.

Mendenhall, M. E., Dunbar, E., and Oddou, G. "Expatriate Selection, Training and Career-Pathing: A Review and Critique." *Human Resource Management*, Vol. 26, No. 3, Fall 1987, pp. 331–345.

Cost-Benefits of Services

Aschkenasy, J. "Culture Shock: Expatriate Benefits are Getting Squeezed as Companies Tighten Their Belts." *International Business,* Feb. 1997, pp. 20–27.

Blake, B. F., Heslin, R., and Curtis, S. C. "Measuring Impacts of Cross-Cultural Training," In D. Landis and R. S. Bhagat (eds.), *Handbook of Intercultural Training.* (2nd ed.) Thousand Oaks, CA: Sage Publications, Inc., 1996, pp. 165–182.

Carnevale, A., and Schultz, E. "Return on Investment: Accounting for Training." *Training & Development Journal,* July 1990, Special Supplement.

Fisher, S. G., and Ruffino, B. J. *Establishing the Value of Training.* Amherst, MA: HRD Press, 1996.

Grove, C., and Hallowell, W. "Cost-Effective Expatriate Training." *International Insight,* Summer, 1996, pp. 1–3.

Grove, C., and Sever, P. "Estimating Financial Savings from Intercultural Training." Unpublished paper, 1990, available from Cornelius Grove, 442 47th Street, Brooklyn, NY 11220.

Payne, I. C. "Defining and Measuring Success in International Assignments." *Mobility,* Feb. 1997, pp. 73–75.

Phillips, J. J. "Level 4 and Beyond: An ROI Model." In S. M. Brown and C. J. Seidner (eds.), *Evaluating Corporate Training: Models and Issues.* Boston, MA: Kluwer Academic Publishers, 1998, pp. 113–140.

Phillips, J. J., and Pulliam, P. F. "Dispelling the ROI Myths." *Corporate University Review,* Vol. 7, No. 3, May/June 1999, pp. 32–36.

Schell, M. S. *Measuring the Value of an Expatriate Program.* Paper based on a presentation by Michael Schell on Apr. 6, 1998, New York: Windham International, 1998.

Schmidt, W. J. "Cost-Benefit Analysis Techniques for Training Investments." In J. H. Woods and J. W. Cortada (eds.), *1998 ASTD Training and Performance Yearbook.* New York: McGraw-Hill, 1998, pp. 269–274.

Solomon, C. M. "Measuring Return on Investment: Do You Know What Your International Assignments Are Worth?" *Workforce,* Vol. 78, No. 3, Mar. 1999, pp. 24–29.

Thomas, D. C., and Ravlin, E. C. "Responses of Employees to Cultural Adaptation by a Foreign Manager." *Journal of Applied Psychology,* Vol. 80, No. 1, 1995, pp. 133—146.

Wederspahn, G. M. "How Does Cultural Awareness Affect My International Business Success?" *Business Facilities*, Sep. 1998, pp. 10–12.

Best Practices

Arthur Andersen and Bennett Associates, *1997 Global Best in Class Study*, Chicago: Arthur Andersen/Bennett Associates, 1997.

Bhagat, R. S., and Prien, K. O. "Cross-Cultural Training in Organizational Contexts." In D. Landis and R. S. Bhagat (eds.), *Handbook of Intercultural Training*. (2nd ed.) Thousand Oaks, CA: Sage Publications, Inc., 1996, pp. 216–230.

Caudron, S. "Training Ensures Success Overseas, *Personnel Journal*, Dec. 1991, pp. 27–30.

The Conference Board. *Managing Expatriates' Return: A Research Report, Report Number 1148–96-RR*. New York: The Conference Board, Inc., 1996.

Derr, C. B., and Oddou, G. "Internationalizing Managers: Speeding Up the Process." *European Management Journal*, Vol. 11, No. 4, Dec. 1993, pp. 435–442.

Dolins, I. L. "Best Practices VI: In-Country Assistance." *Mobility*, Feb. 1998, pp. 27–29.

Frazee, V. "Send Your Expats Prepared for Success." *Workforce*, Vol. 78, No. 3, Mar. 1999, pp. 6–11.

Gates, S. *The Changing Global Role of the Human Resource Function: A Research Report, Report Number 1062–94-RR*. New York: The Conference Board, Inc., 1994.

Harris, P. R., and Moran, R. T. *Managing Cultural Differences*. (5th ed.) Houston: Gulf Publishing Company, 2000.

Jones, D. "U.S. Managers Earn Global Credentials." *USA Today*, Feb. 26, 1997, pp. 1B–2B.

Kenyon, H. S. "Cross-Cultural Training Par Excellence." *Corporate University Review*, Vol. 6, No. 2, Mar./Apr. 1998, pp. 10–18.

Mackiewicz, A., and Daniels, N. *The Successful Corporation of the Year 2000*. Research Report, New York: Economist Intelligence Unit, 1994.

National Foreign Trade Council and Selection Research International, *International Sourcing and Selection Practices 1995 Survey Report*. New York: NFTC, Sep. 1995.

Naumann, E. "Organizational Predictors of Expatriate Job Satisfaction." *Journal of International Business Studies*, Vol. 24, No. 1, 1993, pp. 61–80.

Organization Resources Counselors, *1998 North American International Assignment Policies and Practices*, New York: ORC, 1999.

Organization Resources Counselors, *1999 Survey of Expatriate Assignments in the United States.* New York: ORC, 1999.

Scott, R. E. *Expatriate Adjustment & Performance: A Research Report.* Abilene, TX: Integrated Resources Group, 1997.

Shilling, M. "Avoid Expatriate Culture Shock." *HR Magazine*, July 1993, pp. 58–63.

Swaak, R. A. "Expatriate Management: The Search for Best Practices." *Compensation & Benefit Review*, May/June 1995, pp. 21–26.

Tung, R. *1997 Study of the Expatriation/Repatriation Process.* Chicago: Arthur Andersen, 1997.

Wederspahn, G. M. "Controlling Costs of Expatriate Assignments." *Journal of International Compensation and Benefits*, Jan. 1995, pp. 55–59.

Wederspahn, G. M. "Cross-Cultural Savvy: The Exporter's Competitive Edge." *The Exporter*, Dec. 1996, pp. 35.

Wederspahn, G. M. "Global Business Protocol: Curriculum for Success." *Mobility*, Oct. 1997, pp. 71–72.

Windham International, National Trade Council and Institute for International Human Resources. *Global Relocation Trends: 1999 Survey Report.* New York: Windham International, 1999.

Windham International, National Trade Council and Institute for International Human Resources. *Global Relocation Trends: 1998 Survey Report.* New York: Windham International, 1998.

In-House Promotion of Services

Donnelly, E. "The Need to Market Training." In J. Prior (ed.), *Gower Handbook of Training and Development.* (2nd ed.) Brookfield, VT: Gower Publishing Company Limited, 1994, pp. 73–88.

Mitchell, G. *The Trainer's Handbook: The AMA Guide to Effective Training.* (3rd ed.) New York: AMACOM Press, 1998. See "Marketing Training," pp. 364–404.

Munson, L. S. *How To Conduct Training Seminars: A Complete Reference Guide for Training Managers and Professionals.* (2nd ed.)

New York: McGraw-Hill, 1992. See "Building a Positive Climate for Training," and "How To Gain Support of Management," pp. 9–28.

Rogers, J. L. "Helping Clients Make Training Decisions." In J. H. Woods and J. W. Cortada (eds.), *1997 ASTD Training and Performance Yearbook*. New York: McGraw-Hill, 1997, pp. 121–126.

Bibliography of "Classics"

The following books, all published before 1990, have had a significant influence on the development of the field of intercultural services. Omitted from this bibliography are other landmark books that have been published as revised editions since 1990 and that are referenced in the resource lists at the end of various chapters.

Aitken, T. *The Multinational Man: Role of the Manager Abroad.* New York: John Wiley and Sons, 1973.

Althen, G. *American Ways: A Guide for Foreigners.* Yarmouth, ME: Intercultural Press, 1988.

Althen, G. (ed.). *Learning across Cultures: Intercultural Communication and International Educational Exchange.* Washington, DC: National Association for Foreign Student Affairs, 1981.

Asante, M. K., Gudykunst, W. B., and Newmark, E. (eds.). *Handbook of International and Intercultural Communication.* Newbury Park, CA: Sage Publications, 1989.

Austin, C. N. (ed.). *Cross-Cultural Reentry: A Book of Readings.* Abilene, TX: Abilene Christian University Press, 1986.

Austin, C. N. *Cross-Cultural Reentry: An Annotated Bibliography.* Abilene, TX: Abilene Christian University Press, 1983.

Barnett, R. J., and Muller, R. E. *Global Reach: The Power of the Multination Corporation.* New York: Simon and Schuster, 1974.

Bartlett, C. A., and Ghoushal, S. *Managing across Borders: The Transnational Solution.* Cambridge, MA: Harvard Business School Press, 1989.

Binnendijk, H. *National Negotiating Styles*, Washington, DC: US Department of State, Foreign Service Institute, 1987.

Bock, P. K. (ed.). *Culture Shock: A Reader in Modern Cultural Anthropology.* Washington, DC: University Press of America, 1970.

Brislin, R. W., and Segall, M. H. *Cross-Cultural Research: The Role of Culture in Understanding Human Behavior.* New York: Learning Resources in International Studies, 1975.

Brislin, R. W., Cushner, K., and Cherrie, C. (eds.). *Intercultural Interactions: A Practical Guide.* Beverly Hills, CA: Sage Publications, 1986.

Casmir, F. L. (ed.). *International and Intercultural Communication Annual, Vol. 1.* New York: Speech Communication Association, 1974.

Casmir, F. L. (ed.). *International and Intercultural Communication Annual, Vol. 2.* New York: Speech Communication Association, 1975.

Casmir, F. L. (ed.). *International and Intercultural Communication Annual, Vol. 3.* New York: Speech Communication Association, 1976.

Casmir, F. L. (ed.). *International and Intercultural Communication.* Washington, DC: University Press of America, 1978.

Casse, P. *Training for the Cross-Cultural Mind.* (2nd ed.) Washington, DC: SIETAR, 1981.

Casse, P. *Training for the Multicultural Manager.* Washington, DC: SIETAR, 1982.

Casse, P., and Deol, S. *Managing Intercultural Negotiations: Guidelines for Trainers and Negotiators.* Washington, DC: SIETAR, 1985.

Chesanow, N. *The World-Class Executive: How To Do Business Like a Pro around the World.* New York: Rawson Associates, 1985.

Cleveland, H., Mangone, G. J., and Adams, J. C. *The Overseas Americans.* New York: McGraw-Hill, 1960.

Condon, J. C., and Yousef, F. *Introduction to Intercultural Communication*, Indianapolis, IN: Macmillan, 1975.

Copeland, L., and Griggs, L. *Going International: How To Make Friends and Deal Effectively in the Global Marketplace.* New York: Random House, New American Library, 1985.

Davey, W. G. (ed.) *Intercultural Theory and Practice: Perspectives on Education, Training and Research.* Washington, DC: SIETAR, Georgetown University, 1979.

Fisher, G. *International Negotiation: A Cross-Cultural Perspective.* Yarmouth, ME: Intercultural Press, 1980.

Furnham, A., and Bochner, S. *Culture Shock—Psychological Reactions to an Unfamiliar Environment.* New York: Methuen & Company, 1986.

Geertz, C. *The Interpretation of Culture.* New York: Basic Books, 1973.

Glover, G., and Shames, G. W. *World-Class Service.* Yarmouth, ME: Intercultural Press, 1989.

Gross, J., and Rayner, S. *Measuring Culture.* New York: Columbia University Press, 1985.

Gudykunst, W. B. (ed.). *Intercultural Communication Theory: Current Perspectives.* Newbury Park, CA: Sage, 1983.

Gudykunst, W. B., and Kim, Y. *Communicating with Strangers: An Approach to Intercultural Communication.* Reading, MA: Addison-Wesley, 1984.

Gudykunst, W. B., and Kim, Y. (eds.). *Methods for Intercultural Communication Research.* Beverly Hills, CA: Sage, 1984.

Gudykunst, W. B., and Ting-Toomey, S. *Culture and Interpersonal Communication.* Newbury Park, CA: Sage, 1989.

Hall, E. T. *Beyond Culture.* Garden City, NY: Anchor/Doubleday, 1976.

Hall, E. T. *The Dance of Life.* Garden City, NY: Anchor/Doubleday, 1983.

Hall, E. T. *The Hidden Dimension.* Garden City, NY: Anchor/Doubleday, 1966.

Hall, E. T. *The Silent Language.* Garden City, NY: Anchor/Doubleday, 1959.

Hall, E. T., and Hall, M. R. *Understanding Cultural Differences.* Yarmouth, ME: Intercultural Press, 1989.

Harman, W. *Global Mind Change.* Indianapolis, IN: Knowledge Systems, Inc., 1998.

Harwood, A. (ed.). *Ethnicity and Medical Care.* Cambridge, MA: Harvard University Press, 1981.

Harris, M. *Cultural Materialism: The Struggle for a Science of Culture.* New York: Vintage Books, Random House, 1980.

Harris, M. *The Rise of Cultural Theory.* New York: Crowell, 1968.

Harris, P. R. (ed.). *Global Strategies for Human Resource Development.* Alexandria, VA: ASTD, 1984.

Heenan, D. A., and Perlmutter, H. V. *Multicultural Organization Development.* Reading, MA: Addison-Wesley Publishing Co., 1979.

Henderson, G., and Primeaux, M. (eds.). *Transcultural Health Care.* Reading, MA: Addison-Wesley Publishing Co., 1981.

Hoffman, J. *The International Assignment: Is It for You?* Foster City, CA: D.C.W. Research Associates Press, 1982.

Hoopes, D. S., and Ventura P. (eds.). *Intercultural Sourcebook, Cross-Cultural Training Methodologies.* Washington, DC: SIETAR, Georgetown University, 1979.

Hoopes, D. S., Penderson, P. R., and Renwick, G. W. (eds.). *Overview of Intercultural Education, Training and Research, Vol. II: Education and Training.* Washington, DC: SIETAR, Georgetown University, 1978.

Hoopes, D. S., Penderson, P. R., and Renwick, G. W. (eds.). *Overview of Intercultural Education, Training and Research, Vol. III: Special Research Area.* Washington, DC: SIETAR, Georgetown University, 1979.

Hoopes, D. S., Penderson, P. R., and Renwick, G. W. (eds.). *Overview of Intercultural Education, Training and Research, Vol. I: Theory.* Washington, DC: SIETAR, Georgetown University, 1977.

Illman, P. E. *Developing Overseas Managers and Managers Overseas.* New York: AMACOM, 1980.

Kennedy, G. *Doing Business Abroad.* New York: Simon and Schuster, 1985.

Kleinman, A. M. *Patients and Healers in the Context of Culture.* Berkeley, CA: University of California Press, 1980.

Kluckhohn, F., and Strodtbeck, F. *Variations in Value Orientations.* New York: Basic Books, 1973.

Korzenny, F., and Ting-Toomey, S. *International and Intercultural Communication Annual, Vol. 13.* Newbury Park, CA: Sage Publications, 1989.

Landis, D., and Brislin, R. W. (eds.). *Handbook of Intercultural Training, Vol. I, Issues in Theory and Design.* New York: Pergamon, 1983.

Landis, D., and Brislin, R. W. (eds.). *Handbook of Intercultural Training, Vol. II, Issues in Training Methodology.* New York: Pergamon, 1983.

Landis, D., and Brislin, R. W. (eds.). *Handbook of Intercultural Training, Vol. III, Area Studies in Intercultural Training.* New York: Pergamon, 1983.

LeVine, R., and Campbell, D. *Ethnocentrism: Theories of Conflict, Ethnic Attitudes, and Group Behavior.* New York: John Wiley, 1972.

McCaffree, M., and Innis, P. *Protocol: The Complete Handbook of Diplomatic Official & Social Usage.* Washington, DC: Devon Publishing, 1985.

Moran, R. T., and Harris, P. R. *Managing Cultural Synergy.* Houston, TX: Gulf Publishing Company, 1982.

Morrison, M. A., White, R. P., and Van Velsor, E. *Breaking the Glass Ceiling—Can Women Reach the Top of America's Largest Corporations?* Reading, MA: Addison-Wesley, 1987.

Pusch, M. D. (ed.). *Multicultural Education: A Cross-Cultural Training Approach.* Yarmouth, ME: Intercultural Press, 1979.

Renwick, G. W. *Evaluation Handbook.* LaGrange Park, IL: Intercultural Network, Inc., 1979.

Rhinesmith, S. H. *Cultural-Organizational Analysis: The Relationship of Value Orientations and Managerial Behavior.* Cambridge, MA: McBer and Company, 1971.

Ricks, D. A., et al. *International Business Blunders.* Washington, DC: Transemantics, 1974.

Ricks, D. A. *Big Business Blunders: Mistakes in Multinational Marketing.* Dow Jones-Irwin, 1983.

Rossman, M. L. *The International Businesswoman: A Guide to Success in the Global Marketplace.* New York: Praeger Publishers, 1986.

Ruben, B. *Handbook of Intercultural Skills, Vol. 1.* New York: Pergamon Press, 1983.

Samovar, L. A., Porter, R. E., and Jain, N. C. *Understanding Intercultural Communication.* Belmont, CA: Publishing Company, 1981.

Seelye, N. H. *Teaching Culture: Strategies for Intercultural Communication.* Belmont, CA: Wadsworth Publishing Company, 1987.

Simons, G. F. *Working Together: How To Become More Effective in a Multicultural Organization.* Los Altos, CA: Crisp Publishing, 1989.

Smith, E. C., and Luce, L. F. *Toward Internationalism: Readings in Cross-Cultural Communication.* New York: Harper & Row, 1979.

Snowdon, S. *The Global Edge: How Your Company Can Win in the International Marketplace.* New York: Simon and Schuster, 1986.

Spradley, J. P., and Rynkiewich, M. A. (eds.). *The Nacirema, Readings on American Culture.* Boston: Little, Brown and Company, 1975.

Stewart, E. C. *American Cultural Patterns: A Cross-Cultural Perspective.* Yarmouth, ME: Intercultural Press, 1972.

Stopford, J. M., and Well, L. T. *Managing the Multinational Enterprise*. New York: Basic Books, 1972.

Terpstra, V. *The Cultural Environment of International Business*. Cincinnati, OH: South-Western College Publishing, 1978.

Tung, R. L. *The New Expatriates: Managing Human Resources Abroad*. Cambridge, MA: Ballinger Publishing Company, 1988.

Tyler, V. L. *Intercultural Interacting*. Provo, UT: Brigham Young University, David M. Kennedy Center for International Studies, 1987.

Useem, R. H. (ed.). *Third Culture Children: An Annotated Bibliography*. East Lansing, MI: University of Michigan Press, 1975.

Valentine, C. F. *The Arthur Young International Business Guide*. New York: John Wiley and Sons, Inc., 1988.

Webber, R. A. *Culture and Management*. New York: Penguin Books, 1977.

Weeks, W., Pederson, P. P., and Brislin, R. W. *A Manual of Structured Experiences for Cross-Cultural Learning*. Yarmouth, ME: Intercultural Press, 1977.

Weinshall, T. (ed.). *Culture and Management*. Homewood, IL: Richard D. Irwin, 1969.

Werkman, S. L. *Bringing Up Children Overseas: A Guide for Families*. New York: Basic Books, 1977.

Wight, A. R., Hammons, A., and White, W. L. *Guidelines for Peace Corps Cross-Cultural Training*, Vols. I-IV. Washington, DC: US Peace Corps 1970.

Work, J. W. *Toward Affirmative Action and Racial/Ethnic Pluralism: How to Train in Organizations*. Arlington, VA: Belvedere Press, 1989.

Wurzel, J. *Toward Multiculturalism: A Reader in Multicultural Education*. Yarmouth, ME: Intercultural Press, 1988.

Index

A

abroad, defined, 20
academic approach, intercultural
    learning, 159
Academy of Management Review,
    15
accompanying partners, 20
adaptation factors, expatriates,
    58–59
Adir, Red, 232
Adler, Nancy J., 15, 72, 91–92
affordability of services, 315
African vendors, 265–266
aim of book, 3
ALCOA, 300
American cultural baggage, 36
Amoco Corporation, 116
Aon Consulting
    profiling of expatriates, 210
    Survey of Human Resource
        Trends, 303
arm gestures, 51

Arthur Andersen, 1997 successful
    expatriate traits research, 39,
    57, 303
Asia-Pacific vendors, 258–259
assessing need for intercultural
        programs, 137–139, 183
    assessment tools, 148–149
    critical case analyses, 150
    direct observation, 150
    focus groups, 147
    gap analysis, 141
    interviews, 145–146
    needs statements, 143
    prioritizing needs, 151
    questionnaires, 144
    service provider roles, 152
    visualization stage, 140
associate US vendors, 250–256
Association of Medical Colleges,
    1998 medical school cultural
    training statistics, 14
AT&T, 300

Atlas Van Lines, 302
attributes of trainers, 235
attrition rates of expatriates,
299–306
audiotapes, 209

B

background of trainers, 228
BAFA BAFA cross–cultural
simulation game, 12
Barsoux, Jean-Louis, 82
basic value contrasts, 39–40
behavioral objectives, intercultural
learning, 156
Bennett Associates, 303
Bennett, Milton J., intercultural
sensitivity stages, 36, 53
Berlitz International, failed
expatriation costs, 300
Bhagat, R. S., 43, 313
billing issues, 277–278
Bird, Allan, 301
Black, S. J., 313
body contact, 51
body language, 50–51
boss-employee relationships, 83
Brake, Terrence, 78
Brooks, Ann K., 15
Buffet, Warren, 300
Business Council For International
Understanding, 9
business orientation services, 189
business workshops for intercultural
employees, 178

C

Caldwell, Larry, 308
Caldwell, Philip, 270
Canadian Business Review, 314
Canadian vendors, 264
Caribbean vendors, 265
Carrol, Lewis, 173
Casse, Pierre, 226
causes of cross-cultural stress, 55–56
CD-ROM, 15, 207–208

Center for Research and Education,
10
1981 intercultural training
statistics, 11
centrally-based US vendors,
247–249
Centre for International Briefing, 9
CFO magazine, 303
China, high–context communication,
50
CIO magazine, 295
clashes in values, 40
coaching services, 184
color issues, 52
Columbia University, cross-cultural
joint venture failures, 70, 306
comfort with cultural adjustment, 58
communication cross-culturally,
46–51
company orientations, 291
competence in cultural adjustment, 58
Conference Board, intercultural
training advantages, 311–316
repatriation report, 115
conferences, ASTD, ERC, SHRM,
SIETAR, 18
conflicts in corporate
practices/behavior, 83
Confucius, 38
consultants, 17, 185, 273
content-focused communications, 48
context-focused communications, 48
contracts, cross-cultural joint
ventures, 88
Coopers and Lybrand/Yankelovich
survey, 307
coping with cultural adjustment, 58
Copeland, Lenny, 12
corporate culture
"Eiffel Tower" model, 81
"family" model, 80
"guided missile" model, 81
"incubator" model, 82
costs of relocation, 300
counseling services, 184
country profiles, 187, 207
critical analyses, intercultural needs
assessments, 150

"Eiffel Tower" model, corporate
culture, 81
Elashmawi, Farid, 308
employees
evaluations, 85
motivations, 84
rewards, 86
Ernst & Young, barriers to overseas
expansion, 309
ethical issues, 88, 235
*Ethnicity and Race: Making
Identities in a Changing World*,
76
European Training Foundation,
118
European vendors, 260–263
evaluating intercultural services,
281–287
expatriates, 20
adaptation factors, 58–59
services, 176, 188
US, *see* US, expatriates
experiential approach, intercultural
learning, 160
Experiment for World Learning
(International Living), 9
export/import stage, globalization of
organizations, 73
eye contact, 51

F

facial expressions, 51
facilitated programs, 210
failed expatriation, 300–305
"family" corporate culture model,
80–82
family expatriate services, 188
fee negotiations, 272, 277
feedback to providers, 288–290
Ferraro, Gary P., high-context/
low-context country rankings,
50–51
focus groups, intercultural needs
assessments, 147
focus questions
cross-border roles, 114
cross-cultural communications,
52

cultural adaptation, 59–60
cultural context of business, 38
cultural differences, 45
cultural synergy, 94
exploring intercultural services
possibilities, 24
global managers, 119
globalization, 76
intercultural learning, 158, 167
intercultural services, 191, 211
needs assessment, 153
organizational relationships, 90
provider performance, 293
rationale for purchasing services,
319
supplier relationships, 280
supplier suitability, 232
trainer qualifications, 236
vendor presentations, 242
Fontaine, Gary, 120
Forbes, 308
Foreign Service Institute (US State
Department), 9
foreigners, 20
Fowler, Sandra, 166

G

Galagan, Patricia, 72
games and simulations, 207, 210
Gandhi, Mahatma, 32
gap analysis, intercultural program
needs assessment, 141
generalizations about cultures, 41
generalizations vs. stereotypes, 41
General Motors, 315
Germany, low-context
communications, 50
global management seminars, 178
global managers, 115–119, 134
"Global Relocation Trends 1998
Survey Report," intercultural
training trends, 311
global stage, globalization of
organizations, 75
globalization stages, 20, 72–76
Globalizing Management, 77, 102,
114
Global Workforce magazine, 306, 308

N

O

P

conflicting practices and behavior,
    83
differences in corporate culture,
    80
dissimilar work culture stages, 79
relationships, 78
transnational stage, globalization of
    organizations, 75
trends in intercultural services, 14
tribal corporate culture model, 82
Trompenaars, Fons, corporate
    culture models, 80
Tucker, Michael F., 223

U

United States
    cross-cultural clashes, 40
    cultural values, 36
    expatriates, difficult assignment
        countries, 42
    low-context communications, 48
USA Today, 307

V

value clashes, 40
Vargo, Ed, 281

vendors, *See* providers; resources
videos, 209
"village market" corporate culture
    model, 82
visualization stage, intercultural
    program needs assessment, 140
Viswesvaran, Chockalingam, 313
Volvo, 306

W

Walker, Danielle, 78
Ward's Automotive International,
    306
well-oiled machine corporate culture
    model, 82
Westinghouse, 30
Wight, A. R., 10
Windham International
    1998 cross-cultural training
        statistics, 12, 188, 311, 318
    difficult US expatriate assignment
        countries, 42
workbooks on countries, 208
workplace
    decorum, 84
    diversity programs, 181–182
workshops, 178–179
world trade centers, 18

Gary M. Wederspahn is a well-known consultant, trainer, speaker, and writer in the intercultural business field. He has lived and worked overseas for 16 years in 7 countries. For most of that time he was a senior in-country executive responsible for the productivity and morale of more than 100 US expatriates. In that role he purchased a wide variety of intercultural services and products and oversaw the performance of intercultural service providers.

During the past 20 years, he has designed and delivered cross-cultural training services for hundreds of international assignees and business travelers of major global corporations. He is the author of 70 articles in trade and business publications and he has made more than 100 presentations at international conferences. Business travel has taken him to 32 countries.

Mr. Wederspahn's formal education in cross-cultural studies began as an undergraduate at the University of Washington, and continued with an MA degree from Stanford University and self-directed studies and Harvard. In addition, he studied law for two years at Universidad Libre in Bogotá, Colombia. He is currently living in Geneva, Switzerland.

*For Product Safety Concerns and Information please contact
our EU representative GPSR@taylorandfrancis.com Taylor & Francis
Verlag GmbH, Kaufingerstraße 24, 80331 München, Germany*

T - #0007 - 230425 - C0 - 234/156/20 [22] - CB - 9780877193449 - Gloss Lamination